JAMES BALDWIN, TONI MORRISON, AND THE RHETORICS OF BLACK MALE SUBJECTIVITY

James Baldwin, Toni Morrison, and the Rhetorics of Black Male Subjectivity

Aaron Ngozi Oforlea

THE OHIO STATE UNIVERSITY PRESS • COLUMBUS

Library of Congress Cataloging-in-Publication Data
Names: Oforlea, Aaron Ngozi, 1969– author.
Title: James Baldwin, Toni Morrison, and the rhetorics of black male subjectivity / Aaron Ngozi Oforlea.
Description: Columbus : The Ohio State University Press, [2017] | Includes bibliographical references and index.
Identifiers: LCCN 2016048345 | ISBN 9780814213285 (cloth ; alk. paper) | ISBN 0814213286 (cloth ; alk. paper)
Subjects: LCSH: American fiction—African American authors—History and criticism. | Baldwin, James, 1924–1987—Criticism and interpretation. | Morrison, Toni—Criticism and interpretation. | African American men in literature. | Subjectivity in literature. | Masculinity in literature. | Rhetoric.
Classification: LCC PS153.N5 O36 2017 | DDC 810.9/896073—dc23
LC record available at https://lccn.loc.gov/2016048345

Cover design by Janna Thompson-Chordas
Text design by Juliet Williams
Type set in Adobe Minion Pro

♾ The paper used in this publication meets the minimum requirements of the American National Standard for Information Sciences—Permanence of Paper for Printed Library Materials. ANSI Z39.48–1992.

9 8 7 6 5 4 3 2 1

For my parents, Ernest Ike and Victoria Veronica

I was never what you said I was, I the black. Which means that you were never what you thought you were. And I can prove it, because I watched you when you did not see me.

—JAMES BALDWIN

It's in black men despite the reasons society says they're not supposed to have it . . . what you have is somebody who is fearless and who is comfortable with that fearlessness. It's not about meanness. It's a kind of self-flagellant resistance to certain kinds of control, which is fascinating.

—TONI MORRISON

CONTENTS

ACKNOWLEDGMENTS

FIRST, I thank God for giving me all the (in)tangibles I needed to complete this project and make it thus far in life and my career. Everything I do and am is through Him!

IN THE early phases of developing this book, I was lucky to have scholars to consult with who believed in the significance of this project as not only an intellectual endeavor, but also as a cultural project about the insights, persistence, and intelligence of African American men. In this vein, I am indebted to Professors Valerie Lee, Patrick B. Mullen, and Lewis Ulman at The Ohio State University for providing support, feedback, and invaluable advice; also, my friend and colleague Vandana S. Gavaskar for encouraging me to pursue my vision for this book.

My colleagues in the English Department at Washington State University were extremely supportive as I completed this book project. Here, I want to express deep appreciation to colleagues who provided various feedback as I worked on this project: Peter Chilson and Debbie Lee welcomed me into their writing circle, read chapters, and shared their insights. Not only am I appreciative of Peter's and Debbie's collegiality, I value them as friends who listened and gave sound advice and for being available for great conversations. In later stages of development, Carol Siegel, Donna Campbell, and Desiree Hellegers pushed me to refine my arguments and develop my ideas. Thabiti Lewis and Pavithra Narayanan provided moral support as I worked feverishly to complete this project. Thank you Sue Shipman, a manager in the Holland/Terrell Library, for assisting me in locating the necessary texts to complete this and other research projects. Thank you to my former students Shavon Hayes, Terrence Lee, Khalil Pettway, and Nahom Abraha, whose intellectual curiosity motivated me to create challenging independent studies in which theirs and my projects blossomed. Most importantly, I want to acknowledge the late WSU President Elson S. Floyd whose leadership and commitment to higher education remains with me in Carter G. Woodson's words, "the mere imparting of information is not education."

Outside of WSU, conversations about race, subjectivity, and sexuality with Professors Fred Moten, Warren Carson, and the late John E. Maxwell and Rudolph P. Byrd ignited my thinking as I worked to realize the potential of this project. Dr. John S. Foster's fantastic production of August Wilson's and James Baldwin's plays inspired me to investigate literary representations of African American masculinity and subjectivity.

Once OSU Press accepted my manuscript, I learned the important roles that acquisition and managing editors play in transforming the typed manuscript into a published book. I especially appreciate Sandy Crooms for accepting my manuscript and sending it out for the first reviews. Unfortunately, Sandy left OSU Press after the initial reviews were returned; however, Lindsay Martin readily moved my project through the review process and to contract. Her expertise and availability made all the difference in my experience publishing this book. Also, Tara Cyphers patiently and professionally guided me through the editorial production process. OSU Press obtained insightful and intelligent scholars that were simultaneously encouraging and tough-minded, and in this way they assisted me in increasing the rewards of this book in the final revisions.

A well-known African American literary scholar expressed the following sentiment about trust, sincerity, and accountability in the academia. To paraphrase her, always remember your friends and family are outside the academy. While I don't wholeheartedly accept her opinion, as I have made friends in the academy, I understand her perspective. On many occasions, I turned to my "homies," E. Miles Sr. and Jermaine Sullivan, for support. Other friends who heartened me during critical times include April Scott and Christine McClain. Tina Hayes grounded and reminded me to remember the significance of my work and the Hayes' treated me like "Family." Thank you Nordia Daley for keeping me sane through the tenure track process. Thank you Melinda Bogarty for being the best friend a "brotha" can ask for!

Most important, I would not have undertaken this project, much less completed it, without the love and support of my family. My parents, to whom this book is dedicated, inspired me to pursue a career as a scholar. I don't think they realize how much the way they conducted themselves in their lives and their careers—with honesty, dignity, and courage—inspired me in my career. My siblings (Veronica, Daniel, and Mardella), thank you for understanding the commitment that completing this project required and for forgiving me (at times even encouraging me to go home and write) when I missed family gatherings. My niece, Zipporah, and nephews, Ian, Josef, Zyaire, and Ethan, and extended family served as inspiration as I completed graduate school and this book. In closing, I only hope that my family and friends accept this book as a down payment on the enormous debt that I owe them.

INTRODUCTION

Negotiating

"Innocence," "Romance," and the Discursive Divide

> You come from a sturdy, peasant stock, men who picked cotton and dammed rivers and built railroads, and in the teeth of the most terrifying odds, achieved an unassailable and monumental dignity.
>
> —JAMES BALDWIN, *THE FIRE NEXT TIME* (1995, 10)

> TM: Because they are fabulous! They're fabulous! There ain't nothing like them on the earth! Nothing!
>
> Q: But why do we have such a bad time?
>
> TM: Because of that. You don't know how fabulous you are. It's like the adage goes, "If you knew who you are, you would get up off your knees!" [laughter].
>
> —TONI MORRISON, *CONVERSATIONS WITH TONI MORRISON* (1994A, 121)

BLACK MEN and their experiences have been variously ignored, idealized, demonized, and forced into categories against which they must continually struggle to resist and strive to put behind them. The fiction of James Baldwin and Toni Morrison engages this daily work of crossing what I call "the discursive divide," of moving from being the object of discourse to an empowered agent.[1] As the epigraphs above suggest, although black men

1. The long tradition of theories about black male subjectivity is beyond the scope of this introduction, but two significant figures should suffice to illuminate the scholarship that primarily examines the black and white dialectic. Consider W. E. B. Du Bois and Frantz Fanon, who both analyze the slippage between self and other or oppressed and oppressor (Du Bois's "double consciousness" and Fanon's "fact of blackness"). Du Bois's double consciousness achieves its meaning exactly as the agent of dual meanings: African and African American and slave and freedman. Insofar as double consciousness provides a theoretical lens for engaging the contentious or strained historical and social relationship between the black and white worlds, Du Bois charts double consciousness as having an origin in slavery through emancipation. Fanon is mostly concerned with how black males experience their blackness or black skin

are marginalized in society, Baldwin and Morrison believe that black men have access to discursive strategies that enable them to resist oppression and overcome obstacles that they encounter on a daily basis. In this book, I will explore the rhetorical strategies that the black male characters in the writings of Baldwin and Morrison employ as they move or negotiate among discourses of race, class, gender, and sexuality, navigating the discursive divide that separates representations of black men in dominant discourses from a decolonized and empowered subjectivity. On one side of the discursive divide are the dominant constructions about black men that emerged from Eurocentric descriptions of Africa as primitive and culturally underdeveloped and of Africans as childlike and illiterate. Within American society, these negative representations circulate through laws, stereotypes (depictions of black men as brutes, rapists, Uncle Toms), and visual texts (movies, television, and the Internet) that marginalize black men, creating an invisible boundary between how black men are seen, imagined, and experienced in dominant culture and how they understand themselves in American society.

Across the discursive divide, African American men are free to realize not an essential self, but a complex self that is aware of both racialized discourses about black humanity and African American cultural discourses about survival, resiliency, and achievement. Homi Bhabha's third space is a starting place for thinking about this side of the discursive divide, but it is inadequate to fully capture the journey across the discursive divide as a liberating quest. Bhabha's third space describes where oppressed and oppressor come together (even momentarily) without expectations and invest in their own and are interested in each other's "particularity." In *Location of Culture,* Bhabha's third space is non-constitutive, arbitrary, and not defined by colonial discourse. It is the realm of the beyond or the moment of transit where space and time cross to produce complex figures of difference and identity, past and present, inside and outside, and inclusion and exclusion, "a third space—where the negotiation of incommensurable differences creates a tension peculiar to borderline existence" (Bhabha 2012, 312). In this space, individuals experience disorientation and a disturbance of direction.

Bhabha's third space is a fact for much of contemporary diasporic people and cultures. Similar to Bhabha's third space, I define the subjectivity construction process as a difficult and demanding one not only because the dominant culture expects African American men to behave as if they are second-class citizens, but also because the dominant culture wants them to ignore their feelings of class, political, and racial alienation. However, unlike Babha's third

and the debilitating effects of racism. Racism fragments the black self. The fact of blackness and double consciousness plays out in the lives of Baldwin's and Morrison's male characters.

space, I consider a subjectivity construction process that envisions subjects moving beyond colonial or racialized discourses to a space where they are free to define themselves or articulate their subjectivity in any way they choose. Since African American men have served America in many ways (as a major labor force, fought in many American wars, and entertained in places they weren't allowed to patronize), I argue that residing in a third space where subalterns frequently must negotiate colonial discourses isn't the final desire for African American men. African American men don't want to live in empty spaces, static time, closed borders where they meet resistance each time. They want self-definition, self-hood, and communal consciousness.

These objectives, I argue, inform Baldwin's and Morrison's black male subjects. Their black male subjects (including Paul D Garner, Gabriel Grimes, Macon Milkman Dead, Leo Proudhammar, William "Son" Green, and Alonzo "Fonny" Hunt) perceive the cultural dissonance they encounter in society as an opportunity to construct a counter subjectivity that will enable them to negotiate the discursive divide. Once they cross the discursive divide, Baldwin's and Morrison's black male characters demonstrate an awareness of how they are socially, culturally, and geographically positioned in society. They are strategic about when and how they want to appropriate and subvert dominant ideologies, and they show an awareness of how whiteness functions as a system of particular social, political, and economic privileges predicated on particular historical and cultural constructs, attitudes, and assumptions. Lastly, they acknowledge that whiteness undermines the extended black family structure and exacerbates the animosity or contention between black men and women. After crossing the discursive divide, Baldwin's and Morrison's black male subjects no longer see themselves as isolated objects of legal, economic, and material conditions but as subjects and as members of families and communities. Crossing the discursive divide is, then, implicitly or explicitly a gateway toward participation in community building and collective struggles for racial injustice.

This chapter explores black male inscription and resistance, but not to systematically trace the multiple ways dominant discourses define black men, review all the nuances of racial inscription, or examine the multiple ways black male characters resist racialized language. Instead, it is to argue that Baldwin's and Morrison's black male subjects are positioned in a discursive divide, which they must jump over or pass through in order to realize an empowered black complex self. While the individual chapters in this book explore the strategies of resistance that Baldwin's and Morrison's black male subjects employ to construct counter discourses about themselves and their experiences, this introduction describes the narratives and ideologies that comprise the discursive divide and the places or spaces where black male subjects have the greatest possibility for change or opposition.

However, before exploring the discursive spaces where opposition occurs, I make three important rhetorical moves: I establish a critical context for my discussion by defining the critical terms that are essential to my study of black male subjectivity construction. While I draw on postmodern renderings of subjectivity as non-static and always changing, I privilege articulations of subjectivity that are concerned with the conditions or predicaments of black subjectivity, as these scholars always define it as a product of the African American experience and announced by the vernacular (as I detail later). Secondly, I argue that strategies of resistance are timeless. Not only do strategies of resistance defy Western concepts of time, objectivity, and history as linear, but they are also social, political, linguistic, and non-linguistic and are crucial in contesting socially and historically dominant discourses, including innocence and romance that pose a threat to black men's quest for self-realization. Thirdly, besides showing how black male subjects oppose all discursive positions that cast them as Other, I suggest that Baldwin and Morrison challenge heteronormativity (the normalization of heterosexuality) by presenting intimacy between men on a continuum that does not restrict it to sexual expression. My objective here is to address in simple terms the following: how do Baldwin's and Morrison's black male subjects contend with ideological barriers of race, class, gender, and sexuality as they attempt to cross the discursive divide?

Rather than delve into the murky and dangerous territory of attempting to determine intentionality, I instead argue that Baldwin and Morrison represent strategies of resistance that directly critique and respond to discourses of innocence and romance in the lives of black men. In positing whiteness as an ideology, Baldwin and Morrison resituate whiteness from its unspoken (perhaps unspeakable) status to displace and replace it. They show how whiteness operates in particular locales and webs of social relations. They situate whiteness(es) in time and space, tracing rather than merely asserting its embeddedness in particular histories and class formations, in masculinity and femininity. Together, they explain how whiteness moves from its state of innocence to romance and from its state of romance to innocence.

By juxtaposing these two twentieth-century literary authors, it becomes clear, for instance, that Baldwin and Morrison are two of the most widely read and influential literary figures of the twentieth century, writers who in many ways have set the terms for other black fiction writers.[2] This notoriety

2. As "literary allies" and critics of each other's work, Baldwin and Morrison comment on each other's style and thematic concerns. Baldwin appreciates Morrison's use of allegory and

and respect is evident in the letter that prominent African American authors wrote to the *New York Times* to celebrate the life of James Baldwin and protest the omission of Toni Morrison's *Beloved* from the National Book Award and National Book Critics Circle Award. In addition, in their nonfiction, Baldwin and Morrison articulate the inner workings of the dominant discourses that marginalize black male subjects and define black male subjectivity in opposition to hegemonic masculinity. This comparative analysis of Baldwin and Morrison therefore sheds light on how black subjugation is maintained through rhetorical practices that enable white Americans to benefit from racism without having to take responsibility for black oppression.

Besides being influential African American authors, there are other reasons for doing this comparative study. Although a considerable amount of literary criticism exists on the different novels I examine, only a handful of scholars have attempted to compare Baldwin and Morrison's art and imagination.[3] This critical oversight is quite surprising given the similarity and

myth, and Morrison appreciates Baldwin's insights into the intimate relationships between African American men and women (Baldwin 1989, 284; Morrison 1994a, 77). Their fiction draws on the narrative genres of African American music (*Jazz* and "Sonny's Blues"); moreover, biblical names, events, and Christian experiences are central storylines or themes (*The Bluest Eye, Song of Solomon, Go Tell It on the Mountain,* and *The Amen Corner*). In incorporating the African American folk tradition as narrative structures of the African American experience, Baldwin and Morrison use African American linguistic traditions to articulate perspectives from within the African American context.

Both writers focus on the hermeneutics of African American language and experience as the key to constructing subjectivities. Baldwin argues for African American emphasis on rhetorical performances of subjectivities: "I realize that it was a cadence; it was not a question of dropping s's or n's or g's, but a question of the beat" (Baldwin 1989, 4). Similarly, Morrison says that black language is more than the use of "'dis and dat'; it is the way words are put together, the metaphors, the rhythm, the music—that's the part of the language that is distinctly black to me when I hear it" (Morrison 1994a, 96).

3. Only recently have authors begun to examine the literary friendship between Baldwin and Morrison and the thematic similarities within their works. Lovalerie King and Lynn Orilla Scott's coedited *James Baldwin and Toni Morrison: Comparative Critical and Theoretical Essays* (2006) is an important collection for any Baldwin and Morrison project; however, this comparative collection lacks an essay on black male subjectivities and contains only one essay that is devoted to black masculinity. In addition, there are several journal articles and edited collections (which are the most recent studies) devoted to exploring the literary, social, and cultural insights of Baldwin and Morrison. For example, other recent examinations—*James Baldwin Now* (1999), edited by Dwight McBride, and *The Cambridge Companion to Toni Morrison* (2007), edited by Justine Tally—draw on literary or postmodern paradigms to look at Baldwin's or Morrison's fiction and nonfiction: examining a specific theme (i.e., sexuality, gender) or incorporating a creative expression (jazz, blues, folklore). La Vinia Delois Jennings's recent book *Toni Morrison and the Idea of Africa* (2008) and Katherine Lawrence Balfour's *The Evidence of Things Not Said: James Baldwin and the Promise of American Democracy* (2001) examine Baldwin's and Morrison's fiction in relationship to larger cultural histories and experiences. Roland Murray (2007), Robert F. Reid Pharr (2007), and Andrew Shin and Barbara Jud-

complexity of Baldwin's and Morrison's art, imagination, and treatments of subjectivity. To date there isn't a single monograph that launches an extended comparative analysis of Baldwin's and Morrison's canons. The one coedited collection, *James Baldwin and Toni Morrison: Comparative Critical and Theoretical Essays,* by Lovalerie King and Lynn Orilla Scott includes two essays on masculinity that explore folkloric archetypes as the origin for black masculinity and counter heteronormative subjectivities. However, critics haven't adequately examined what Baldwin and Morrison perceive as rhetorical threats to the construction of black male subjectivity, and they have overlooked the discursive strategies that Baldwin's and Morrison's black male characters employ to define themselves in a society that is antagonistic to black men and their experiences.

Studying Baldwin's and Morrison's canons together also helps illuminate their shared commitment to using nonfiction as a platform for their deliberations on liberation, racial domination, and intracultural communication. "Supplement" is a useful concept for considering the complex and intricate relationship between their fiction and nonfiction. Taken from *Of Grammatology,* the concept "supplement" places binaries "sous rature" (under erasure) while identifying a shared and irrevocable relationship between two quantities. Derrida's notion of "supplement" proposes that two quantities complete, define, and give depth and significance to each other without undermining

son (1998) examine how Baldwin and Morrison challenge gender, identity, and sexual politics. Trudier Harris's *Black Women in the Fiction of James Baldwin* (1985) explores the function of historical and social discourses in the lives of his characters and the performance of sexuality. In this regard, Harris is an important text that must be consulted in any major project on Baldwin and black feminism.

Morrison has received a significant amount of attention from feminist critics. The black male characters and experiences are mostly read as ancillary to the female characters and experiences. In fact, some of the most recent essay titles indicate the extent to which women and women's experiences are placed at the center of the critiques: "'As if word magic had anything to do with the courage it took to be a man': Black Masculinity in Toni Morrison's *Paradise*" by Andrew Read (2005) and "To Love and Be Loved: Considering Black Masculinity and the Misandric Impulse in Toni Morrison's *Beloved*" by Nancy Kang (2003). In addition, Susan Neal Mayberry's *Can't I Love What I Criticize?: The Masculine and Morrison* (2007) is a close read of several of Morrison's male characters. Mayberry explores the complexity of Morrison's black male characters but does not examine the rhetorical strategies they employ to construct themselves as men. Missing from the critical analyses of the Baldwin and Morrison corpus is how the male characters attempt to fashion subjectivities beyond negative stereotypes of black male identity. The absence of an exploration of how African American male characters survive social racism and construct their own subjectivities reinforces arguments that support traditional misunderstandings of black male subjectivities. Without positing alternative ways that black male characters construct subjectivities, one could easily assume that subverting or internalizing stereotypes is the only possibility for African American subjectivities.

each other's significance. Derrida writes, "the supplement supplements. It adds only to replace. It intervenes itself in the place of; if it fulfills, it is as if one fills a void. If it represents and makes an image, it is by the anterior default of a presence" (Derrida 1997, 145). Derrida's notion of "supplement" is a suggestive theory for discussing the relationship between Baldwin's and Morrison's nonfiction and fiction at multiple levels and as cultural projects.

Baldwin's and Morrison's cultural project is to explore subjectivity construction through language and material experiences. What may appear to be gendered or stereotypical performances for black men could constitute active resistance. The extent to which their black male subjects are able to construct and maintain a positive self-identity establishes the limitations and possibilities of manhood. "Play" best captures this relationship because it accounts for the economy between black male subjectivity and dominant discourses and black male subjectivity and material experiences. Play, according to Derrida, is "a metaphor of energy—where two opposed forces playing against each other constitute the so-called identity of a phenomenon" (Derrida 1997, xlii). Baldwin sees self-creation as a combination of resolve and determination: "You have to impose, in fact—this may sound very strange—you have to decide who you are, and force the world to deal with you, not with its idea of you" (Baldwin 1989, 5–6). For Morrison, a crucial component of black men self-creation is the ability to identify the locations of real social threats: "We've had to distinguish among you [white people] because our lives depended on it. I'm always annoyed about why black people have to bear the brunt of everybody else's contempt" (Morrison 1994a, 256). Although black men "bear the brunt of everybody else's contempt" and recreate themselves against experiences of being black, they struggle (sometimes successfully) to construct a life for themselves and their family members. This struggle demonstrates the central concern of their fiction.

Before I articulate how the discursive divide functions in Baldwin's and Morrison's writings, I will first discuss the terms that are significant to this study: hegemonic masculinity, subjectivity, positionality, and materiality. Besides enhancing the theoretical framework for this book, these terms provide a way to understand the sociopolitical character of the discursive spaces that black men occupy within and without African American communities. The fact is that these terms resist resolution and a single definition is a source of strength not weakness. Resistance to closure makes possible the ongoing mediation of meaningful, legitimate difference.

RESISTING SUBJECTIVICATION

Hegemonic masculinity refers to white male subjectivity construction, which occurs at the expense of African American men, culture, families, and communities. Scholars borrow the concept hegemony from Antonio Gramsci's prison writings. While in an Italian prison in the 1930s, Gramsci developed a complex theory for mapping inequalities that amplify contemplations on race, class, and gender. As Gramsci argues, hegemony endures primarily through the ruling groups winning the consent of the subaltern, lower class. Hegemony is always fragile because the dominant group must convince others of its legitimacy, even as subaltern groups struggle to resist their own marginalization. Hegemonic domination occurs when the dominant group persuades others of a particular rational perspective of society that confirms their social status but appears to be neutral and natural. In terms of whiteness, many have struggled to make hegemonic ideals appear natural, particularly through positioning it as normative—racially neutral, American. This normalizing occurs through laws, social behaviors, and institutional treatment. As Gramsci wrote, the dominant culture's real strength does not lie in its ability to exercise violence but through the ideologies passed through its institutions. Ideologies produce and continue the common sense that rationalizes and integrates inequalities of race, class, and gender into a larger structure of hegemonic control.

Contemporary scholars have imported Gramsci's hegemony to develop their own theories about inequality. For example, R. W. Connell introduces the concept of hegemonic masculinity to explain how men, depending on their race, class, and sexuality, are positioned in society in relation to the hegemonic, or accepted, ideal of masculinity (Connell 2005, 79). Within this system of gender relations many African American men find themselves marginalized or forbidden from pursuing, achieving, and enjoying the social benefits or freedoms that are typically related to being a man or to masculinity. African American masculinity openly or indirectly challenges hegemonic masculinity by embracing competing strategies that allow men to redefine and embody masculinity. However, they don't always resist accepted expressions of hegemonic masculinity, but instead embrace the existing system of dominant masculinity. In this sense, they are complicit within the logic of hegemonic masculinity—accepting the dominant definition of masculinity with the belief that they will benefit from it or because they accept black male inferiority as commonsense. Thus, although African American men are positioned differently because of their race and/or sexuality, they, to some degree, gain some advantages from the overall structure of masculinity, which sanctions physical aggression and intellectual manipulation to maintain power over women.

I adapt Connell's paradigm to explore how hegemonic masculinity and the discourses of whiteness frame Baldwin's and Morrison's representation of the experiences of black men. Whiteness, like masculinity, consists of ideologies that, because of cultural difference and experiences such as race, class, and gender, locate whites as the hegemonic ideal of masculinity. While not all white men represent these standards, given differences with respect to class status and sexual preferences, they have access to capital, employment, and technology. Detailing how class and sexuality, for example, define men outside of hegemonic masculinity would necessitate an exhaustive examination of multiple masculinities and subjectivities, which is clearly not within the scope of this project. Instead, I am concerned with how the rhetorical strategies of oppression that are inherent in practices of hegemonic masculinity impact black men's decision-making processes on a number of levels, with implications that, at their most acute level, bear on questions or matters of life and death.

Aligned with Marxists, feminists, and postcolonial articulations that take into consideration the paradox, contradictions, and the culturally unspoken assumptions that define the subject, Baldwin's and Morrison's representations of subjectivity and positionality highlight how images, history, memories, and experiences coalesce to form one's self-image. One's subject position is mostly designated by dominant discourses, but redefined or challenged by the subject. Thus, when I use the terms subjectivity and positionality, I am not conflating these concepts nor am I making rigid distinctions. I understand subjectivity to account for the shifting consciousness of an individual and positionality to refer to the physical, social, or metaphorical space characters purposefully or unintentionally occupy or are placed in at a given time. Subjectivity refers to a subject's shifting consciousness.

In treating black male subjectivity as a process (always changing), this book has been deeply influenced by work in history, sociology, literary theory, and cultural studies that treats subjectivity construction as a contested arena. Louis Althusser's notion of interpellation as the linguistically mediated process through which individuals become subject to the ideology of the dominant culture provides the best theoretical framework for discussing the relationship between language and ideology. Althusser writes, "I shall then suggest that ideology 'acts' or functions in such a way that it recruits subjects among the individuals (it recruits them all), or transforms individuals into subjects (it transforms them all) by that very precise operation which I have called interpellation or hailing and which can be imagined along the lines of the most commonplace everyday police (or other) hailing: 'Hey, you there!'" (Althusser 1994, 144). The response to being hailed is automatic. Through the act of hailing, individuals are transformed into subjects. Subjects learn to imagine time, space, and other experiential domains in ways that have become conventional within their community. In the process, some individuals surrender to these ways of imagining their experiences without, necessarily, becoming permanent prisoners to them.

Frantz Fanon's writings demonstrate the significance of interpellation as a domination of the racially marked subject through the white gaze, leading to a problematic sense of self. In Fanon's articulation of racial interpellation, the black body enters into the symbolic order where it is already pathologized, criminalized, and degenerated. By replacing Althusser's hypothetical "hailing" of the police scene with an event from his life, Fanon describes an encounter with a young white boy who points at him and yells, "'Mama, see the Negro! I'm frightened!' Frightened! Frightened! Now they were beginning to be afraid of me" (1967, 112). Besides emphasizing the always already-existing imaginary visual and symbolic discourses that subjectivate the black body, Fanon conveys the power of language and ideology to fix black bodies in a position where through a disciplinary hegemonic gaze a child (who presumably doesn't know about systemic racism) possesses the power to racialize the black body. The ease in which the child discursively determines Fanon's body also draws attention to the boy's subject position. By identifying Fanon with the same racial logic that colonizers and slaveholders employed to create the darker Other, the boy encircles himself in white privilege and marks himself as more superior to Fanon and other racially different subjects. As a result of this type of racializing, Fanon and Other black subjects speak from an oppressive but ironically advantageous subjugated position. Donna Haraway maintains that "subjugated standpoints . . . promise more adequate, sustained, objective, transforming accounts of the world," noting that "how to see from below is a problem requiring at least as much skill with bodies and language, with the mediations of vision as the highest technoscientific visualizations" (1988, 584). Black male subjectivity refers to the cultural, social, political, and psychological processes that shape and situate subjects in the world. I consider how the black self was denied autonomy or self-consciousness and was defined by the social and cultural situation in which the black subject was placed—in slavery, chain gangs, dilapidated communities, and low social status in America.

One's subjective position is always constrained by others and always changes, which is especially true for African American men whose subjective position has been defined and redefined since slavery. Unfortunately, this process of subjectification occurs to some black men at a much too early age—before they develop a sense of self or an understanding about themselves and their place in the world. Baldwin states, "When a Negro child is fourteen, he knows the score already. There is nothing you can do. And all you can do about it is try . . . is pray really that this will not destroy him. But the tension that this creates within the best of the Negro men is absolutely unimaginable, and something this country refuses to imagine, and very, very dangerous" (1989, 9). Morrison picks up on the resistance that black men confront as they struggle to live in a country that celebrates masculinity but devalues black manhood. Morrison focuses on the weight of oppression: "Black men . . . are reacting to . . . external pressures . . . For one thing they have an enormous responsibility to be men. There's something very large in that word. Men define masculinity by other men" (1994a, 7). While it appears that Morrison and Baldwin are making distinct arguments about black male resistance (Baldwin suggests black men should look within themselves for a strategy of resistance, and Morrison argues that black men find resistance in the company of other men), they both argue that black men shouldn't rely on others for definition or recognition and for the importance of discerning society from a black male perspective. The black male characters in Baldwin's and Morrison's fiction struggle to have their own experiences validated in a world that is openly hostile and violent to them, their families, communities, and institutions. In this sense, black male subjectivity is rooted in the experiences of subjugation and violence.

Baldwin's and Morrison's use of subjectivity and positionality highlights the connections between intentionality, subjectivity, and objectivity. While many of Baldwin's and Morrison's characters thrive despite racism or social alienation, some refuse to live under the constraints of racism. Baldwin's character Rufus, a jazz musician, jumps off a bridge to his death rather than live in a racist society, and Morrison's Milkman leaps off a cliff into the arms of his brother. In both instances, the black male subjects sacrifice their lives to be free, embracing suicide as an act of resistance. However, death doesn't release individuals from language. In fact, in *Another Country*, the act distinguishes Rufus from the other characters in the novel, who remember him as someone who succumbed to social oppression. Thus, the other characters couldn't imagine Rufus's suicide as an act of resistance. Freeing oneself from language is impossible, considering how individuals (including members of the dominant culture) are inscribed by multiple discourses and benefit from the deep structure (rules that underlie usage) of language. To Baldwin and Morrison, language is rich with racial coding that benefits or privileges white subjects, placing them outside of the confines of laws and alleviating them of their social responsibility to black subjects. Baldwin's and Morrison's tropes of innocence and romance, respectively, are examples of how language perpetuates racial oppression at a level of awareness that is often unrecognized by writers and speakers.

Materiality, another significant critical term in this study, refers to the physical and economic conditions by which society oppresses black men, barring, for example, access to employment, living wage jobs, and equal education. Baldwin and Morrison represent the materiality of black men's lives across regions, communities, and institutions in America. Most concerned with the contradictions between the letter of the law and black men's material experiences, Baldwin and Morrison depict how, throughout the late twentieth century, though they were legally free, the material conditions of African Americans' lives evinced little improvement since the era of legalized slavery. State and federal governments passed civil rights laws and promoted liberties for blacks; however, city, state, and county authorities didn't enforce them. This inequality impeded African Americans' progress and further defined them as second-class citizens. Black Codes (laws to discourage vagrancy in the South) were used in horrifying ways to imprison innocent African American men and force them into chain gangs that basically replicated the experience of slavery. In addition, rulings such as *Plessy vs. Ferguson 1896* legislated "separate but equal" in public spaces but in fact sanctioned the institutionalization of separate and highly unequal conditions.

In Baldwin's and Morrison's writings, however, black men meet Houston Baker's "legal Xing" with discernment and fortitude (1995, 35). They focus on the disparity between legal definitions and representations of black men and their own self-images, and they draw on a legacy of resistance that is endemic to African American experiences. After Baldwin left America, he gained a sense of agency, recognizing, "If I can do it, I may do it. . . . [B]ut in the years I grew up in the U.S., I could not do that. I'd already been defined" (1989, 236). Morrison focuses on black men's ability to endure challenging circumstances. She writes, "There is a certain amount of feistiness in black men that nobody has been able to wipe out. But, everybody has tried" (1994, 18). Black men change their surroundings and look inward for strength and self-actualization. These quotes suggest that social oppression arrests black men's agency, but it doesn't prevent them from realizing a sense of self, from reimagining themselves and their relationships to larger discourses and social struggles. In a very real way, the constraints that dominant society places on black men forces them to deconstruct their social status and plan an approach for survival and—ultimately—for justice.

Internalized hate manifests as fear, desire, and violence in Baldwin's and Morrison's writings. For example, in Baldwin's *Another Country,* Rufus, a frustrated musician, accepts that he will never realize his dream to be a successful jazz artist. At once succumbing to his pain and embracing what seems his only pathway to freedom, he jumps off a bridge to his death, as discussed previously. Neither his sister nor friends can save him from his own feelings of inferiority. In *The Amen Corner* and *Sonny's Blues*, Baldwin's characters combat sorrow with music and Christian teachings. The degrees of sexism and color consciousness within Morrison's black fictional communities in *Paradise* and *The Bluest Eye* represent two manifestations of internalized racism: intergenerational shame and self-loathing. Projecting self-hate onto black women in the form of physical and psychological abuse, the black male characters replay white racism and misogyny in the African American context. The black male characters attack the black female characters, revealing their own insecurities about being black and male in a racist society. The black men in *Paradise* violently attack the women in the convent to protect their role as patriarchs in their families and communities. The men's actions are unforgivably hateful and misogynistic. *The Bluest Eye* provides another example of how black men perform internalized racism as phallocentric aggression and self-loathing. Morrison depicts elementary school–age black boys dancing around Pecola, teasing her about the color of her skin, which makes her feel inferior. The actions of the men in *Paradise* and the boys in *The Bluest Eye* represent racism's lasting effects, even when no noticeable occurrences of discrimination are happening, or when the lives of individuals seem distant from larger, structural expressions of racism.

Black men possess the greatest possibilities of change or transformation when they carefully and incisively interrogate their subject position. Confronting this ideological nexus presents an opportunity to move against oppressive boundaries of race, sex, and class domination. As one moves "out of one's place," bell hooks states, one must consider and recognize "the realities of choice and location" (1990, 45). Choosing to move from a place of oppression to one of liberation means that one merges the political with the personal and accepts the legal and social benefits and ramifications of representing themselves as conscious black subjects. As Baldwin's and Morrison's black male characters acquire consciousness of self, society, and community, they reflect on the effectiveness of their survival strategies.

DIACHRONIC SUBJECTIVITIES

This discursive divide challenges Western concepts of time and death that our existence is limited, death itself connotes temporality as well as the nature of human subjectivity. In his definition of the individual human subject, Martin Heidegger asserts that "no one can relieve the other of his own dying" (1992, 310). Similarly, Jacques Derrida observes in the *Gift of Death* "Death is very much that which nobody else can undergo or confront in my place. My irreplaceability is therefore conferred delivered, given one can say, by death" (1995, 41). Finally, Zora Neal Hurston writes, "Two things everybody's got tuh do fuh theyselves. They got tuh go tuh God, and they got tuh find out about livin' fuh theyselves" (1990, 205). Baldwin and Morrison construct a counter-discourse to Heidegger's, Derrida's, and Hurston's claim that human subjectivity and individuality depends on the unshareability of death or that death is the grand equalizer that one experiences individually and alone. In exploring black male experiences in various material and psychological struggles (the fight for humanity, freedom, civil rights, social and legal equality, family, and community), Baldwin and Morrison present black subjects as inhabiting what Orlando Patterson (1982) refers to as a "social death," a terminal state that black men experience across historical periods. Suffering from a social death (not accepted as fully human by the wider fictional society), black men represent a peculiar kind of atemporality, or not being in time. An unchangeable social condition for black men over time in the United States permits them to share death. This keen awareness of shared mortality (the predictability of one's own and one's family and community members' deaths in and across time) is perhaps the most profound and stirring thematic thread in African American literature—and in African American history.

Synchronic examinations of black masculinity (such as Rolland Murray's *Of Our Living Manhood*, Martin Anthony Summer's *Manliness and Its Discontents*, and Darieck Scott's *Extravagant Abjection*, to name a few) that represent the material experiences of black men within a given era or literary period provide an opportunity for us to examine the structural relationship between masculinities and the survival strategies of men within a particular historical and material context. However, diachronic analyses highlight the significant similarities of rhetorical strategies and creative expressions over time. Although there were some changes to how black men were viewed in eras ranging from the colonial period to post-war America, the dominant ideological constructions of black men remain the same. In response to this predicament, black men revise rhetorical strategies to address the specific threats that the conditions within a particular era pose to black humanity, freedom, and progress. Baldwin and Morrison demonstrate this when they incorporate a trope or creative expression from earlier texts in their novels. As evidence of this, one can consider the reappearance and function of rhetorical strategies (like signifying, the dozens, and sermons) and creative expressions (i.e., folktales, slave quilts, and soul food) in fiction. The trope of the mask appears in

Langston Hughes's poem "We Were the Mask" published in the 1920s (Hughes 1959) and in Baldwin's *Tell Me How Long the Train's Been Gone* published in 1940. At the turn of the century, Du Bois wrote about sorrow songs in *Souls of Black Folk* and in 1987 Morrison incorporated them in her *Beloved.*

Such a temporal and political dynamic—of the past inhabiting the present—occurs throughout the African American literary tradition. In the late 18th and early 19th century, Phyllis Wheatley's poems in traditional Western style and forms and Frederick Douglass's and Harriet Jacob's narratives corresponding claim about styles and forms subverts the master-slave relationship and foreground literacy as a site for resistance. In protest literature, Ann Petry's and Richard Wright's novels object to constraints on human life and question the poor living and working conditions of black people. West and East Coast hip hop artists transform the themes and concerns from the protest tradition into verses and rhymes over music. Contemporary writer Colson Whitehead's explorations of identity and colorism are reminiscent of Harlem renaissance writers Zora Neal Hurston's and Wallace Thurman's concerns with how "passing" reveals the uncertainties of the constructedness of race. Spoken word or slam poetry artists' deliberations on social experience such as oppression, alienation, and disenfranchisement suggest the influence of Black Arts poets. Several African American literary artists, including Gwendolyn Brooks and Bebe Moore Campbell, revisit Emmett Till's murder, reminding readers that African American men like Trayvon Martin and Jordan Davis are still victims of racial violence.

In problematizing traditional understandings of time, subjectivity, humanity, and morality, Baldwin's and Morrison's novels challenge Aristotle's argument that time is the measure of change and that it cannot exist without change by marking time in accordance to how much social change has occurred for African Americans in America. Time, then, is based on African American progress as opposed to the era in which the novel is written or story takes place. In this way, the consciousness of the characters reflects the sentiments of real people within the African American community; many African Americans argue that their present feelings of oppression feel very much like their past experiences with oppression, and if change is not implemented the future will feel like the past and present. Dr. Martin Luther King Jr. speaks to this sentiment when he discuss why "wait" almost always means "never":

> For years now I have heard the word "wait." It rings in the ear of every Negro with a piercing familiarity. This wait has almost always meant "never." . . . I guess it is easy for those who have never felt the stinging darts of segregation to say "wait." But when you have seen vicious mobs lynch your mothers and

> fathers at will and drown your sisters and brothers at a whim . . . when you see the vast majority of your twenty million Negro brothers smothering in an airtight cage of poverty in the midst of an affluent society . . . then you will understand why we find it difficult to wait. (1994, 91)

The characters in Baldwin's and Morrison's novels echo King's concept of time in terms of changes in society or lived conditions when they speak about how theirs and other African American material conditions remain static. For example, in *Sonny's Blues* the narrator, a school teacher, reflects on how much he sacrificed to escape poverty: "But houses exactly like the houses of our past yet dominated the landscape, boys exactly like the boys we once had been found themselves smothering in these houses, came down into the streets for light and air and found themselves encircled by disaster. Some escaped the trap, most didn't. Those who got out always left something of themselves behind, as some animals amputate a leg and leave it in the trap" (1965, 112). In contrast, in Morrison's *Sula*, Jude complains about how difficult it is to make a living in a racially unjust society: "'Hey, Jude. What you know good?' 'White man running it—nothing good.' . . . 'Same old stuff,' he replied and told them a brief tale of some personal insult done him by a customer and his boss. . . . He ended it with the observation that a Negro man had a hard row to hoe in this world" (2004a, 102–3). Baldwin's and Morrison's male characters aren't static, and they find ways to improve their conditions despite the seemingly unchanging nature of their social and racial surroundings. Over and against a Deleuzian model of temporal suspension and "alterity," Baldwin's and Morrison's fiction—and, I argue, African American literature as a whole—must be read as "coeval," to use Johannes Fabian's anthropological term; that is, simultaneously occurring at the same time, being of the same era, and being influenced or influencing present-day canons, cultures, economies, and temporalities (Fabian 1993, 167; Deleuze 2007, 29).

ATEMPORAL SUBJECTIVITIES

One way to understand how rhetorical strategies transcend historical periods is through research in social learning theory, such as Lev Vygotsky's work on survival strategies, cultural mediation, and interpersonal communication. As a psychiatrist, Vygotsky argues that "language mediates knowledge, promotes thinking, develops reasoning, and supports cultural activities like reading and writing" (1978, 118). Through language, individuals learn to navigate the nuances of society. Language at its core is a communicative tool that evolves within a specific sociohistorical context. Vygotsky argues that children learn basic survival skills (riding bicycles, pouring glasses of water, and closing doors when leaving the room) through engaging in these activities every day in society. Experiencing racism is part of life for African Americans. Therefore, they must acquire effective (but non-threatening) survival strategies. Elaine Richardson's critical work on hip hop and Vorris L. Nunley's research on community literacies reminds us that African American rhetoric provides a way for individuals to safely and confidently situate themselves in a variety of nonviolent or non-threatening contexts. Without a doubt, Baldwin and Morrison know that individuals learn and refashion a survival strategy so that it fits their own needs within their specific material and historical circumstances.

Houston A. Baker provides a more culturally specific approach for considering African American subjectivity and rhetoric as atemporal. In *Blues, Ideology, and Afro-American Literature: A Vernacular Theory* (1984), Baker defines the vernacular as strategies for understanding the African American experience through the expression of the blues. Stressing the formal definition of the vernacular as referring to the localness and language of the slave or proletariat, Baker employs the term to connect his own critical methodology to the modes of knowledge of African American culture. My own use of the term is in line with critical traditions that intentionally privilege an African American worldview as the center of interpretation: folklore, literature, and rhetoric. My use of the term vernacular is guided by Baker's appropriation of the word as the practice of the powerless and those who speak a critical language grounded in local concerns, not the language of elites or academics that oftentimes comprise a discourse community that excludes the poor and the undereducated. Both localness and language point to the specific situation of vernacular theory that I want to stress. I use the term to speak to subjectivity formation as a cultural practice or way of knowing that originates from within African American contexts or consequence experiences.

By way of example, Baldwin and Morrison discuss constructing a critical perspective from African American history, creative expressions, and ruminants of their own experiences. Baldwin talks about drawing on the vernacular expression of music.

> Listening to Bessie Smith helped me to "recreate" a subjectivity that I had known as a child and from which I had spent so many years in flight. Bessie Smith, through her tone and her cadence . . . helped me to dig back to the way I myself must have spoken when I was a pickaninny, and to remember the things I had heard and seen and felt. I had buried them very deep. . . .

> I had never listened to Bessie Smith in America (in the same way that, for years, I never touched watermelon), but in Europe she helped me to reconcile myself to being a nigger. (1989, 4)

In the same way that the vernacular connects Baldwin to an African American way of understanding and perceiving, the vernacular connects Morrison to African American ways of feeling and imagining. Morrison suggests that drawing on the vernacular helps one to locate a position of power from which to speak about one's relationship to power and give one courage to remove the veil aside of "proceedings too terrible to relate." She continues that "these memories within" enable her to fill in the gaps with other recollections and her own imagination (1994a, 92). In incorporating the vernacular, Baldwin and Morrison represent an intense local commitment to the experiences that forge African American sensibilities.

I am arguing that the vernacular provides a critical term and approach for thinking about the atemporality and relationship between subjectivity and rhetoric. My observation of rhetoric as atemporal is confirmed by the most recent studies that present the African American rhetorical tradition across multiple generations. Geneva Smitherman argues that rhetoric is "language . . . a tool for ordering the chaos of human experience . . . a great amount of comfort comes from being able to 'name events and things' and that to use words to give shape and coherence to human existence is a universal human thing—a linguistic fact of life that transcends cultural boundaries" (1986, 77). This relationship between power and language determines who speaks, who listens, and what can be said about authority, supremacy, and dominance as evidenced by recent studies. In *African American Rhetoric(s): Interdisciplinary Perspectives,* edited by Elaine B. Richardson and Ronald L. Jackson II (2004), the authors cover a century and a half of thought. Scholars' engagement with African American rhetoric highlights the transcending qualities of language practices, *African American Rhetoric(s)* contain essays that historicize, suggest pedagogies, and illustrate contemporary research projects in African American rhetoric. By including essays that are concerned with the evolution and sociopolitical function of African American rhetoric, the editors present it as cultural practices that defy temporality as language practices for interrogating and challenging racialized discourses in public spaces across temporality.

In the introduction to *African American Rhetoric(s),* Keith Gilyard's survey of research in African American rhetoric is especially valuable because he shows how rhetorical strategies, expressions, and conventions are refitted to fight racism, sexism, and gender and sexual oppression. Gilyard highlights studies that examine anti-slavery speeches and sermons that appropriate traditional rhetorical conventions and (when necessary) subvert racially charged themes with a nationalist flavor in the Civil Rights and Black Power movements. Other essays in the collection explore rhetoric and the vernacular in law, technology, classrooms, and communities. From slavery to the present, African American rhetoric combines Western and Eastern rhetorical traditions with African American language and experiences to reach and persuade audiences.

Another important study on rhetorical strategies of resistance is Vershawn Ashanti Young's *Your Average Nigga: Performing Race, Literacy, and Masculinity,* which argues for language use that meshes or intermingles black English vernacular with standard American English. Code meshing provides a means for students to combine dialects, Englishes, and other languages with Standard English in formal writing and speaking contexts and in casual conversations. Young writes that code meshing "integrate[s] identity and linguistics," and it "links literacy to culture in a way that's more in line with how people actually speak and write" (2007, 713). "Code-meshing," he argues, "provides individuals a rhetorical way to push against the artificial ideological walls between language varieties" (xii). Intermingling Englishes and other languages with Standard English permits students to express their complex identities, experiences, and familial and cultural histories and represent themselves in various contexts without denying their home culture.

Vorris L. Nunley's *Keepin' It Hushed: The Barbershop and African American Hush Harbor Rhetoric* and "From the Harbor to Da Academic Hood: Hush Harbors and an African American Rhetorical Tradition" explores the geographical spaces and places where rhetorics "traverse generations and genres" (2011, 7). Hush harbors refer "to cane breaks, bush arbors or hush harbors" where they "untie their tongues, speak the unspoken, and sing their own songs to their own selves" (2004, 223). In hush harbors, slaves reinterpreted biblical stories, employed folklore, and communicated about political events (Civil War), social movements (abolition efforts), and cultural upheavals (rebellions and escape plans). Beyond slavery, hush harbor rhetoric takes place in barbershops, "beauty shops, African American sororities and fraternities, porches, taverns, and other sacred or secular Black spaces and places serve as geographies or sites of resistance where countless known and unknown Black bards temporarily escaped the hegemonic gaze of Whiteness to make themselves a world" (2004, 223). African Americans use rhetoric to explicate new racism as a socially constructed reality, one that integrates historical arguments about black inferiority with the contemporary practices of colorblind racial arguments.

To further underscore the time defying dimensions of rhetoric, I am concerned with subtle rhetorical strategies such as those used to fight for constitutional rights and employed to outmaneuver gatekeepers in institutions such as universities, corporations, and government. To this point, two groundbreaking early studies of African American rhetorical strategies represent rhetoric as subtle but powerful modes of persuasion and resistance. Haig and Hamida Bosmajian's *The Rhetoric of the Civil-Rights Movement* examines the effectiveness of non-violent protest sit-ins, freedom riders, picketing, marches, wade-ins, read-ins, and jail-in speeches, songs, and pamphlets to persuade the government to desegregate public spaces and institutions. Nonviolent protest privileges the strategy over the goals. Besides the will to defy and the capacity to resist as central to nonviolence, nonviolent strategies appeal to an individual's conscious and insist on seeing the self in the other as opposed to revenging physical assaults with violent aggression. Lastly, nonviolent strategies of resistance transform conflicts onto a plane of interaction entirely alternative to how the military recognizes the goals and missions accomplished. The object of nonviolent strategies is not to seek victory over the opponent, but rather conquest over the conflict that separates people from one another. Except for the few scenes in *Tell Me How Long the Train's Been Gone* where Leo Proudhammar and his lover Christopher support or participate in the Civil Rights and Black Power movements as speakers and organizers, Baldwin and Morrison mainly represent subtle strategies of resistance as the best defense against power.

This project builds on early and contemporary African American rhetoric research projects by investigating the multiple places and spaces within and without African American contexts where Baldwin's and Morrison's characters seek, retreat to, or are relegated to a particular region, occupation, or community where they find refuge in a hush harbor. In hush harbors, black male characters in Baldwin's and Morrison's novels are quite clearly engaged in the practice of crossing the discursive divide. They reflect on the power of the white gaze to define and deconstruct their bodies to the extent that they are mindful of their gestures and mannerisms, and they purposely and consciously manage their bodies (how they position their eyes, legs, hands, heads, etc.). In this state of hyperawareness of whiteness, they seek a break in dominant discourses, a place where they can employ liberatory discourse that would enable them to realize their potential.

The novels included in this study represent black male subjectivity construction across literary periods and beyond temporal and geographical borders or barriers and in multiple contexts and experiences with attention to slavery and its consequences, emancipation and its failures, the Great Migration and its promises, the pitfalls of assimilation and integration, Christian teachings, and nationalist ideologies. I include black male subjects at different ages and stages in life. They are slaves in the South, freedmen in the North, incarcerated in the North and alienated in the South, and socially conscious in the North and decultured in the South. The complex and multidimensional black male characters reflect on their responsibilities to their families, communities, and themselves. Ambitious and well intentioned, their black male characters are flawed subjects who struggle to rise from the most abject circumstances to relative peace, independence, and self-sufficiency and are united by their desire to completely cross the discursive divide.

INNOCENCE, ROMANCE, THE DISCURSIVE DIVIDE

While crossing the discursive divide, black subjects recognize whiteness as a social construction or an understanding of white subjects as a product of the social, economic, and political forces of a particular time period. Whiteness changes according to the historical period, but its primary function as the center of the structure of power remains the consistent position from which white subjects engage society, each other, and people of color. This understanding of the limitation of whiteness as the struggle to hang on to power and exercise power over non-white people is represented in David Roediger's *Black on White: Black Writers on What It Means to Be White* and Veronica Watson's *The Souls of White Folk: African American Writers Theorize Whiteness.* Besides highlighting the very seldom studied literary and scholarly tradition of African American writers decentering whiteness or turning the black gaze on white people and culture, Roediger's and Watson's books investigate the psychological and emotional impact of the racial divide on identity and subjectivity formation from the perspective of African Americans. While many African American writers turn their oppositional gaze on white people and culture, Baldwin and Morrison explore whiteness as a rhetorical strategy that maintains the spaces that exist between white identity and black subjectivity.

In "Whiteness: A Strategic Rhetoric," Thomas K. Nakayama and Robert L. Krizek argue for an understanding of whiteness as subtle discursive strategies or expressions between white subjects that reaffirm their power and social standing. Everyday interactions such as race-related asides in conversations, strategic eye contact, and jokes strategically situate and resituate whiteness as the center of social structures and confirm white subjectivity as the universal subject (1995, 298). Besides relating traditional (read racist) ways of thinking to the white subject, these "discursive strategies of whiteness" reinscribe white dominance or superiority in the absence of oppressive institutions like slavery and colonization. Unmarked racist rhetoric provides white Americans a way to benefit from or refuse to trade on their skin color without having to acknowledge their racial, social, or economic inequalities with African Americans. By way of example, very shortly after their arrival in the United States, European immigrants learn the "race talk" or "the negative appraisals of the native-born black population" (Morrison 1993, 57). Once they learn the rhetoric of "racial estrangement" not only do they complete the experience of assimilation, but, as Baldwin and Morrison demonstrate in their critical essays, immigrants also become representative of white privilege as a discourse on denial of or idealization of racial difference.

In "Stranger in the Village," James Baldwin explores how African American subjectivity experiences the practice of traditions that otherwise could be understood as racist (in the form of folklore traditions). In a remote Swiss village, the villagers have never set eyes on a black man; they do, however, have a folk festival where extremely Nordic-looking children paint their faces, wear horsehair wigs, and go door to door to collect money for the missionaries in Africa. The folklore festival gives the villagers knowledge about Africans but not experience, a condition that defines, for Baldwin, Western intellectual "innocence." In their representation as African children they embody the "saved" African children; however they remain innocent of their complicity in the conditions from which these children must be saved. When they see Baldwin, who is there writing *Giovanni's Room,* they exclaim "Neger! Neger!" When they see him sitting in the sun, they reach up and touch his hair and rub his arm to see if the color will come off. In the Swiss villagers' eyes Baldwin is an African demonstrating the results of "saving" or a historical anomaly—how can a savage so clearly in need of ministration be in the Swiss Alps living in a chalet as a writer? In these and other ways, "Stranger in the Village" is a tour de force into African American subjectivity.

Although the Swiss children that yell "Neger! Neger!" as Baldwin walks down the street do not realize how deeply these words penetrate his psyche, his readers become aware of the depths to which it affects him when he utters under his breath the same phrase he shouted at young New York white boys when he was younger: "your mother was a nigger" (1998b, 162). Baldwin is aware of two things: one, the Swiss boys do not mean any harm; and two, that "James Joyce is right about history being a nightmare—but it may be the nightmare from which no one can awaken. People are trapped in history and history is trapped in them" (163). In "Stranger in the Village," African American subjectivity is explored: How are Europeans able to remain innocent of a history that they are largely responsible for? What narrative do white Americans explain to themselves and each other about the complex history they share with African Americans? And how are African Americans positioned as the ones who must understand and negotiate white subjectivity?

From this vantage point, Baldwin and Morrison reread literary texts by white authors and point out a peculiar type of thinking about African American identity that does not represent how African Americans imagine themselves or their cultural experience. In *Playing in the Dark* and "Unspeakable Things Unspoken: The Afro-American Presence in American Literature," Morrison explores the literary and cultural implications of the discursive strategies that American literary authors employ to construct African American characters. Morrison argues that discursive strategies construct African American characters in one-dimensional, stereotypical, and dehumanizing ways through a careful reading of novels by Mark Twain and William Faulkner. The significance of Morrison's critical work is the way her deconstructive project retrieves African American subjectivity from the margins of these canonical texts. Of Twain's and Faulkner's novels she asks, "What words do Twain and Faulkner allow or do not allow their characters to speak?" In addition, she asks, "What movements and choices do Twain and Faulkner allow, or not allow their African American characters to make?" As a literary technique, the use of the determining capabilities and qualities of racialized discourses make American audiences consciously (or unconsciously) aware of how and when a particular character is performing a cultural role.

Baldwin defines innocence as white Americans' tendency to project onto African American people and culture all desires or proclivities they want to deny in themselves, identifying black people and culture as unenlightened and damned. A rhetoric of innocence reaffirms white dominance through language, blames black people for the systemic forces that shape their lives and communities, obscures the patterns of domination and subordination in society, and obfuscates the ways in which whites are menaced by racist practices and ideologies. In his nonfiction, Baldwin constructs an etymology for "innocence" that originates from within the larger American context. Drawing from the standard definition of innocence as free from wrongdoing, Baldwin defines innocence as a refusal to recognize how one's actions affect others and how one's happiness is achieved at the expense of others. For Baldwin, innocence is a rhetorical strategy—"a deliberate ignorance, a form of moral insulation that allows Americans not to confront the deep injustices that define society" (Balfour 2001, 76).

To illustrate how white Americans benefit from a rhetoric of innocence, Baldwin posits his conversation with Norman Mailer about how power functions in the lives of black men. Reflecting on his conversation with Mailer, Baldwin writes:

> The thing that most white people imagine that they can salvage from the storm of life is really, in sum, their innocence. It was this commodity precisely which I had to get rid of at once literally, on pain of death. I am afraid that most of the white people I have ever known impressed me as being in the grip of a weird nostalgia, dreaming of a vanished state of security and order, against which dream, unfailingly and unconsciously, they tested and very often lost their lives. (1993b, 217–18)

As an example of white innocence, Mailer is oblivious to the heavy price that black people paid (and still pay) for white Americans' ruthless pursuit of economic and political freedoms resulting in the loss of their sense of ethics, morality, and reality. Placing the acquisition of goods and power over humanity and civil rights, white Americans pursued a vision of America that excluded any cultural experiences that challenged Eurocentricity. In this way, Mailer exemplifies Baldwin's notion of innocence, for Mailer refuses to acknowledge his and other white men's relationship to power, and he presents a weakened white male identity that is related to black identity only in that white men can learn how to deal with their own feelings of white angst by observing how black people benefit from their existential/ist existence on the margins of society. Baldwin's contention is that the narratives that white Americans spin about their own experiences don't acknowledge the obvious ways in which power structures perpetuate white dominance and black subjugation and that the American history that white Americans embrace is nothing more than a historical and discursive fabrication. Baldwin is most critical of these historical fictions because they ultimately inform the dominant discourses that black men struggle to define themselves against.

Like Baldwin, Morrison is concerned with how language is in the service of reaffirming white male identity at the expense of black male subjectivity. However, unlike Baldwin's preoccupation with how white authors deposit white angst and anxiety on black culture and people, Morrison explores the representation of blackness and the constructions of African American characters in the fiction of white American writers and in literary landscapes that are overrun with Africanist presence. Morrison uses the word Africanist as "a term for the denotative and connotative blackness that African peoples have come to signify as well as the entire range of views, assumptions, readings, and misreadings that accompany Eurocentric learning about" people of African descent (1992, 6–7). In short, Morrison's use of Africanism speaks to white conceptions (or more accurately, misconceptions) about African American people, conceptions that are rooted in the projections of white authors, of their fears, desires, and conflicts.

According to Morrison, issues of canonicity (defined not just in terms of what is taught and talked about but in terms of the imaginative and historical terrain on which early American writers journeyed) are in large measure shaped by the presence of the racial other. In pursuit of their quest, white American writers project symbolic meanings onto their black characters, which have to do with white subjectivity alone—with conquering their "primitive" urges, getting in touch with their sexuality, and avoiding coming to terms with their own sadism. In Morrison's view, blackness or black identity was the terrain on which white identity was constructed, romanticized, and sentimentalized. Instead of confronting whiteness, white authors use blackness metonymically—as discourses about human freedom (romance):

> There is [no] romance free of what Herman Melville called "the power of blackness," especially not in a country in which there was a resident population, already black, upon which the imagination could play; through which historical, moral, metaphysical, and social fears, problems, and dichotomies could be articulated. The slave population, it could be and was assumed, offered itself up as surrogate selves for meditation on problems of human freedom, its lure and its elusiveness. This black population was available for meditations on terror—the terror of European outcasts, their dread of failure, powerlessness, Nature without limits, natal loneliness, internal aggression, evil, sin, greed. In other words, this slave population was understood to have offered itself up for reflections on human freedom in terms other than the abstractions of human potential and the rights of man. (1992, 38)

This quote locates Morrison's definition of romance in the Western intellectual tradition. Highlighting how whiteness is constructed on the principles of the Enlightenment values of rational progress and equality before a just law (regardless of history), Morrison argues that Enlightenment principles maintain white domination and black subjugation. She argues that the "romance" of idealized fiction incorporates white constructions of black identity that are in the service of model white subjectivities.

Morrison holds that a romanticized white subject and a sentimentalized view of black characters are defining tropes in the American literary canon. These consciously or unconsciously unacknowledged dialectics of black and white, Morrison writes, speak to the belief that ignoring the dynamics of race is a "graceful even generous, liberal gesture" (1992, 10). Thus, the innocence and romance so prized in America and American literatures are grounded in the rhetorical contradictions within the discursive divide that determine black men's material experiences. Morrison anatomizes the discursive contradictions that, in multiple ways, simultaneously oppress and celebrate black men and masculinity. For example, the dominant culture appreciates black men's strength and athletic ability and attempts to control and police black masculinity. The dominant culture believes that black men are exceptional entertainers and accuses black men of affectation. The dominant culture celebrates black music as passionate and emotional but ignores the extent to which these prized qualities originate from social oppression. Innocence and romance are the discursive pitfalls that black men navigate as they cross the discursive divide. Baldwin and Morrison emphasize that language is not merely a self-governing system of symbols, but a nexus of imperatives including modes of performing, existing, and becoming.

Through language and ideology, the dominant culture influences how black men understand themselves, their culture, and community in relation to American society. Even when they aren't experiencing racism at a particular moment, they still feel inferior because they have come to believe, or have internalized, the dominant society's message that they are different and do not belong. Consequently, some black men live in a state of self-hatred and inevitable self-destruction, always negotiating or repressing what the conscious mind does or does not want to acknowledge as weak or perplexing. It is in this incomplete repression that we find the beginning of the process of abjection:

> The unconscious contents remain here excluded but in strange fashion: not radically enough to allow for a secure differentiation between subject and object, and yet clearly enough for a defensive position to be established. . . . As if the fundamental opposition were between I and Other or, in more archaic fashion, between Inside and Outside. As if such an opposition subsumed the one between Conscious and Unconscious. (Kristeva 1982, 7)

The abject is that which "draws" the subject "towards the place where meaning collapses" (Kristeva 1982, 2). Any attempt to repress negative discourses may reject unwanted thoughts but only temporarily, for the ideas aren't locked away in a closed box (as Freud suggests). Rather, they dance around the borders of the subject's self-definition, always ready for the moment in which they are employed to complete or fragment the subject's definition of self. In this sense, self-definition is never a completed process and is always shaped by the wanted and unwanted thoughts about self, family, society, or community. The subject embraces a defensive posture, but not one that is completely divorced from the world around it. The subject tries to steady itself as a center from where reason flows, but discourses are shaping and reshaping the subject so that consciousness is never stable and significant. Abjection accounts for the process by which the subject incessantly tries to establish itself, persistently repelling those discourses that relentlessly contest its possibilities: "Unflaggingly, like an inescapable boomerang, a vortex of summons and repulsion places the one haunted by it literally beside himself" (Kristeva 1982, 1). The study of abjection is, especially in the African American context, a study of the looming presence of slavery and its consequences and repercussions on the black conscious and unconscious, including but not limited to black subjects in society and whiteness in the black mind. The festishization of blackness or the viewing of black skin (or ideas or images associated blackness or black people) with a mixture of horror and desire produce a confluence of fears, anxieties, and repressed desires. In considering the abject in my analysis, I consider how the denotative and connotative meanings of blackness, black subjects, and culture factor into black subjectivity construction.

ABJECTION AND THE DISCURSIVE DIVIDE

In engaging the discursive divide, black subjects encounter not only racialized discourses of innocence/romance, but also the history of associating black people and culture with the image of the dangerous Other—who is at once ill and infectious, damaged and damaging—serving as the focus for the projection of anxiety concerning the self. The power of such "ever-receding images should not be underestimated," writes Gilman. "They remain impressed on a culture as on a palimpsest, shaping and coloring all of the images that evolve at later dates" (Gilman 1985, 239). And indeed in *White Racism: A Psychohistory,* Joel Kovel agrees with Gilman's psychopathological analysis of black people and culture, "comments that few groups have suffered the appellation of filthiness so much as blacks" (1984, xlv). In an aversion to white racism, where there is a sense of disgust at the dirtiness of black bodies and black people, Kovel finds "a quintessential fantasy of Otherness—for the black body from which the white ego flees is his own body" (xlv). African Americans, in other words, have served as the container for white shame—that is, for projected fears and anxieties that the self is defective and dirty; moreover, the darker-skinned and poor black has become the "dangerous Other" for lighter-skinned and middle-class blacks in the African American community.

In *Extravagant Abjection: Blackness, Power, and Sexuality in the African American Literary Imagination,* Darieck Scott explores the connection between abjection and concepts of race, gender, and sexuality. Pondering blackness as a starting point or place of reference for discovering strategies of resistance, Scott questions if the turning toward or away from blackness in art, society, and literature makes the black past appear to be simultaneously "useless" and usable for black subjects (2010, 5). To quote Scott, "If we are racialized (in part) through domination and abjection and abjection and humiliation, is there anything of value to be learned from the experience of being defeated, humiliated, abjected?" (6). Of course, Scott answers his own question with a resounding yes and proposes that one can learn how black subjects define themselves or confirm their existence from blackness. In other words, Scott argues that if one studies blackness as a starting point for subjectivity construction, then one has the opportunity to ascertain the strategies that individuals draw on to construct a subjectivity against a shameful past. In his book, Scott offers strategies that African Americans employ to "access freedom" from "domination and defeat" (9). As Scott imagines black sexuality as a vehicle for freedom or empowerment, I propose that a careful analysis of the discursive divide reveals strategies of resistance that Baldwin's and Morrison's characters embrace to confront the dilemma of the shameful past: What do you do with your shameful past? Should you embrace or push against it?

Baldwin and Morrison illustrate that self-respect and self-degradation are intrapsychic occurrences that simultaneously shape individuals' relationships with their family and cultural history. Significantly, the black family and community can be the source of the sickness or antidote for black shame or the shame of being black that fractures psyches. Baldwin and Morrison are equally troubled with how the historical perceptions of Africa as primitive and backwards engenders shame in individuals and causes individuals to distance themselves from their ancestry (Gilman 1985, 132). Africa, as a source of "humiliation and self-humiliation," signifies a racist code that seals individuals in their own skin (Baldwin 1989, 143). Baldwin recalls how he and his family members considered being called black a degrading epithet: "It was an insult to be called black in those years when I was growing up, and part of my father's disaster and part of the danger which menaced the entire family was our relationships toward our own blackness, which was very painful. It was a matter of shame and humiliation which was not my father's fault and not our fault. It was the context in which we were born," where most African Americans accepted Eurocentric renderings of Africa as less than or opposite Europe (143). The stigma of Africa as the netherside of Europe and Afrocentric features as exaggerations of Eurocentric features (eye, hair, and skin color) represent the African "stain" in Morrison's writings that "signify the polar opposite of love and repulsion" (Morrison 1994a, 282). Black people, as a group, theorizes Morrison, signify the polar opposites of love and repulsion. On the one hand, they represent loyalty, harmlessness, and protectors. On the other hand, black people epitomize disorder, irrationality, and forbidden sexuality (xv). Ultimately, it is dialectics (fixity with fluidity, determination and over-determination) or perpetual irresoluteness that circumscribes shame to one's blackness and progress and regress endlessly, each phase of ascent and descent saddled with the historical past and present experiences, each iteration engraving itself more permanently into practice and memory. For example, Baldwin demonstrates that Gabriel Grimes's self-abhorrence, which surfaces as a rabid patriarchal authority, and Morrison that Soaphead Church's self-loathing, which manifests as sexual perversion, are a result of a disassociation from African cultural values. Gabriel's and Soaphead's assault against their families and communities are a reflection of what they "learned about how whites refer to 'the other' in their families (for whites the other is of course African Americans), and so they imported the white system rule into [their] families" (Rosenblatt 2014, 63). Looking on their families and communities with the "white gaze," Gabriel and Soaphead put into service patriarchy, paternalism, and white supremacy in their families. In a very real way, Gabriel and Soaphead want the people in their families and communities to feel less than them.

Both Morrison and Baldwin explore the family unit as a source of chronic sadness, intense anger, and feelings of regret as part of the inward/outward subjectivity construction process. In his research on racism and humiliation in the African American novel, Rosenblatt argues that abusing, demeaning, and castigating family members are all common responses of African American characters that are "made to feel less than, degraded, discredited, dishonored, humbled, or shamed" (64). From the Harlem Renaissance to contemporary African American novels, Rosenblatt reveals that while black characters frequently repress shame and humiliation in the presence of whites, they release their emotions to family members in several ways that often have dire consequences on the people close to them. While living in a society in which men are valorized for their "strength, independence, and invulnerability," black men (because of their race and class status) interact with the world as if they are "weak, inadequate, or helpless" (Harris-Perry 2011, 123). Baldwin explains the generational impact of "rage" and "anguish" on black subjectivity:

> One has got to consider . . . the dilemma and the rage and the anguish of a Negro who, in the first place, is forced to accept all kinds of humiliations in his working day, whose power in the world is so slight he can not really protect his home, his wife, his children, when he finds himself out of work.

> And then he watches his children growing up, menaced in exactly the same way he has been. (1989, 9)

Baldwin's generational explanation of the ramifications of shame and humiliation speaks to his treatment of black families in *If Beale Street Could Talk* and Morrison's depiction of colorism in *Tar Baby.*

According to Baldwin and Morrison, negative representations of Africa engender shame and humiliation in African American subjects. For Baldwin and Morrison, the source of the shameful past is the physical and emotional estrangement from Africa. Baldwin suggests that the ambivalence that black American subjects experience is a result of their estranged relationship to Africa and Africans: "An American Negro, however deep his sympathies, or however bright his rage, ceases to be simply a black man when he faces a black man from Africa. . . . I am suggesting that one of the prices an American Negro pays—or can pay—for what is called his acceptance is a profound, almost ineradicable self-hatred. This corrupts every aspect of his living, he is never at peace again, he is out of touch with himself forever. And, when he faces an African, he is facing the unspeakable dark, guilty, erotic past which the Protestant fathers made him bury—for their peace of mind, and for their power—but which lives in his personality and haunts the universe yet" (Baldwin 1998b, 268). However, Morrison states (and I believe that Baldwin echoes this sentiment) that African Americans must embrace these feelings of ambivalence, for black subjects cannot discover or achieve fulfillment outside of the black community or in the absence of his gender counterpart (African American men and women need each other to survive). On several occasions, Morrison made clear that her idea of community includes Africa. She writes that the gap between "Africa and Afro-America . . . does not exist and challenges the idea that the black self can grow without remembering the past or drawing on the creative spirit of the community" (1994a, 247). There is a necessity for remembering the horror, but of course there is a necessity for remembering it in a manner in which it can be digested, in a manner in which memory is not destructive. The act of writing the book is one way of confronting it and making it possible to remember (248).

Media texts reinforce white supremacy by offering a place for the dominant culture to retreat when they want their own subjectivity affirmed. Still within these confluences of ideologies, black subjects find agency by returning the gaze. In discussing how the media function as a place of agency, bell hooks argues that the gaze is intrinsic and extrinsic: "Spaces of agency exist for black people, wherein we can both interrogate the gaze of the Other but also look back, and at one another, naming what we see. . . . Subordinates in relations of power learn experientially that there is a critical gaze, one that is oppositional" (1990, 289). Baldwin writes, "You go to white movies and, like everybody else, you fall in love with Joan Crawford, and you root for the Good Guys who are killing off the Indians. It comes as a great psychological collision when you realize all of these things are really metaphors for your oppression and will lead into a kind of psychological warfare in which you may perish" (1989, 5). Morrison writes, "Popular culture, shaped by film, theater, advertising, the press, television, and literature, is heavily engaged in race talk. It participates freely in this most enduring and efficient rite of passage into American culture: negative appraisals of the native-born black population. Only when the lesson or racial estrangement is learned is assimilation complete" (2008b, 145). Whiteness is not about being white; instead, it is a commitment to white superiority. These media texts are one reason black subjects question the dominant culture's commitment to work toward racial equality.

In the state of abjection or space of ambivalence where black male subjectivity construction occurs, subjects are pushed and pulled between multiple competing discursive systems. Between multiple linguistic systems where black subjectivity is defined and contested and reaffirmed and rearticulated, black subjects within and without African American cultural contexts navigate various positionalities. More specifically, the theoretical work of Hortense Spillers (2003), Fred Moten (2003), and Marlon Ross (2004) reminds us that subjectivity construction is always an inward/outward process and references the past, present, and future of the subject's experiences. Spillers's exploration of the "non-self-referential mulatto/a" as a political identity reminds us that one has to take into account a multitude of competing factors when attempting to define individuals in public and private spaces and distinguishing the subject from his/her objectification. Spillers writes, "The mulatto/a just as the nigger tells us little or nothing about the subject buried beneath the epithets, but quite a great deal more concerning the psychic and cultural reflexes that invent or invoke them" (2003, 302). Along these lines, Moten argues for an approach to exploring subjectivity construction as an inward/outward process that resists closure and the tendency to conflate subjectivity with personhood. Moten states that "while subjectivity is defined by the subject's possession of itself and its objects, it is troubled by a dispossessive force objects exert such that the subject seems to be possessed—infused, deformed—by the object it possesses" (2003, 1). Moten's concern with the phonic materiality of the subject is not completely beyond the scope of this book, for Moten sees the African American vernacular as expressions of blackness that are irreducible. The vernacular represents the break or an interruption in dominant discourses where African American subjectivity improvises a black worldview. Lastly,

I found Ross's research on the public spaces and practices where black men challenged and reformulated notions of back manhood and pushed against traditional notions of gender and sexuality helpful for imagining black male agency in institutions and through rhetorical practices (2004, 2). The break, mullattoness, and the arbitrariness of the gender line not only gives a nod to the ever present complexity of black male subjectivity formation, it also suggests a space, place, or standpoint from which black men form rhetorical strategies of resistance to engage the discursive divide.

TOWARD A RHETORIC OF AFRICAN AMERICAN MALE SUBJECTIVITY

In considering the rhetorical strategies of resistance that black men employ to negotiate the discursive divide, my thinking has been sharpened by scholars who examine the ways that African American men and women collaborate to challenge the politics of racism, sexism, and sexuality. In particular, the gender criticism of Michael Awkward and Athena D. Mutua is concerned not only with how black men are complicit or benefit from male privilege, but how many of them work to destabilize patriarchal domination. Drawing on Hortense Spillers's notion of the "liberating possibilities" of the feminist within the black male subject, Awkward proposes a male feminism that is more than a self-referential discourse by men about how they struggled against and were victimized by patriarchy and in return victimized women (1995, 54). Awkward argues for a "sympathetic" approach to examining black male patriarchy that considers the ways in which black men internalized the domination that they experienced, thus, projecting it onto black women, children, and communities. Awkward provides a critical lens for black male critics to not only explore how they have been menaced in the struggle to fulfill hegemonic masculinity, but also to discover a critical lens for "reconceptualizing the black male subject" (2001, 190).

In this way, I draw a connection between Awkward's black male feminist project and an Afrocentric approach that highlights the means by which black men work to "deconstruct or destroy the ideological foundations, social categories and institutional power of race" (Marable 1995, 227). Mutua reconfigures Afrocentricity so that it not only posits a black masculinity that is pro-black, anti-racist, and anti-sexist, and anti-homophobia, but one that "isn't dependent or predicated on the subordination of others" and that "promote[s] human freedom for all, both in the context of their personal lives and in the outward manifestations of those personal lives in social, cultural, economic, and political contexts" (2006, 7). Mutua's idea of "progressive masculinity" highlights the significance of exploring the ways in which African American men and women work together to eradicate racist and sexist oppression. For Mutua, challenges to gender oppression are more successful when men and women collaborate across gender and sexuality to build strong communities and institutions. She states that "progressive black masculinities are both about a stance against domination and a commitment to the valuation and empowerment of black humanity" (25). Unfortunately in the past, this collaboration has taken place to a lesser degree in sociopolitical movements like Civil Rights and Black Power. However, African American people and communities have grown immensely as a result of the critiques of the lack of gender inequality and anti-homophobia stances in these movements. As comrades in the fight against gender oppression, African American men and women stress the importance of family and community relationships and social, economic, and political reform within and without African American communities. Awkward's and Mutua's research is suggestive for conceptualizing black male subjects as insightful and intentional in how they define themselves in public and private spaces. While traversing the discursive divide, black male subjects contend with social patterns of oppression that are interrelated and bound together and influenced by the intersectional systems of society.

In articulating the rhetorics of black male subjectivity construction, this book builds on research that posits gender as a socially constructed category of identity. In his research on middle-class black masculinities, Martin Summers rereads the extensive sex role literature and critiques the model of multiple masculinities and power relations. In his analysis, he argues that the masculinity and power relations model was integrated into a systematic sociological theory of gender, which emphasizes that gender isn't a compilation of intrinsic qualities and characteristics. Instead, gender refers to how men and women are socially defined, consider themselves as gendered subjects, perform their gender subjectivity, and are reproduced in society through language and entrenched throughout economic, political, and cultural institutions. Thus, individuals possess gender identities, while society and culture produce gender conventions. Through conventions, society situates and governs men and women within a historical and culturally specific structure of hierarchal social interactions. Black men are more than the attributes and characteristics that society imposes on their bodies; they are also the individual's performances of resistance and negotiations among specific beliefs and values within a given society. Gender ideologies are comprised of not only a combination of values and attributes that society inscribes on an individual's physical body, they are also the individual "acts of conforming to, contesting, or negotiating the gender conventions of a particular society" (Summers 2004, 10). In this sense, gender is not fixed or stable. Rather, it is a fluid and dynamic process. The social constructionist approach also emphasizes that gender is constructed in relation to others. Summers writes, "In the process of defining oneself as masculine individuals within specific historical contexts use identifiable characteristic against which to construct their manhood" (10). Not only does sex determine these qualities, but also "class and skill level" and "race," "sexuality," "ethnicity," and "nationality" (10).

The many experiences that Baldwin's and Morrison's black male subjects face can't be accounted for within static boundaries of race or gender discrimination as black male experiences are dynamic, complex, and complicated by class, region, and sexuality. Moreover, the intersection of racism and sexism factors into black men's lives in ways that cannot be captured wholly by looking at the race and gender dimensions of personal experiences. I draw on Kimberly Crenshaw's observations that ideologies and other discrete forms and expressions of oppression actually shape, and are shaped by, one another and determine black men's lives. Intersectionality, Crenshaw argues, accounts for the study of how differences such as race, class, gender, and sexuality and other social, cultural, and political categories interrelate and perpetuate black subjugation. While I don't present intersectionality as a totalizing theory of black male subjectivity construction, I believe that it provides a sophisticated critical lens for engaging the representation of black male experiences in Baldwin's and Morrison's writings where they seek to denaturalize categories of analysis and separate the statistical from the morally determined.

What is the process by which black male subjects resist discursive inscription? First, Toni Cade Bambara argues that resistance requires that the black self-undergo a revolution or transformation. Bambara writes, "Revolution begins with the self, in the self. The individual, the basic revolutionary unit, must be purged of poison and lies that assault the ego and threaten the heart" (2010, 124). Literally or figuratively, the black self appropriates dominant ideologies for its own purposes, overthrows the ideology that situates it in its oppressive circumstance, and eradicates the ideologies that define the subject. Baldwin's and Morrison's black male characters display an awareness of how they are positioned, and they question the cultural norms and values that maintain their positionality. More than simply negating a negativity or affirming oneself in the face of external forces or oppositional discourses, George Yancy describes resistance as a moment in which one rejects "a form of freedom predicated upon the denial of the freedom of others . . . structurally dependent upon the oppression of the Black body or defined parasitically in relationship to the oppression of the Black body" (2008, 113).

Similar to Yancy's rhetorics of independence and affirmation, Baldwin and Morrison propose a rhetoric of resistance that doesn't require permission but rather is predicated on values such as justice, liberty, and freedom. Baldwin and Morrison suggest a black male resistance that counters outward constructions and questions the source of knowledge. Baldwin recalls, "I was born fifty-five years ago. In a sense I was born in the nightmare of the white man's mind. All of my growing up and all my early youth was first that discovery and then the bloody struggle to get out of that mind, to destroy that frame of reference for myself and for those coming after me" (1989, 181). Resistance in Morrison's work is self-affirming, complete, and individually satisfying: "When a man is whole himself . . . and he's not proving something to somebody else—white men or other men and so on—then the threats of emasculation, the threats of castration, the threats of somebody taking over disappears" (1994a, 17). Here, Baldwin and Morrison suggest that events or incidents that threaten black men physically and emotionally engender resistance. Black men learn the value of looking "beneath appearances," taking "nothing for granted," hearing "the meaning behind words" (Morrison 1994a, 17). Black male subjectivity construction takes place simultaneously within and without the African American context and in romantic and non-romantic relationships between men.

Second, resistance occurs whenever heterosexuality or homosexuality is challenged as the primary mode of intimate expression between men. Human sexuality cannot be completely understood in terms of such limited concepts as homosexuality and heterosexuality. Eve Sedgwick's *Between Men* offers an appropriate paradigm for examining males and male culture in Baldwin's and Morrison's fiction. Sedgwick views sexuality as a continuum that includes different forms of sexuality and comprises countless erotic inclinations involving homo-social relations.[4] In the context of male culture, she presents the diverse expressions of male sexuality—a continuum that encompasses homosocialism or male bonding, homoeroticism or male desire, and homosexuality—which can be implicitly or explicitly expressed among men in a hetero-

4. In articles and essays, feminist scholars highlight the multiple ways women characters are defined by patriarchy and the ways in which Morrison's women characters resist conforming to social patriarchal expectations. Specifically, Barbara Smith contends that Morrison's *Sula* "works as a lesbian novel not only because of the passionate friendship between Sula and Nel but because of Morrison's consistently critical stance toward the heterosexual institutions of male-female relationships, marriage, and the family. Consciously or not, Morrison's work poses both lesbian and feminist questions about black women's autonomy and their impact upon each other's lives" (1995, 138). I believe that black feminist criticism offers a unique insight into the rhetorical function of maleness and manhood in the fictional lives of Baldwin's and Morrison's women characters.

sexual, patriarchal, and especially homophobic culture (Sedgwick 1985, 4–5). This continuum of male sexuality and homoerotic desires in men is evocative for considering, firstly, the relationship that Baldwin and Morrison create with their male characters; secondly, the homo-social bond between men in their novels; and thirdly, the emasculating or masculinizing process that runs through their work.[5] Baldwin and Morrison challenge readers to consider expressions of love between black men on a continuum by presenting black men as multidimensional—including in the sexual domain and extending to the emotional and psychological. In other words, relationships where men centralize the emotional and psychological needs of other men can be characterized as a homo-social continuum or post-sexuality "sex that is taking place beyond the socially constructed senses of sexuality that have dominated the twentieth century" (Dieveler 1999, 163).[6] In their novels, intimacy is not about sex as much as it is about unconditional love and acceptance. Blurring the line between intimacy and intercourse serves a dual purpose: it accounts for the historical discourses that cast black men as dangerous and lascivious, and it serves as a counter-narrative to narrow or two-dimensional ways of thinking about black male sexuality. Concerned that the binary of homosexuality and heterosexuality reduces sexuality to the biological sex of one's partner, or in psychological terms, the object of one's affection, I argue that there are a host of other factors that make up human sexual desire, and there are multiple ways that men express intimacy and emotion in non-sexual ways.

Considering intimacy as a range of expressions directs attention to the socially constructed boundaries and categorizations that Baldwin frequently spoke against throughout his life. On multiple occasions, Baldwin responded to questions about his sexuality and sexual politics in general (from within

5. The reaction to this among critics varies from a keen interest in the relationship between Baldwin's personal life and his writings (mainly his insights about being a black gay man used as a critical context for exploring his novels) and sexuality as a determining factor of social experiences for Baldwin's black gay or bisexual male characters. Most recent essays give attention to the nexus of racism and sexism as the primary force of oppression in the lives of Baldwin's gay and bisexual black male characters. For example, Warren Carson states: "For Baldwin, the bonding of males—and for African American males in particular—is a natural process toward a shared sense of unity and fraternity, but one whose development has been inhibited, if not altogether thwarted, by society's sexism, racism, and unrealistic expectations for men" (2000, 216). Of course, David, a bisexual white male character in *Giovanni's Room,* struggles with his sexuality, but it is more about what it means to fulfill a white male norm. One could make this about race as well by saying a significant aspect of the definition of a normative white male is heterosexuality; however, I contend that whiteness does not make David vulnerable to social oppression.

6. Post-sexuality suggests a post-categorical, post-structural concept of sexuality. Although Dieveler employs "post-sexuality" to explain the contemporary relevance of Baldwin's ideas about sexuality, I am extending this to Morrison's novels because I believe that she pushes her audience to engage black male love beyond or outside the bedroom.

and without the black community). In one interview Baldwin notes, "homosexual, bisexual, heterosexual are 20th century terms which, for me, really have very little meaning. I've never, myself, in watching myself and watching other people, watching life, been able to discern exactly where the barriers were" (1989, 54).[7] This critique is evident in *Just Above My Head* (1979); Arthur Montana's sexuality isn't a determining factor in whether he will survive or live a productive life. Consider this analysis of Arthur as an example of how "Baldwin treats homosexuality as a normal or supernormal behavior and he sharply differentiates between phallic confrontation and overt effeminacy" (Lash 1977, 49). Arthur "is homosexual, but seen sentimentally, continually as a member of a family, the doting younger brother, the loving son. He is meant to be a kind of artist hero, hardworking, dedicated, tragically undone by the rages of lives" (Pinckney 1988, 163). In addition, in *Go Tell It on the Mountain,* John's journey of sexual self-discovery, including most notably his relationship with Elijah, coincides with his spiritual salvation and his father's shortcomings.

Similarly, Morrison explores how men establish and cross or violate one another's boundaries. In *Song of Solomon,* Milkman's search for his family legacy is interlaced with a story about strife between him and his best friend, Guitar. Their once understanding and supportive friendship, in which they unquestionably accepted, protected, and expressed their love for each other, turns into an acrimonious relationship, complete with mistrust and revenge. The novel ends with a climactic suicide scene in which they die in each other's arms. In *Beloved,* Morrison represents love and intimacy between Sweet Home men who are "All in their twenties, minus women, fucking cows, dreaming of rape, thrashing on pallets, rubbing their thighs, and waiting for the new girl" (1987, 18). Unlike Charles Nero, who argues that the bestiality the Sweet Home men engage in "reveals her inability to imagine gay relationships among heroic characters," I believe that *Beloved* depicts dimensions of black love and sharing between men (2000, 402). Throughout *Beloved,* love and intimacy transcends the boundaries of intimacy and sexuality. It is unrestricted and on a spectrum. Baldwin's and Morrison's novels challenge readers to think about intimacy between black men as boundless and borderless, defying social, regional, and geographical restraints.

In their writings, Baldwin and Morrison represent a variety of black male expressions in order to discern the full complexity of gender dynamics in the African American context. They demonstrate that age, social status, and marital status interact with race, gender, and sexuality to produce a complex multi-

7. See Baldwin's comments in *Conversations with James Baldwin* about Eldridge Cleaver's homophobic public attack in *Soul on Ice.*

dimensional map of power relations, which by no means privileges all men or subordinates all women. By moving away from a concept of gender defined entirely in terms of a male-female binary, they deepen traditional interpretations of patriarchy and recuperate a range of gender relationships. Thus, while harshly criticizing the patriarchal practices within African American culture, Baldwin and Morrison represent dominant constructions of black male subjectivity as irrevocably tied to female subjugation and posit that patriarchy functions repressively in the lives of black men. Casting black male and female characters as mutually dependent on each other and equally oppressed by patriarchy (albeit differently), Baldwin and Morrison highlight relationships between black men and women as a site of resistance. Baldwin states that black men are indebted to black women for holding black families together when men were unable or refused to be involved with their offspring and communities (Baldwin 1989, 196–97). Morrison also acknowledges that while some black men haven't been involved in black families and communities, but there must be a more complex understanding of the roles of black women in black culture and American society. Morrison argues, "I wasn't impressed with much of the rhetoric of Black men about Black women in the Sixties, I didn't believe it. I don't think they meant it. I was distraught by the gullible young Black women who got caught up in it . . . in spite of duress, the relationship between Black men and Black women in those days was much more a comradeship than the romantic love it got to be later as a result of the infiltration from the other culture" (1994a, 72). In my analysis of Morrison's fiction, I examine these complex gender relations with a particular focus on the legacy of cooperation and community building between black men and women.

Bell hooks describes this shared work history as a significant aspect of the African American experience and important to the survival of black families. Cooperation across gender lines is apparent in *If Beale Street Could Talk* and *Sula,* which challenge representations of male-female relationships as violent love-hate companionships dependent on sexual gratification as a means of psychological release from relational stress. Although Fonny expresses his feelings to Tish more overtly than Ajax does to Sula, Tish and Sula share Fonny's and Ajax's dreams, including Fonny's desire to be a carpenter and Ajax's goal to be an airplane pilot. Tish and Sula don't simply function to fulfill roles defined by Fonny and Ajax. The romantic relationships are presented as more than sexual, superficial, or skin deep. Unfortunately, racism interrupts their courtships and lives when Fonny is falsely imprisoned for rape and given that Ajax wants to be a pilot more than he wants Sula. Nonetheless, the idea that black men and women can be "comrades in the struggle" challenges dominant ways of thinking about black male subjectivities and black men.

Besides exploring the politics of gender and the representations of gender experiences, I also examine the difficulty Baldwin's and Morrison's male and female characters encounter when they attempt to build a life together. In considering the relationships between black male and female characters in Baldwin and Morrison writings, I read Baldwin's and Morrison's black male characters as inheritors of patriarchal discourses without the inherited privileges. Black male characters have clearly been excluded from many of the rights and privileges that white men enjoy. As ex-slaves and descendants of slaves, the black male characters are mostly unable to protect or provide for their families, and they live in fear for their lives as well as those of their loved ones. Having a family includes taking the chance that one day they might not be able to protect loved ones from physical abuse or, worse, death. Thus, performing masculinity requires coming to terms with the psychological and emotional fallout of systematic degradations and modes of emasculation. My approach, however, neither ignores how Baldwin's and Morrison's male characters benefit nor how they are emasculated by patriarchy.[8] I argue that patriarchy limits black men and women—it doesn't excuse black men from being accountable in gender oppression. However, it does point out the limitations of patriarchy to function as an emancipatory discourse for black men and women. Most importantly, complicating patriarchal norms and imperatives opens up dialogue about how black men can work with black women to challenge multiple and intersecting systems of oppression. It provides an opening to explore how black men and women can support each other in building strong families and communities.

In order to pass through the discursive divide, Baldwin's and Morrison's black male characters develop three ways of knowing: knowing how they feel about themselves, knowing their own experiences, and knowing how others experience them. These ways of knowing allow for black male characters to define themselves against negative ideologies that signify a damaged, aberrant, inferior, and abject masculinity and that cast black men as brutes, rapists,

8. In *Negotiating Difference,* Michael Awkward articulates the rhetorical move that African American men must make in order to "destroy" or destabilize sexist and dominant discourses about masculinity and patriarchy. David Ikard found Awkward's methodology useful for highlighting the phallocentric structures within African American literary texts. In *Breaking the Silence,* Ikard forefronts the women's voices and demonstrates how Bob Jones is complicit in oppressing the women characters. However, illuminating sexist and patriarchal practices isn't the only critical approach for demonstrating the limitations of the patriarchal discourses that seek to divide and oppress African American men and women. A literary critical reading should also highlight how black male characters resist embracing patriarchal practices and explore the rhetorical strategies that male characters employ to construct themselves as men and as "comrades" to women in the fight against racism and oppression.

and uncle toms. That cast them, in a phrase, as the racial Other. Essentially, Baldwin and Morrison show how black men employ language subversively to liberate themselves from oppression. For example, Baldwin and Morrison make available to their black male characters the same creative expressions that slaves produced as a response to bondage (spirituals, folktales), that African Americans embraced to express pain and suffering (jazz, rap, biblical Word), and that African Americans sacrificed as the cost of the experiences of being black and oppressed (mask, silence). As a whole, these creative expressions comprise the rich history of African American artistic, musical, and folkloristic achievements.[9] As the characters draw on these traditions and other alternative discourses to define themselves and to negotiate their relationships with other characters, they "reconfigure and refashion a self that . . . counter[s] conventional constructions and tenets" (Clark 2002, 10). This new Self is aware of its positionality, the positionality of others, and its complicity in gender oppression. In their novels, rather than drawing on simple and familiar stereotypes, Baldwin and Morrison represent black male subjectivities as never static and constantly produced in the midst of social relations that are themselves in flux and at times paradoxical.

In their fiction, Baldwin and Morrison present black men in dialectics with other characters or as outward and inward processes that together, and sometimes contrarily, constitute black masculinity vis-à-vis white men, vis-à-vis black women, and vis-à-vis Others.[10] The following chapters explore the

9. Patrick B. Mullen (2008) recognizes folklore as a vehicle for communication, whether lore is recorded during an ethnography project or captured in literary texts. Mullen's insight about the relationship between literature and ethnography is helpful for understanding how folklore functions as rhetorical strategy in African American literary texts. Mullen argues that literature and ethnographies have similar aims. In Baldwin's and Morrison's novels, folklore (as community values and beliefs) provides a culturally specific critical lens on which the story develops and pivots. They include tales, fables, song, legends, and proverbs as literary devices that drive the action and communicate the intentions and worldview of the characters. For example, in Baldwin's *The Amen Corner* (1998a) Brother Boxer is torn between the Word of God and earning a living as a delivery driver for a beer distributing company, and Son in Morrison's *Tar Baby* (2004b) refers to Jadine as an example of a tar baby. Baldwin and Morrison use folklore as alternative critical lenses for reading black male subjectivity.

10. By focusing on the economy within the multiple dialectics that shape African American male subjectivities (subjectivities vs. man, subjectivities vs. woman, subjectivities vs. community, etc.), I read African American male subjectivities for how they resist or appropriate dominant stereotypes about black male identity. In many ways, my methodology is similar to early researchers who explored the intersections of rhetoric, folklore, and literature and mapped and elucidated the rhetorical performances of African Americans. For example, Geneva Smitherman's dozens (1986), Houston Baker's blues matrix (2007), Henry Louis Gates Jr.'s signifyn' (1980), and most recently Richard Majors and Janet Mancini Billson's cool pose (1992) have provided culturally specific paradigms for exploring the intersection of literature and rhetoric and black male subjectivity as resistance. These texts are more concerned with the encounter or dialectic between dominant culture and rhetorical strategies as opposed to exploring how black

rhetorical strategies that Baldwin's and Morrison's black male characters use to challenge dominant discourses and reposition themselves on the other side of the discursive divide. Although critics have addressed the dynamics of black men moving from places of oppression to liberation (both physically and psychologically), I extend the discussion of this movement within Baldwin's and Morrison's works to examine what black male characters draw on to redefine themselves as men, sons, fathers, husbands, and lovers. In this investigation, I question the discourses and scenes that show characters moving back and forth between the black and white world and traversing regions and contexts.

Drawing on contemporary critical theory, I argue that each chapter is concerned with a particular instance of the construction of historical and intellectual modes of resistance and cooptation. The black male characters are neither totally imperiled nor constituted (i.e., determined entirely by the social or linguistic structures around them), nor are they completely individualistic or self-constituting (i.e., the source or agent of all meaning), but rather, they are both constituted and constituting. Baldwin's and Morrison's black male characters wrestle with the nuances of racism and struggle to redefine themselves in opposition to these discourses. Their fictional characters draw on cultural materials to construct self-defined voices and subjectivities that transcend or reframe culturally damaging categories: slave and freed man, saint and sinner, northern inheritance and southern heritage, individual desires and community responsibility, personal ambitions and social limitations, and dependence and autonomy. In negotiating these categories, the characters represent the potential for a more nuanced understanding of constructions of black male subjectivity and the material experiences of Baldwin's and Morrison's black male fictional characters.

In chapter 1, I argue that Morrison's *Beloved* posits silence as a counter-discourse about black needs, concerns, and identity. Counter-discourse is a subversive system that challenges the production of knowledge and power. As a system of counter-ideologics that resituates the nature of slaves and redefines their relationship to the society or communities in which they live and exist, counter hegemony acts as a powerful tool to undermine ideologies, cultural norms, and value systems. Silence is the strategy of strategic endurance that

---

males construct a life beyond dominant discourses. In placing language as a black male subjectivity construction at the center of my inquiry, my book is similar to James Wilmouth Coleman's *Black Male Fiction and the Legacy of Caliban* (2001), David Holmes's *Revisiting Racialized Voice: African American Ethos in Language and Literature* (2004), and Vershawn Ashanti Young's *Your Average Nigga: Performing Race, Literacy, and Masculinity* (2007). I provide a firm cognitive grounding for contemporary interests in the rhetorical function of black masculinity in places and spaces, particularly the verbal and nonverbal ways black males negotiate institutions and ideologies.

Paul D employs to challenge oppressive discourses and represent his experiences as a slave. As a rhetorical strategy, silence represents the "unspeakable" (degrading, debasing, or humiliating) experiences of the daily atrocities-of plantation life. Silence is also a significant metaphor for the condition of duress under which the slaves live, and it shows an awareness of the emasculating actions that are deemed masculine.

In chapter 2, I argue that Baldwin's *Go Tell It on the Mountain* articulates a counter-history of Christian innocence—one that suggests that Pentecostalism since Emancipation has had a damaging impact on black male subjectivity formation. Whereas Pentecostalism imagines spiritual fulfillment via the construction of patriarchal domestic and political formations, Baldwin's novel stresses Pentecostalism's failure to create emancipatory potential in either domain. Gabriel is in the discursive divide of the secular and spiritual. Therefore, what Baldwin highlights is not his success or failure as a father and preacher but the processes by which he attempts to fulfill these roles. The discourses that Gabriel draws on to redefine and reposition himself speak to his desire to fulfill what he imagines as God's favor to him: a family, an heir to his "throne," and pastor of his own church.

In chapter 3, I explore African American male subjectivities as a nuanced performance of the Self in Baldwin's *Tell Me How Long the Train's Been Gone*. Using Homi Bhabha's (1984) powerful redefinition of mimicry as a cultural strategy, I argue that Leo's decision to be an actor allows him to utilize the rhetorical strategy of mimicry in a space where discourses are endlessly repeated. As the terrain for the construction of subjectivities, mimicry distinguishes not between representation and reality, but between one representation and another. It is precisely this distinction that constitutes the discursive divide and allows the reader to move from the consensus that Leo does not know who he is to an appreciation of his self-knowledge regarding representation as reality and reality as representation.

Chapter 4 examines Milkman as a symbol of the first generation of southern migrants born in the north. Situated between Macon's and Pilate's northern and southern value systems, Macon (Milkman) Dead III leaves the comforts of his upper-middle-class lifestyle in the north to search for his family inheritance in the south. His willingness to travel from the north to the south to retrieve his birthright speaks to the importance he places on family duty and commitment and also makes him susceptible to the influences of the discourses and the narratives that are instrumental to African American migrants' process of redefinition. Secondly, although a major impetus for the Great Migration was to achieve a better life, African American men consciously or unconsciously relied on folklore to survive the northern landscape.

In chapter 5, I contend that Baldwin's gay sensibilities are relayed through the insights of his female protagonist Tish Rivers, who witnesses the carnivalesque and the shifting and competing subject positions that each character occupies at a given moment. Disassembling these moments through critical concepts that account for the turmoil that racial oppression engenders in African American families, I offer a queer reading of *If Beale Street Could Talk* that suggests the dynamics of black expression—the potential of black masculine performance as dynamic and honest expressions of their own emotional state. I believe that Baldwin discloses a gay sensibility that is a consequence of intersectionality but is nourished by his own unique take on gender performance as a reflection and resistance of dominant cultures values.

In chapter 6, I contextualize Morrison's novel within larger conversations about subjectivity as a gender "performance of repetitious behavior within the limits of discursive gender requirements—in this case a performance of binary and univocal sex/gender within the framework of compulsory heterosexuality/romantic relationships between men and women. . . . Gender performance, in turn, creates the impression of a given or interior nature, a natural sexual disposition, which, like a textualized intention, is thought to be expressed in and by the performance" (Strozier 2002, 87). Son and Jadine continuously locate each other within a strict gender discourse about expectations for men and women while refusing each other's attempt to locate them in a gender role and performance.

This book emerges out of enjoyment, not hopelessness. It is rooted in my desire to celebrate black male subjectivities and in what I know about the experiences of many black males. Some of the questions I address concern how African Americans create history from memory and folklore, how they adopt discourses of enlightenment and spirituality, and how they define their place in society and family. This research has led me to wonder what happens to our own subjectivities when we start using fiction to consciously search for black males' strategies of resistance in the most dire of circumstances. For example, the scenes in *Go Tell It on the Mountain* where John Grimes recognizes academic literacy and Christian teachings as liberatory discourses and Shadrack designates a special day for despondent, depressed, or dejected blacks to either decide to live in pain or commit suicide, remind me that resistance is a rhetorical and discursive action as well as a state of being. In representing black males crossing the discursive divide, I acknowledge the importance of constructions of black male subjectivities that are empowering, that overcome isolation and despair, and that enable the formations of family and community and, ultimately, collective struggles for justice.

CHAPTER 1

"Help Me This Mornin's Bad"

Songs, Narratives, and Other Rhetorical Acts in *Beloved*

> Got one mind for white folk to see. Nother for what I know is me.
> —LAWRENCE GELLERT, *ME AND MY CAPTAIN*

A SIGNIFICANT INSIGHT for exploring the discursive divide in Morrison's *Beloved* is the diversity of approaches that African American men employ to survive antebellum discourses and confront loss and intimacy. Morrison, as she does with black female characters, presents black male characters on a continuum that includes their ability to show love and tenderness and their willingness to show fear and vulnerability. Case in point is Halle, who hires himself out to save enough money to buy his mother's freedom, but ultimately has a psychological breakdown after watching the rape of his wife; Sixo, who walks thirty miles to see the woman he loves; and Paul D, who cries as he watches another slave closer than a brother burn alive without shedding a tear. Thus, Morrison's sentiment that black men have an enormous responsibility to be men extends to her black male characters (1987, 17). In the face of extreme racism and debilitting oppression, the Sweet Home men maintain a sense of self; they exemplify self-confidence and an incredible autonomy. They are complex and introspective with a desire to be fathers, husbands, and thoughtful sons and possess an "incredible amount of magic and feistiness" (1994a, 17–18). Toward others, Morrison's male characters are sensitive and insensitive, nice and mean, thoughtful and dismissive. Toward Morrison's black women characters, they are chivalrous and patriarchal as well as loving and kind.

While there are other male characters in *Beloved,* I believe that the focus should be on Paul D's struggle to make peace with his past life as a slave and his desire to build a life as a freedman in Ohio. Publications on *Beloved* are primarily interested in Paul D as Sethe's antagonist or a representation of hegemonic masculinity. Thus, while some scholars locate Paul D within the gendered logic of white male inheritance, others centralize the experiences of the black male characters in *Beloved* by examining the dynamics of black male experiences within the novel.[1] For example, Nancy Kang (2003) examines how black masculinity is threatened, under stress, or remains a dynamic force that has been constrained to the extent that it has nowhere to go. Similarly, Susan Mayberry (2007) explores black masculinity as a discourse within the context of the lives of the black women characters but does not consider the role of rhetoric in shaping male subjectivity. Lenore Kitts (2006) draws connections between Paul D's musical expressions and the African American musical tradition but doesn't explore the rhetoric of black male subjectivity to define himself.

While some scholars have examined how Morrison incorporates the African American rhetorical tradition in *Beloved,* many critics have overlooked the recent scholarship that suggests silence as a viable rhetorical strategy of resistance for Paul D. In her groundbreaking book *Unspoken: A Rhetoric of Silence,* Cheryl Glenn argues that silence is an expressive power as opposed to a "passive" or defensive speech act that is often underestimated and read as "nothinness" (2004, 3). "Silence is every bit as important as speech," and it "reveals speech at the same time that it enacts its own sometimes-complementary rhetoric" (3–4). When "employed as a tactical strategy or

1. Deborah Sitter suggests that Paul D's adverse response to the scars on Sethe's back is his desire to, similar to white men's, locate his masculinity on the bodies of black women: "Paul D's denial that Sethe has a tree on her back is a case of phallic assertiveness masking his own insecurity about his own manhood. He imposes his own (male) conception of a tree, measures her tree by it, and finds it lacking." Sitter believes that the way Amy Denver, a white indentured servant, romanticizes the brutality that Sethe experienced is more sensible than Paul D's response because "together, Amy Denver and Sethe create a famine context against which Paul D's image of the tree must be understood" (1998, 171, 195). In contrast, taking into account the institution of slavery, Bernard Bell says, "The scars on Sethe's back signifies the physical and psychic sufferings of slavery that Paul D shares with Sethe" (1998, 177). Trudier Harris characterizes Paul D's response to the spirit that inhabits 124 Bluestone Road as a classic male response to beat it back, which is the superimposition of Paul D's masculinity on Sethe (1998, 130). Harris argues that when Paul D drives the spirit out of the house, he demonstrates that his "masculine will is stronger than her [the female spirit] silent, though sometimes noisy desire" (130). Paul D is seen as exerting his patriarchal authority and continues to be viewed with unmitigated suspicion, but Paul D has no power. These perspectives suggests that Paul D has a direct and natural, as opposed to an indirect or institutional, relationship to white male privilege and uncritically resituates Paul D back in the master/slave dialectic from which Morrison has him struggle.

inhabited in deference to authority, silence resonates loudly along the corridors of purposeful language use. Whether choice or im/position, silence can reveal positive or negative abilities, fulfilling or withholding traits, harmony or disharmony, success or failure. Silence can deploy power; it can defer power. It all depends" (xi).

Morrison represents Paul D's use of silence as a response to the paternalistic discourses on the Sweet Home plantation. Without speaking, Paul D refuses gestures from the plantation owner that might suggest that is willing to be complicit in his oppression. Also, Paul D relies on his "rememories" of stories he shared and conversations he had with other Sweet Home men to define himself against slavery discourses (1987, 112). In the presence of white slave owners, Paul D feigns ignorance but embraces vernacular forms (jokes, signifyin', narratives, and call and response) as an alternative to white male patriarchy and domination. While imprisoned on a coffle and traveling north, he remembers the songs and narratives that fostered a bond between him and other slaves. Drawing on silence and the vernacular, Paul D is able to create a break (albeit a small one) in the dominant discourse to contemplate his options: acting against racial oppression or listening to how white slave owners characterize and categorize him. Within this space, his subjectivity is no longer a direct and inverse reflection of white masculinity; instead, it speaks to his present context and it locates his subjectivity in the African American vernacular tradition. By positing how Paul D negotiates the discursive divide of slavery and freedom, Morrison represents the interior lives of slaves in the form of flashbacks and memories.

In order to gain access to the interior lives of Paul D and the other slaves, Morrison draws on official records (slave narratives and historical records) and her own experiences to represent a particular silence and memory commentary. Not only are events that affect Paul D (such as foiled escape plans, traveling north, and contemplations of manhood) reminiscent of other slave narratives, but other occurrences (for example the withholding of traditions such as slaves naming their offspring and creating families) inform Morison's memories. She describes her memories as profound and deep recollections that shape her consciousness and inform her literary production: "I have memories within that came out of the material that went to make me. The memories within are the subsoil of my work. But memories and recollections won't give me total access to the unwritten interior life of these people. Only the act of the imagination can help me" (1995, 10). In *Beloved,* Morrison remembers "the sixty-million and more" people who were severed from their country, family, and culture and subjected to horrendous conditions and experiences. She contemplates Sweet Home as a site of degradation and oppression where black subjectivity (en)counters dominant discourse, and slaves reconstruct their humanity from the African American vernacular.

What we learn about the other slaves in *Beloved* help us to understand Paul D's past as a slave on the Sweet Home plantation and as a prisoner on a coffle. Morrison subverts traditional representations of characters in novels as foils and heroes by depicting all characters as heroes and survivors who confide in or accept Paul D as a confidant. However, their complex positioning in the text provides more information about Paul D. He bears witness to the pain and sorrow of Sixo (a slave in love), Halle (a father who seeks permission to care for his ailing and aging mother), and Sethe (a mother who is punished for protecting her children). Through showing Paul D sympathetically listening to or watching these characters express their anguish, Morrison draws readers' attention to him as a kindhearted character who not only understands how slavery menaces everyone differently, but also how men and women search for ways to combat or minimize the psychological impact of slavery on their subjectivity. From Paul D's perspective, Morrison describes the value of male slaves as much as the total of how he can be expended. Inasmuch as he could procreate, it was to produce more labor and therefore more wealth: on the plantation, he comes to learn "the dollar value of his weight, his strength, his heart, his brain, his penis, and his future" (1987, 226). Slavery converts and reduces slaves to objects and property. Paul D faces extreme brutality and oppression and perseveres through dire circumstances. He bravely accepts his fate and refuses to surrender to his memories of the degradation he experienced as a slave, and he displays unquestionable courage and an indomitable spirit despite the oppressive and physical restraints placed on him. He is an example of the "magic and feistiness" that Morrison says that black men possess (1994a, 18). As an ex-slave, he commits to caring for mother and daughter, Sethe and Denver, and imagines a life for himself with them as a family—free of humiliation and hopelessness. Paul D symbolizes the redefinition of male subjectivity in the face of the systematic annihilation of culture and family, and he represents the cruel extent to which manhood can be denied, defined, and redefined in the context of slavery.

Through Paul D, Morrison posits silence as a counter-discourse about black needs, concerns, and identity. Counter-discourse is a subversive system that challenges the production of knowledge and power. As a system of counter-ideologies that resituates the nature of slaves and redefines their relationship to the society or communities in which they live and exist, counter-hegemony acts as a powerful tool to undermine ideologies, cultural norms, and value systems. Silence is the strategy of strategic endurance that Paul D employs to challenge oppressive discourses and represent his experiences as a slave. As a rhetorical strategy, silence represents the "unspeakable" (degrading, debasing, or humiliating) experiences of the daily atrocities of plantation life. Willed silence is also a significant metaphor for the condition of duress under which the slaves live, and it shows an awareness of the emasculating actions that are deemed masculine: "To buy a mother, choose a horse or a wife, handle guns, even learn reading if they wanted to—but they didn't want to since nothing important to them could be put down on paper" (Morrison 1987, 125). On the fictional plantation in *Beloved,* these actions are deemed manly; the male slaves are only able to perform them with permission. This reaffirms their status as slaves. Thus, the refusal to speak, to be unintelligible, marks the terrain where African American male subjectivity can be explored. Silenced thoughts and unspoken words constitute the interior lives of the characters (the narrative of *Beloved* is often structured around characters who are thinking things they do not say). As Morrison argues, the unspeakable/unspoken is that inscribed part of subjectivity that is confirmed in the context of specific experiences that reveal "deeper and other meanings, deeper and other powers, deeper and other significances" (1989, 14). In positing the experiences of the slaves on the Sweet Home plantation, Morrison moves attention from an archetype to the primary experiences that embody an archetype and from grand narratives about slavery to the material experiences of characters who experience slavery.

(Re)reading *Beloved* with black male subjectivity construction as the focal point highlights how Paul D uses both language and silence in his attempts to define himself and create a family within a post-emancipation American context. The patriarchal discourse open to the white slave owners is not a readily available context for black male redefinition to take place. Paul D (and other Sweet Home men) is not recognized as a father that had any role to play in the lives of black women with whom he conceived children or befriended within or outside of slavery. Therefore, when Paul D traveled north, and reestablishes his friendship with Sethe (whom he eventually courts), he encounters a problem (simultaneously a result of gender and experience) that makes clear how he experienced slavery differently than her. While Sethe can't forget her crime of infanticide, which was motivated by how Mrs. Garner exploited her and refused to grant her a wedding and Schoolteacher who encourages his boys to rape and "steal her milk" (20, 1987), Paul D's pride in his ability to survive the beatings, degradation, and emasculation at Sweet Home impacts his capacity to empathize with Sethe's decision. Besides being insensitive to Sethe, Paul D's rhetorical missteps (rudeness and thoughtlessness) indicate how much he has to learn about the difference that gender makes to how he and women experienced life on the Sweet Home plantation. For Paul D's subjectivity-construction process includes redefining himself in the face of paternalistic discourses that seek to make him represent negative beliefs about black manhood.

Paternalism accounts for the contradiction inherent in being a Sweet Home man. While slaves were seen as animals or objects, they were also acknowledged as humans deserving care. Paternalism denies human agency to slaves, but claims it does so for their own protection. Subjected to slave codes and relegated to the margins of the Antebellum South, slaves were property and forbidden from matrimony and education because slaveholders believed that family and literacy would make slaves unhappy with their social position and unfit to serve them and God. As property, slaves could be sold, gambled, or given away, or used as collateral; they were listed on tax rolls just like livestock and farm equipment and written in wills as family dependents—a kind of permanent children who supposedly needed the guidance, protection, discipline, and nurturing of slaveholders, masters, and later family members. Slaves were forbidden from freely engaging in activities that would define them as men in public spaces or exercising civil rights that would categorize them as legal citizens. Slaves were to be seen but not heard. Thus, the common belief on plantations such as Sweet Home is that slaves should be given what they need but not the responsibility or freedom of choice.

Sweet Home slaves were not allowed to speak unless spoken to because allowing them to speak necessitates acknowledging them as an equal. In this sense, they are positioned as the inferior Other. Not only does this action of slaveholders privilege their voices over the oppressed—an example of the paternalistic impulses in discourses of slavery—it is also a distinguishing characteristic of Eurocentricity in Western intellectuals who argued that the ability to speak differentiates man from animals and brutes. Of course, this dictum excludes non-white men and women who spoke languages other than English—from Aristotle's "man is a being of the word" and Socrates' pondering why man was given the word to the arguments of Wilhelm von Humboldt, Martin Heidegger, Max Picard, Thomas Mann, and George Steiner that silence constitutes language and reaffirms man's existence (Glenn 2004, 5). In conflating speech with humanity, Western intellectuals establish a false binary (the written over the oral and speech over the non-verbal) and ignore the significance of silence to speech acts.[2]

2. For a fascinating and thorough historical explanation and rhetorical analysis of speech and silence, see Cheryl Glenn's *Unspoken: A Rhetoric of Silence* in which she argues that classical rhetoricians perceived speech as a gift of the gods, a distinguishing characteristic of humans, and the authorized medium of culture and power. Those who lack the ability to speak were designated non-human (animals) and those who were forbidden from speaking in public (slaves, women, and children) were regarded as inferior to men. In challenging Western intellectuals

Although paternalism was a significant ideology in slaveholding states, its limitations were highlighted by the instances where slaves complied while plotting or strategizing ways to subvert plantation life and the institution of slavery. Highlighting subtle but profound acts of resistance, historians and writers draw our attention to the "hush harbors" and hushed spaces where slaves "talked back" by pointing out the tactics or "strategies of strategic endurance" that slaves employed to appear complicit: obedient and subordinate while secretly planning to escape, learning to read, or determining who owns them (Rodriguez 2007, 125). John Hope Franklin reports slaves "loafing on the job, feigning illness in the fields and on the auction block, and engaging in an elaborate program of sabotage" (2011, 160). Similarly, Junius P. Rodriguez states that slaves strategically used the common belief that they were "childlike" and "ill-equipped" as "a form of personal security" and to undermine production on the planation (2007, 126). Lastly, Frederick Douglass provides examples in his narrative of how he subverted the plantation system: he tricked homeless boys into teaching him how to read and write by offering them food from his master's house, practiced writing in his master's discarded copy books, learned to read the *Columbian Orator,* and finally wrote a pass to freedom. Through "strategies of strategic endurance" slaves not only sabotaged plantation life and undermined paternalism, they helped erect a wall between the black and white worlds. The rhetoric of silence challenges ideologies that maintain paternalism.

Geneva Smitherman suggests a model for thinking about Morrison's use of the rhetoric of silence. Smitherman states that rhetoric accounts for the disorganization that ideologies such as racism and sexism introduce in society (1986, 77). Rhetoric is "language . . . a tool for ordering the chaos of human experience . . . a great amount of comfort comes from being able to 'name events and things'" and that "to use words to give shape and coherence to human existence is a universal human thing—a linguistic fact of life that transcends cultural boundaries" (77). This relationship between power and language determines who speaks, who listens, and what can be spoken about

privileging speech as the domain for men and silence as belonging to the uneducated and uneducable, Glenn argues that the hierarchal relationship between speech and silence or the privileging of speech over silence is a false binary that doesn't consider how rhetoricians tactically use silence (punctuate their words or sentences with silence) as emphasis and account for the many ways that European women and people of color appropriate silence at intentional times to undermine oppressive conditions and practices. Speech only gains significance from the strategic use of silence. Glenn states that "it is silence that reveals speech at the same time that it enacts its own sometimes complementary rhetoric" (2004, 3). Paul D strategically uses silence to negotiate the discursive divide of slavery and freedom. Morrison's Paul D is intelligent about the limitations of rhetoric's oppression and knowledgeable about the African American rhetorical tradition. Paul D highlights the interdependence of speech and silence.

authority, supremacy, and dominance and challenges early European rhetoricians who privileged the spoken or speech over silence. In privileging speech over silence, rhetoricians not only ignore the official language and cultural styles of Other cultures, they also overlook the more nuanced and dynamic communication styles, as Morrison illustrates with Paul D, who decides when he wants to speak, and Sixo, who easily melds African and Native American oral traditions.

A signal catalyst to consider in Morrison's approach for representing the process of black male subjectivity construction is African Americans' predisposition to examine their positionality from their own perspective and from the perspective of the dominant culture. In Morrison's (and Baldwin's) novels, African American characters demonstrate an awareness of the split between the Negro that white Americans imagine exists and the black self, which they inhabit and know. This split or double consciousness Du Bois defines as "a peculiar sensation, this double consciousness, this sense of always looking at one's self through the eyes of others. . . . One ever feels his twoness—an American, a Negro, two souls, two thoughts, two reconcile strivings, two warring ideals in one dark body" (1997, 22). According to Du Bois, African Americans possess a subjective realization that originates from their particular experiences (in regards race and gender), and they have a consciousness based on their social experiences (being black). Such a dual awareness enables African Americans to understand and respond in effective ways to the immediate (sometimes dangerous) situation. Morrison makes use of double consciousness in *Beloved* by representing slaves who are aware of the limitations of white subjectivity. The male and female characters demonstrate double consciousness each time they insert their own understanding of white subjectivity and when they show compassion for the suffering of other slaves. In essence, then, double consciousness empowers black subjects to develop or draw on strategic strategies of endurance that will enable them to acquire what they want or communicate what is necessary.

Du Bois's work provides an illuminating pathway into *Beloved*, for the characters are not only aware of the paternalistic discourses that define them on the plantation, they are also knowledgeable about the rhetorical practices that supply them with a voice or vehicle to express their displeasure. Most literary studies on subtle strategies of resistance are on the female characters in Alice Walker's *The Color Purple* and Zora Neale Hurston's *Their Eyes Were Watching God*. These studies comment on the rhetorical means (verbal and nonverbal) by which the female characters resist patriarchal oppression within and without African American contexts or communities. The black male characters in *Beloved* are subjected to the same patriarchal authority as the female characters in Walker's and Hurston's novels. As Celie and Janie challenge patriarchal domination through verbal and non-verbal cues, signs, or words, Morrison's male characters resort to subtle rhetorical forms of resistance to survive brutality and to voice anger, displeasure, and abhorrence with male paternalism.

In considering *Beloved* as an exploration into strategies of endurance, this chapter explores the process of black male subjectivity construction in Morrison's *Beloved*. Thus, the slaveholders' voices only have authority if slaves listen. Here, I differentiate between "to listen," which means to attend or pay attention, and "to hear," which suggests to comprehend. Hence, a saying among African Americans: I hear you, but I ain't listening to you. "Silence is a rhetorical art of empowered action" (Glenn 2004, 156). Slaves achieve a significant amount of power in silence. While silent, slaves take advantage of the discourses in the discursive divide, such as the infatuation with blackness and the romantic notion that slaves were content in bondage. In silence, slaves observe how masters respond to various situations and learn what slave owners know about them and other slaves, note slaveholders' shortcomings and ignorance, and position themselves to stealthily exploit slaveholders' weaknesses. They share and practice strategies of resistance, secretly acquire literacy, and plan insurrections and escapes as Morrison depicts in the slaves laughing at the string that Schoolteacher wrapped all over their heads, "cross my nose, around my behind. Number my teeth. I thought he was a fool. And the questions he asked was the biggest foolishness of all" (1987, 368).

Indeed, silence gives Paul D and the other slaves in *Beloved* a space to disguise their contempt for slavery and enslavers in forms unrecognizable or unintelligible by authority. Morrison represents slaves' acute sensibilities when slaves take advantage of how they are defined. In despair on a chain gain, Paul D and other male slaves speak in unison about the life they have and will never have. They swing their axes at withheld opportunities: "And they beat. The women for having known them and no more, no more; the children for having been them but never again. They killed a boss so often and so completely they had to bring him back to life to pulp him one more time . . . they beat away. Singing love songs to Mr. Death, they smashed his head. More than the rest, they killed the flirt whom folks called Life for leading them on" (210). Besides beating their day and night dreams for teasing them with images of lives that they will never have, they take advantage of what whites don't know.

Lastly, Paul D and the other slaves exploit slave owners' ignorance or inability to recognize or acknowledge their humanity and insistence on defining blackness as native and untameable. It is this romance with blackness that Morrison comments on when she writes in *Beloved*: "White people believed that whatever the manners, under every dark skin was a jungle. Swift unnavigable waters, swinging screaming baboons, sleeping snakes, red gums ready for their sweet white blood" (382). Paul D and other slaves use this romance with blackness to their advantage when they resist domination through various activities such as acquiring passes to freedom and participating in traditions without permission from the slave owners. Feigning to accept the plantation system, Paul D and the other slaves know that slaveholders can't account for slaves' consciousness. In this sense, silence is between feigned and unfeigned. Paul D and the other slaves exploit slaveholders' attempt to appear paternalistic and their romantic notion that slaves are content in bondage.

Slaves get power from not listening to the master because they know that slaves' consciousness is the place where slavery can't reach or change. Hence, a saying among African Americans is I hear you, but I ain't listening to you. Thus, listening is a point of contention for slaveholders because slaves consistently remind slaveholders through subversive acts that bondage happens to their bodies not their minds. Despite the many times slaveholders instruct slaves that they are property, slaves not only resist accepting this classification, they also exercised freedom over themselves. In *Flight to Canada*, Ishmael Reed argues that flight is the most subversive act because the fugitive slave stole his own property (1998, 64). Despite Schoolteacher's numerous attempts to teach the Sweet Home men that they are property, the Sweet Home men continue subversive acts such as running away, feigning sickness to get off work, finding solace in sharing narratives by a large sycamore tree on the plantation that Sweet Home men affectionately refer to as Brother. Silently and faithfully hiring himself out to buy his mother's freedom because he hears (although she doesn't say) that she is tired, Halle subtlety and cunningly represents the "quiet technique" of altering the economy of the plantation. Strategies of endurance are essential for exploring how slaves talked (verbally or nonverbally) back to plantation authorities and undermined plantation culture in the hushed spaces.

•

> The white man is sealed in his whiteness. The black man is sealed in his blackness.
>
> —FRANTZ FANON, *BLACK SKIN WHITE MASKS* (1967, 9)

Fanon identifies the problems that silence mediates as the colonizing gaze. Fanon's concern with the discursive dimensions of colonization illuminates Morrison's representation of Paul D's physical and sexual degradation at the hands of two successive slaveholders. In Fanon's articulation of mutually dependent relationships or the dialectic, individuals gain an understanding of one's self from how each wants to be seen. As an archetype of symbolic and psychological violence and aggression, the dialectic underscores the necessity of the gaze or recognition that transforms black subjects into objects or the colonized. The colonized, then, internalizes (accepts) how the gaze constructs him and turns this gaze inward on himself and outward on other black men. As Fanon states, the colonized is always aware of the gaze: how in a single look his "body schema, attacked in several places, collapsed, giving way to an epidermal racial schema" (1967, 92). This fragmentation is heightened by the visual and irreconcilable difference of the black figure, which becomes a predominant signifier for difference even as the Black male fashions himself to be other than what he is. For Fanon, in order to resist inscription, the colonized must accept the gaze as a permanent presence but not a determining discourse.

Fanon's paradigm is helpful when considering the impact of paternalism on black male subjectivity in *Beloved.* When Paul D reflects on his experience as a slave, he remembers the terrifying effects slavery had on his and the psyches of other slaves. Many slaves he encountered while traveling north were lost souls suffering from extreme disorientation, delusions, and amnesia. He sees "Negroes so stunned, or hungry, or tired or bereft it was a wonder they recalled or said anything. . . . Once he met a Negro about fourteen years old who lived by himself in the woods and said he couldn't remember living anywhere else. He saw a witless colored woman jailed and hanged for stealing ducks she believed were her own babies" (Morrison 1987, 66). Witnessing the stresses and strains on slaves who seem to have traded one nightmarish reality for another, Paul D realizes that these discourses hit ex-slaves simultaneously and continuously and have a long lasting impact on them. In this well-known passage, Morrison writes:

> The more colored people spent their strength trying to convince them how gentle they were, how clever and loving, how human, the more they used themselves up to persuade whites of something Negroes believed could not be questioned, the deeper and more tangled the jungle grew inside. But it wasn't the jungle Blacks brought with them to this place from the other (livable) place. It was the jungle white folks planted in them. And it grew. It spread. In, through and after life, it spread, until it invaded the whites that had made it. Touched them everywhere. Changed and altered them. Made them bloody, silly, worse than even they want to be, so scared were they of the jungle they made. (198–99)

Here, the dynamics of white/black subjectivity formation in relation to the metaphor of the "jungle" is within and without, for both whites and blacks. The distinction of Self and Other feeds off the binary, making "colored people" desperate to prove that they were not as they were defined and encouraging white people to become indulgent of power with its attendant jungle of sadism and humble cruelty. This relationship between Self and Other, master and slave, thoroughly dehumanizes both parties. For Paul D, the cost of dehumanization marks subjectivity formation. Dehumanization is ground zero; Houston Baker defines it as the location where African Americans transform and recuperate the circumstances that "otherwise would X or erase them" (1995, 35). Baker defines this redefining process as combating erasure or the legalized "X-ing" of African Americans through discourses such as the laws that protected slavery. The outcome of this discursive oppression is the deadening and invisibility that Ellison describes in *Invisible Man*. From rock bottom, Paul D wrestles with memories of being a slave and sees himself as a victim on the Sweet Home plantation. At the beginning of the novel when Paul D is standing on the porch of 124 Bluestone Road, he is a newly freed slave with a desire to have a life and family outside of slavery. In order to achieve this peace, Paul D must come to terms with paternalism as a network of discourses that maintained his enslavement. This network is the social aspect of power or the relationship between slave owners' philosophy about servitude and the practices they employed to maintain slavery.

In *Slavery and Social Death*, Orlando Patterson argues that there is a "social aspect of power" that maintains slaves outside of or below the society in which they serve. The "social aspect of power" is employed strategically and emphasizes that power is exercised on a continuum. On one end, "power is acknowledging human force openly, then to humanize it by the use of various social strategies like fictive kinship . . . asymmetric gift exchanges" (1982, 18). On the other end, Patterson says, is the "method of concealment," in which coercion is almost completely hidden or thoroughly denied (18). The slaveholders in *Beloved* represent this range. Mr. Garner benefits from his relationship with Paul D and the other slaves, but the slaves suffer in each interaction with Mr. Garner. Garner "attempts a kindly paternalism, recognizing the humanity and worth of his slaves. Although he refers to them as 'men' rather than boys, his good intentions are illusory" (Fulweiler 2000, 130). While these acts could be seen as opportunities for Paul D to redeem himself or prove his manhood, these acts only reinforce Mr. Garner's status, authority, and paternalistic compulsions. Patterson writes, "By holding out the promise of redemption, the master provides himself with a motivating force more powerful than any whip. Slavery in this way was a self-correcting institution: what it denied the slave it utilized as the major means of motivating him" (1982, 101). Mr. Garner's status is emboldened in the presence of other slaveholders: "If you a man yourself, you'll want your niggers to be men too" is a paternalistic attempt to elevate his slaves above the dominant discourses that define them as chattels (Morrison 1987, 10). To other slave owners, Mr. Garner's insistence that "my niggers are men every one of em. Bought em thataway, raised em thataway" reinforces Garner's masculinity and Paul D's emasculation (10). When other slaveholders see Garner's slaves behaving as Garner had trained them, they will be reminded of Garner's masculinity and his ability to train the untrainable, according to the racial discourses of the time.

While Mr. Garner conducts an experiment to discover the extent to which he could make black subjects fulfill his expectations, Schoolteacher endeavors to tear down all signs that indicated the humanity of slaves, reducing Paul D to the ontological status of non-human. As a contributing factor to the discursive divide, scientific and anthropological discourses about the inherent inferiority of slaves rationalize the inhumane treatment of people of African descent. In studies, experiments, and philosophical treatises, Western scholars record their forgone conclusions about how slaves are fit for or benefit from slavery. In the 19th century, Dr. Josiah Clark Nott, a physician, wrote *Connection between the Biblical and Physical History of Man, Types of Mankind,* and *Indigenous Races of Earth,* texts that defended slavery by arguing that "psychological traits of the African and their physical endurance and limited mental capacity made them a race specifically suited for slavery" (Rodriguez 2007, 117). Nott argues for a racial hierarchy that positions Africans on the bottom and Europeans on the top. Nott's racialized discourse was a foundation for many southern slavery proponents to use to defend slavery. Similarly, Samuel A. Cartwright published papers in the *New Orleans Medical and Surgical Journal* in the 1850s that focused on the ethnology of slave populations in the South. Using science to support his claims and pseudoscience to argue that slaves have specifics attributes, Cartwright argues that "the propensity of slaves to run away was not a natural desire for human freedom but rather a malady" that he called dysaesthesia aethiopica, an illness that caused rascality to appear in some slaves but not in others (Rodriguez 2007, 117). Nott's and Cartwright's flawed research is constructed on problematic scientific arguments with a forgone conclusion.

Schoolteacher exemplifies the methodology of these early scholars when he employs scientific and anthropological discourses to rationalize the use of force in degrading slaves. As a methodology of cataloguing the incipient human traits that are specific to slaves, Schoolteacher measures craniums and checks teeth and the flexibility of limbs. Taken to an absurd extreme, Schoolteacher believes that he can segregate human from animal traits: "No, no. That's not the way. I told you to put her human characteristics on the left; her animal ones on the right. And don't forget to line them up" (Morrison 1987, 193). After conducting his research, Schoolteacher concludes that the intelligence of slaves isn't much above the level of animals. From Schoolteacher's research, Paul D learns that he is only a Sweet Home man at Sweet Home, and when he and other slaves leave, their status changes. They aren't experiments, just simple property that toils when told: "One step off that ground and they were trespassers among the human race. Watchdogs without teeth; steer bulls without horns; gelded workhorses whose neigh and whinny could not be translated into language responsible humans spoke" (125). Under Schoolteacher's authority, Paul D's body is scientifically deconstructed.

Intrigued with the insidiousness of this arrangement, Paul D critically reflects on his relationship to Garner and the institution of slavery: "Paul D tells himself, Garner called and announced them as men—but only on Sweet Home, and by his leave. Was he naming what he saw or creating what he did not?" (Finney 1998, 110). Paul D poses a philosophical question about the intrinsic or cultural qualities of black maleness. If it is cultural then Paul D does not have any positive experiences to build on. And if it is inherent, then Paul D needs to develop a cultural heuristic in order to find that core of masculinity within himself. This enterprise graded the manhood of black subjects within constructed discourses of race, religion, and economic imperatives. Thus, performing manhood in the African American context in *Beloved* requires coming to terms with the psychological and emotional fallout of systematic gradations of emasculation and understanding that white oppressors didn't perceive black subjects as logical inheritors of white patriarchy—a point Robyn Wiegman makes in *The Anatomy of Lynching* when she writes, "patriarchal logic of the dominant culture became the defining mechanism for organizing the newly freed slave" (2001, 357). In the slavery system—authoritarianism in the extreme—Mr. Garner and Schoolteacher drew on all available discourses to maintain hegemony; no "family provider" or black patriarch could be allowed. The attainment of slavery's intrinsic goals was contingent on the fullest and most brutal utilization of the productive capacities of every man, woman, and child (Ya Salaam 2001, 120).

As he struggles for an existence outside slavery, Paul D comes to terms with how he has been already transformed to less than a farm animal named Mister. In clever irony, Morrison names the rooster on the Sweet Home plantation Mister, so that each time Paul D speaks about the rooster he must use a salutation that announces his subordinate position (which affirms his social position and renders him complicit in his own oppression). Paul D says, "Mister was allowed to be and stay what he was, but I wasn't allowed to be and stay what I was. Even if you cooked him, you'd be cooking a rooster named Mister, but wasn't no way I'd ever be Paul D again, living or dead. Schoolteacher changed me, I was something else, and that something was less than a chicken, sitting in the sun in a tub" (Morrison 1987, 72). Here, "Paul D thinks about (but does not speak about) how slavery emasculated [him] beneath the status of the rooster, Mister" (Fulwieler 2000, 120).[3] Socially dead, Paul D is already once transformed. "The life he strives to regain cannot be the life he lost" (Patterson 1982, 98). As a slave, Paul D struggles for freedom and ultimate liberation to discover how to be a "new black man" (a man who doesn't embrace racism and patriarchy) (Neal 2006, 10). He accepts that he can't go back to being how he was before slavery, for he was born a slave and doesn't have memories that are independent of slavery. In order to become a new black man, Paul D must know what to retain and what to forget about slavery. He selectively chooses to remember the memories that move him from "the liminal state of social death" to a state of freedom (Patterson 1982, 39). However, if being free means totally being a part of society, Paul D will never be free, for there isn't a space that he can occupy where he will be looked on as other than an ex-slave.

•

> The white man is always trying to know into somebody else's business. All right, I'll set something outside the door of my mind for him to play with and handle. . . . I'll put this play toy in his hand, and he will seize it and go away. Then I'll say my say and sing my song.
>
> —ZORA NEALE HURSTON, *MULES AND MEN* (1990, 3)

Another manifestation of silence in *Beloved* occurs when Paul D reflects on his relationship with other slaves as a means to mediate the emasculating discourses at Sweet Home. In this case, silence is still rhetorical but speech occurs as thoughts about how other slaves resisted inscription. "Silence is not opposed to language, which I define as the human capacity for vocal and written utterance. Rather, silence and language act in a reciprocal fashion in the construction of knowledge" (Glenn 2004, 5, 8). The relationships that Paul D has with the other Sweet Home men present him with opportunities to gain a more positive understanding of himself. For example, reflecting on Sixo's words and gaze, Paul D remembers how uplifting and reaffirming his rela-

3. For a parallel argument, see Howard W. Fulwieler, "Belonging and Freedom in Morrison's *Beloved*: Slavery, Sentimentality, and the Evolution of Consciousness."

tionship and interaction with Sixo was: "When he looks at himself through Garner's eyes, he sees one thing. Through Sixo's, another. One makes him feel righteous. One makes him feel ashamed" (Morrison 1987, 267). In his relationship with Sixo, Paul D begins to understand how black masculinity is being constructed in a dialectical relationship with white identity and in the cultural context of slavery. He begins to see more potential for himself in Sixo's eyes because in Mr. Garner's terms, he will always be the shadowy (and darkened) image of white masculinity. Paul D says he sees more possibility for himself in Sixo's eyes. In Sixo's eyes, he comes to terms with his social position as an ex-slave, understating the complexity of his situation. Within this space of difference is where decolonization occurs and is "always a violent event" (Fanon 1963, 1). "It is quite simply the substitution of one 'species' of mankind by another. The substitution is unconditional, absolute, total, and seamless" (1). The transformation one undergoes from colonized to uncolonized is a traumatic but necessarily violent process in order to move the colonized from a state of dependency to independence. Fanon doesn't celebrate unnecessary physical or destructive force, for he is more invested in the self-conscious process or the specific ways in which one attempts to rid himself of self-hatred and embrace a doctrine of pride and self-confidence. This is Paul D's predicament. Thus, he must reconcile the inward self with outward constructions.

The manner in which Paul D uses his body suggests another rhetorical performance of silence. Paul D and other slaves communicate their disposition with their body. An example of silence as body rhetoric in *Beloved* occurs when Paul D is sold to Brandywine, a notorious slave trader who is known for debasing and tearing down slaves before selling them to plantations. On the coffle, Paul D witnesses Brandywine and his men beat and sodomize the prisoners. Although Paul D's legs and hands are bound with chains, he still manages to use his body components to communicate with other slaves. In "A Phenomenology of the Black Body," Charles Johnson explains how the black body functions as an instrument for communicating how one feels. He says, "The body is our general medium for having a world. The blind man's stick is no longer alien to him, not a mere object, but his bodily extension . . . if I am downcast, the body gestures accordingly with a dropping posture" (2001, 226). Paul D and the other men stand side by side under the watchful eye of the guard waiting for the order to start work. Since his hands are bound and they are chained together waist to waist, he uses his eyes to communicate how he is feeling: "No one spoke to the other. At least not with words. The eyes had to tell what there was to tell: Help me this mornin's bad'; 'I'm a make it'; 'New man'; 'Steady now steady'" (Morrison 1987, 107). The location of the eyes on the body allows Paul D to see without being seen. Moving his eyes instead of his body allows him to avoid the stare of the prison guard. The eyes see danger. From watching the eyes of each other, the men on the coffle can tell others' mental, spiritual, and physical health. Thus, Morrison shows the sufficiency of the corporeal schema when contextualized within a historical-racial schema.

Also, Morrison represents silence as the dynamic rhetorical play that African Americans employ to subvert or challenge authority. To signify, Henry Louis Gates argues, "is to engage in certain rhetorical games" (1988, 59–60). Signifyin(g) is figurative, suggestive speech; it is a complex rhetorical device that requires the control, ownership, and employment of applicable modes of elucidation and understanding on the part of listeners. For instance, in the following rhetorical act from Mel Watkins's *On the Real Side,* a slave signifies on the institution's distinction between chattel slave and property. "'You scoundrel, you ate my turkey,' the master admonishes. . . . 'Yes, suh, Massa, you got less turkey but you sho nuff got mo' Nigger,'" the slave replies (1999, 32). Since slaves are considered property, they shouldn't be held responsible for eating or damaging other property on the plantation. Holding slaves responsible for consuming property challenges the belief that they are childlike and unable to distinguish right from wrong. Mitchell-Kernan argues that the most important aspect of signifying is the misdirection of the speech acts and the ability to expose that which haunts the dominant consciousness. She continues, "Labeling a particular utterance signifying involves the recognition and attribution of some implicit content or function which is potentially obscured by the surface contents or function. The obscurity may lie in the relative difficulty it poses for interpretation" (1999, 318).

Paul D witnesses a similar interaction between Sixo and Schoolteacher. Similar to Schechter's example above, Sixo shows signifying as silence is a language practice in which speakers smartly comment on a particular situation or incident without revealing all the knowledge they have about it. Here, signifying as silence is the withholding of information to win or clarify an argument. Sixo explains to Schoolteacher the cost of labor and production: When Sixo was asked if he had stolen the shoat, Sixo argues that if he belongs to the master and the shoat belongs to the master then he could not have stolen the pig. But Schoolteacher's rebuttal is that "definitions belonged to the definers—not the defined" (Morrison 1987, 190). In a single dialogue and moment, Sixo reveals that he is aware of how important he and other slaves are to the institution. And, as property, he is required to intensively labor for long hours each day, so it is necessary for him to utilize the resources on the plantation. Besides standing squarely within the African American vernacular tradition, Sixo leaves an indelible mark on Paul D.

By including Paul D's contemplation on Sixo (or the slave and slave dialectic), Morrison points to the inability of paternalism to determine how a slave imagines or identifies himself. In recognizing that his self-definition doesn't originate from or depend on Schoolteacher or Mr. Garner and the arbitrariness of the discursive realm of white psychology, Paul D resists what Arnold Kemp refers to as "genopsycholingisticide . . . linguistic . . . subjugation": how language overwrites one's sense of self (Gilyard 1996, 31). Concurring with Kemp's argument that the dominant literacy and language circulate white supremacy, Keith Gilyard argues that language has a dual function: "as a force either to prevent or foster the development of authentic selves" (31). Gilyard's notion of an authentic self loosely applies here, for Paul D is more concerned with constructing a self-image that does not include or rely on dominant discourses as opposed to striving for an "authentic self" that is free of racial inscriptions (which is impossible). For Paul D, Sixo and the other community of slaves induce apperception whereas each new post-slavery experience absorbs and converts the fragments of past experiences into a new understanding. Strategies of strategic endurance (such as humor, signifying, and oral narratives) that are a regular part of plantation life become a critical lens for surviving diverse circumstances.

Morrison illustrates the complexity of Paul D's subjectivity through his refusal to speak about his past. As a coping mechanism, Paul D chooses to live in silence. The refusal to speak about the past or to succumb to one's past experiences marks the place where Paul D begins to construct his subjectivity. While traveling north to Ohio, Paul D decides that his past experiences at Sweet Home and on the coffle do not define him or his future; therefore, he will not speak about what he experienced as a slave or prisoner, a task that was possible while traveling from place to place: "when he was drifting, thinking only about the next meal and night sleep, when everything was packed tight in his chest, he had no sense of failure, of things not working out" (Morrison 1987, 221), but this proves to be difficult once he reaches the doorsteps of 124 Bluestone Road. Using silence as a strategy for separating the past and present has advantages and disadvantages. The advantage is that by not discussing his past, Paul D can focus on building a future with Sethe. Silence functions as a starting place for Paul D to separate his past experiences as a slave from a future as Sethe's husband. He accepts that "a life with Sethe would change his need to travel from place to place . . . and approaches Sethe with a tentative restraint of a conditional lover" (Powell 2000, 148).

Sethe eyes Paul D suspiciously. His behavior does not match her experiences with other slaves. In wondering what makes Paul D different, she ponders how Paul D succeeded in escaping the discourses that suffocated other men like Halle and Sixo. Unlike other ex-slaves, Paul D's eyes do not suggest his past or signal and beg for the questions that would prod him to discuss his life. This intrigues Sethe. She marvels at his uniqueness while being suspicious of his motivations. In her experience, ex-slaves very seldom forget how they were tortured. Paul D tells her if there is "a way to put it there and there's a way to take it out. I know em both and I haven't figured out yet which is worse" (Morrison 1987, 71). Interested in how he manages to suppress the past, remove the "wildness" that "the bit places in the eyes of most slaves," Sethe focuses attention on Paul D's subjectivity. Sethe prods him about what he remembers most about the bit. Paul D talked about envying the farm animals for how freely they wandered around the yard and in the woods, but he stopped short "because saying more might push them both to a place they couldn't get back from. He would keep the rest where it belonged: in that tobacco tin buried in his chest where a red heart used to be. Its lid rusted shut. He would not pry it loose now in front of this sweet sturdy woman for if she got a whiff of the contents it would shame him" (72–73). Paul D employs silence and memory to decide if, how, or when he wants to use or share his memories.

However, by consciously choosing silence, Paul D thwarts his desire to move forward with Sethe. Paul D uses silence to deal with the pain of seeing his enslaved brothers tortured. Sethe consistently asks him about the whereabouts of her husband, Halle. Paul D knows what happened to Halle but in speaking about it he acknowledges the circumstances under which black male slaves were unable to fulfill definitions of manhood. Paul D's memories of the same event are of Halle suffering because he could not protect Sethe and his children from Schoolteacher. When Paul D tells Sethe that Halle broke down after witnessing Schoolteacher's and the boys' assault on her, Paul D centralizes the unspeakable nature of male slaves' experiences and the inadequacies of language in explaining their helplessness. Refusing to allow Sethe to accept that Halle failed her because he did not intervene in Schoolteacher's assault, Paul D points out the emotional toll that enslavement has on male subjectivity. Responding adversely to Sethe's suggestion that "Halle found another way to live" (Morrison 1987, 69), Paul D emphatically states the limitation of black male subjectivity: "Let me tell you something. A man ain't a goddamn ax. Chopping, hacking, busting every goddamn minute of the day. Things get to him. Things he can't chop down because they're inside" (69). Paul D is overwhelmed with "the patriarchal notion that women must be protected by men; however, he can't resist emulating the macho sexism of his white counterparts rather than working toward a more natural and healthy equality between the sexes" (Bell 1988, 171). The quandary is that if Paul D talks too much, he risks reenacting that white patriarchal domination. However, if he doesn't speak, he risks another kind of damage. This leaves a narrow space within which to construct black male subjectivity. At pivotal times, Paul D thinks about but does not speak his deepest and sincerest feelings to Sethe. As he reflects on the possibilities of creating a family with Sethe he contemplates what it means to love as a slave and as a freeman. If Paul D utilizes a definition of manhood he learned as a slave, he would continue to "love just a little bit; everything, just a little bit, so when they broke its back, or shoved it in a croaker sack, well, maybe you'd have a little love left over for the next one" (Morrison 1987, 45). In his current situation facing life after Sweet Home, Paul D desires to love and procreate without the fear that his children will be taken and sold. Paul D is sincere when he declares his love for Sethe because he wants her to "make a life with him" and "beat back the past" (73). Paul D wants to be Sethe's confidante, protector, and rescuer. He is willing to "catch" her before she falls to her "knees" from the weight of grief, and he wants to provide Denver the home that her father was unable to (45). While Sethe clings to the past (making it a palpable presence in the house), Paul D imagines a future with her and Denver. It is this difference (in their way of reconciling their past lives with their present identities) that reinforces how each uses the past to construct their subjectivity.

This silence extends to black women too. Again Paul D is silent, but not to be subversive as he is with white men, but to listen to the black women's concerns and experiences. As he struggles to be a "comrade" to women or "a friend of [their] mind" in the fight against racism and oppression, Paul D employs silence to redefine himself as a man, friend, husband, and lover for African American women and families (Ikard 2007, 299). Besides being one of the most important qualities that Paul D displays in the novel, this use of silence suggests an additional way to fulfill Michael Awkward's notion of black male feminism (that black men should attempt to destabilize sexist and oppressive dominant discourses). In using silence to represent Paul D's subjectivity, Morrison represents the possibilities of black male subjectivity by establishing his concern with the material conditions of black girls and women. The patience and understanding that Paul D demonstrates marks a standard for caring relationships between black men and females:

> Women saw him and wanted to weep—to tell him that their chest hurt and their knees did too. Strong women and wise saw him and told him things they only told each other: that way past the Change of Life, desire in them had suddenly become enormous, greedy, more savage than when they were fifteen, and that it embarrassed them and make them sad; that secretly they longed to die—to be quit of it—that sleep was more precious to them than

> any waking day. Young girls sidled up to him to confess or describe how well-dressed the visitations were that had followed them straight from their dreams. (Morrison 1987, 17)

Fulfilling what he believes to be his role as a black man, Paul D is silent and attentive while listening to the girls' and women's painful memories. As this passage shows, Paul D knows that girls and women suffer differently than boys and men. Paul D appropriates what is often thought of as a woman's role—listening—to redefine black male subjectivity within the narrow space between the dominance of white racist patriarchy and the kind of submission he was forced into as a slave.

Beloved complicates this process. When Paul D meets Beloved, he is learning how to understand and empathize with black women and their experiences, but is unable to because she refuses to share her memories. She remains silent but discovers subtle ways to undermine his relationship with Sethe. Beloved's presence disrupts not just his courtship of Sethe but his strategy for relating to women in a nonpatriarchal way. She appears without a history or story to share and slowly but consistently demands Sethe's attention. Most critics argue that Beloved is a baby ghost, a reincarnation of Sethe's murdered daughter who returns to remind or punish her for her crime. They point to Sethe's response to Beloved: Sethe grieves to the extent that she is unable to remain employed or care for herself or Denver. She spends quiet moments confiding with Beloved about her feelings of regret and helplessness. Beloved listens—she doesn't talk much but her intent is clear, and her presence is felt and known. Beloved demands and consumes all of Sethe's attention. She refuses to answer Paul D's questions in front of Sethe, and she throws a tantrum when Paul D presses her for information about where she is from. Beloved changes and controls the dynamics in the house. With Beloved as part of the household, Paul D is unable to take Denver and Sethe to carnivals, spend time singing around the house doing handy work, or enjoy Sethe's delicious dinners with his developing family (Sethe, Denver, and himself). Paul D no longer has the space to talk endlessly and into the late night with Sethe about their future together. As he does with Mr. Garner and Schoolteacher, Paul D attempts to endure and outlast Beloved's mystical and dominating power, and he struggles to retain a sense of separateness from her machinations. However, Beloved has an insidious nature like Mr. Garner and Schoolteacher. Similar to the slave owners who regulated Paul D's life, Beloved neutralizes Paul D's manhood. She determines where and with whom Paul D sleeps. Literally, Beloved terrorizes Paul D's mind—causing him to live in fear at 124 Bluestone Road as he lived as a slave on Sweet Home plantation.

As the reembodiment of white subjectivity outside of Sweet Home, Beloved neutralizes Paul D's manhood and interrupts his process of subjectivity construction. Thus, to Paul D, Beloved is not a woman. Paul D's suspicion of Beloved and his curiosity to know her mysterious origins gets the better of him: "he had never known a woman who lit up for nobody in particular, who just did it as a general announcement" (65). More than once in the shed, Paul D calls Beloved's name, thus satisfying her sexual desires. After being enslaved by two different slave owners, Paul D experiences a great deal of shame at being so easily dominated by Beloved. He contemplates telling Sethe that Beloved coerced him into having sex with her, but he realizes that "he cannot say to this woman who did not squint in the wind, 'I am not a man'" (128). Paul D recognizes the first-hand gender experience that Derrick Bell refers to in "Sexual Diversion": Bell explains that black women's opinions of black men are not formed in a vacuum but as a result of first-hand experience. Black women do not accept social ills such "as racism as the reason for sorry behavior—they have experienced it first hand and for them it is an excuse, not a justification" (2001, 171). To tell Sethe about his sexual encounter with Beloved is to admit to her and accept in himself that he lacks self-control. He assumes that Sethe wouldn't believe that a girl young enough to be his daughter could overpower him and his imagination. Accepting that there is no longer a place for him at 124, Paul D temporarily seeks refuge and home in a church cellar alone, refusing to speak about his struggles at Bluestone. He eventually returns to Bluestone Road.

As a result of his relationship with Sethe, Paul D comes to accept a more dynamic understanding of himself and alternative ways to express himself. He uses the vernacular to indirectly speak about his experiences. Although he speaks with the vernacular, he still practices a rhetorical practice that isn't authorized or viewed as legitimate, but rather linguistically inferior to speech. Thus, since the dominant class doesn't accept the vernacular as an official language or rhetorical style, I argue that the vernacular serves as a linguistic alternative to speech. It occurs at the periphery and affirms the subjectivity of the oppressed. Paul D embraces the vernacular as an alternative to talking directly about his experiences. Memories and folksongs are narratives about his past. He recalls these narratives in quiet contemplation and while completing chores around the house. The vernacular allows him to speak the unspoken without breaking his silence. Glenn argues that "muted groups demonstrate linguistic resistance to linguistic domination in a number of ways, from speaking out and telling to talking back" (2004, 26). Here, Glenn borrows from bell hooks the idea that black women developed a rhetorical style that compelled others to listen. Talking back, according to hooks, is "speaking as an equal to an authority figure" (2014, 5). Hooks offers talking back as an African American rhetorical style that responds to the silence that black women receive whenever they encounter unbending patriarchy. Talking back also works in the case of Paul D as he or his labor is valued the same as Sethe on the Sweet Home plantation. Not only are they positioned the same as slaves with no voice, thoughts, or memories worth hearing, they are also struggling to find the correct register in which they can release themselves from their past.

Paul D's memories are primarily narratives about living with other slaves and watching slaves as close to him as brothers die brutal deaths. Intersecting many of his memories are moments in which he learned by listening to other slaves talk about life and death as a slave. These stories fulfill Elliot Oring's criteria for folk narratives reflecting both the past as well as the present and reflecting both the individual and community (1986, 123). In *Beloved,* folk narratives are the stories that connect Paul D and the other slaves to the community of slaves on the Sweet Home plantation. Sixo's narratives connect Paul D to Sixo's Native American folklife before slavery and suggest an attainable relationship between Paul D and the traditions of Sixo's fictional but not depicted Native American community. It is the tradition or the suggestion of tradition within the narratives that shapes Paul D. For "tradition involved a negotiation between individuals and their various communities, often about alterations to the traditions responding to conditions at the time of the enactment" (Bronner 2005, 26). The narratives that Paul D learns provide a means for him to negotiate plantation life and connect him to a community outside Sweet Home. Besides connecting him to a Native American tradition off the Sweet Home plantation, these narratives instruct Paul D about alternative beliefs and values about manhood. The memories that come to mind, whether he summons them or not, are thoughts about the laughter and brutality he shared and suffered with the Sweet Home men. These narratives suggest to Paul D ways to think about himself as a man outside of slavery. He recalls laughing as Sixo told him stories about the healing power of love, at pursuing love in spite of the slave masters.

Paul D's memories about his life as a slave on Sweet Home and prisoner on a coffle are ingrained and part of his self-identity. Not only does he reflect on how he was infantilized and dehumanized, he also recalls the humor and acceptance that occurred between him and the other slaves on Sweet Home. From these memories, he constructs a counter-discourse about what it means to be an ex-slave. Narratives about watching slaves as close to him as brothers burned alive intersect with stories about feigning working and outsmarting plantation owners and with his own memories of slaves performing acts of brotherhood. In *Beloved,* folk narratives connect Paul D to the Native American community and traditions that Sixo represents each time he spoke about dancing "among trees at night . . . to keep his bloodlines open," the healing power of love, and pursuing his love interest—the Thirty-Mile Woman—despite threats from Schoolteacher. Sixo tells Paul D about how he dodged the whip of a white man and woman in a buggy upon returning from one of his many visits with the Thirty-Mile Woman (Morrison 1987, 24). Sometimes after hearing a story, they would laugh together. However, their laughter should not be interpreted as amusement, for as Aristotle states, "At times when old and young men feel pity 'laughter' . . . is the opposite of querulousness . . . imagining that anything that befalls any one else might easily happen to them" (1927, 86). Positioned differently in these situations, Sixo is the language-user or bearer whereas Paul D is a listener. If Garner or Schoolteacher would have walked up on this scene they most likely would have concluded that slave laughter is an indication of how happy they are—their contentment. Many plantation owners romanticized slavery and argued that slaves' singing, dancing, and laughter were clear signs of their innocent, natural, and inherent natures.

As a strategy of endurance, humor foregrounds a façade of naiveté and curiosity and conceals the wit and intelligence that many slaves had during slavery. The laughter that Paul D shares with other slaves as Sixo narrates his mistreatment reinforces Mel Watkins's and Paul Beatty's argument that the subversive nature in most black humor brings to light deeply held ideologies about race, class, and gender. Through humor, slaves recast their lives so that the lunacy of the other party is more apparent than their own humiliation. "As an effective palliative for the injuries to body and psyche which bondage inflicted, and a medium for articulating hopes and fantasies of freedom," humor provides a way for slaves to be optimistic in a pessimistic present (Sterling 1997, 347). It also provides a way for slaves' communication in the presence of planters to go unnoticed or remain indecipherable. Taken from Watkin's *On the Real,* the example below depicts slave humor as sarcastically wicked:

> "Pompey, how do I look? the master asked.
>
> "O, massa, mighty. You looks might."
>
> "What do you mean 'Might,' Pompey?"
>
> "Why, massa, you looks noble."
>
> "What do you mean by noble?"
>
> "Why, suh, you looks just like a lion."
>
> "Why Pompey, where have you ever seen a lion?"
>
> "I saw one down in yonder field the other day, massa."

> "Pompey, you foolish fellow, that was a jackass."
> "Was it, massa? Well, suh, you looks just like him." (1999, 67)

Similarly, slaves outsmart or trick slave owners through signifying and humor:

> One morning, when Ike entered the master's room to clean it, he found the master just preparing to get out of bed. "Ike," he said, "I certainly did have a strange dream last night."
>
> "Sez yuh did, Massa, sez yuh did?" answered Ike. "Lemme hyeah it."
>
> "All right," replied the master. "It was like this: I dreamed I went to Nigger Heaven last night, and saw there a lot of garbage, some old torn-down houses, a few old broken-down, rotten fences, the muddiest, sloppiest streets I ever saw, and a big bunch of ragged, dirty Negroes walking around."
>
> "Umph, umph, Massa," said Ike. "Yuh sho' musta et de same t'ing Ah did las' night, cause Ah dreamed Ah went up ter de white man's paradise, an' de streets wuz all ob gol' an silvah, and dey wuz lots o' milk an' honey dere an' putty pearly gates, but dey wuzn't uh soul in de whole place." (39)

While acknowledging their "lowly position in society," the above slaves point out the inanity and brutal nature of white men and the hypocrisy of "that peculiar institution" (Watkins, 1999, 30–32). In *Shadow and Act,* Ralph Ellison says that African Americans have a "special perspective" that incorporates comic vision as a means for coping with America's social and political predicament. Ellison continues that this experience has given black people a different way to look at African American culture and people against American history and the landscape. Thus, it is humorously heartbreaking to think about adult males punishing other adult males for sneaking off a plantation to visit a woman they love (1995, 131–32). Simultaneously looking from within and without, slaves' language-play questions the fundamental tenet of slavery: that slaves needed a white father figure to guide them through the tumultuous and unpredictable experience of life.

While humorous narratives have an empowering function in Paul D's subjectivity construction, work songs and chants align his subjectivity with African American laborers who embrace song as a vehicle for managing and articulating their pain, triumphs, frustrations, and aspirations. In preserving the beliefs, values, and feelings of a people and its culture, the music and words counter dominant discourses by presenting a bottom-up perspective of slavery. Houston Baker states that the "ironic repudiation of the American system" (celebrations of escapes from chain gains and complaints of the inhumanity of overseers) that we find in work songs is a characteristic that distinguishes African American literature (1990, 13). Lars Eckstein describes the function of work songs and chants as follows: "Cathartic expression of the unspeakable pains comes only in music, in the blues and its predecessor, the collective work song. This is put forth in Paul D's experiences on the Georgia chain gang, where the men survive by singing their lives in the typical call and response patterns rooted in West African field songs" (2006, 208). The song that Paul D sings, while repairing the table and chair he repeatedly slammed against the wall in an effort to chase the baby ghost away, hearkens to Henry Truvillion's song "Sis Joe" (Morrison 1987, 40). In his recorded lecture "Railroad Songs: Work Songs for Rail Trampling and Track Laying," John Lomax describes Truvillion as the "head track-layer for Wier Lumber Company in a remote region between Texas and Louisiana." In order to keep the black men who worked under his supervision "united, cooperative, and in good humor," Truvillion led his crew in singing hollers and work songs (Kitts 2006, 505). Although he is not leading a work crew, Paul D motivates himself with the song about working on the railroad: "Lay my head on the railroad line / Train come along, pacify my mind / If I had my weight in lime / I'd whip my captain till he went stone blind" (Morrison 1987, 40). "Sis Joe" functions as another method for Paul D to "beat back the past" and build a future with Sethe. In positing "Sis Joe," Morrison connects Paul D to the African American male railroad workers who embraced the African American rhetorical tradition. African American laborers changed the lyrics to songs as they worked to articulate their feelings at a given moment. In ruminating about changing the words while singing, Paul D exemplifies the composing process of African American workmen in fields and railroads.

Besides providing a "psychic" relief and "physical stabilization" while performing tedious tasks, Paul D finds solace in work songs for they provide him with comfort in the idea that he might be able to have a family that slavery denied him (Levine and Belfield 2005, 212). As Paul D sings "Sis Joe," he thinks about having a life with Sethe, but admits that she is not "a normal woman in a normal house" (Morrison 1987, 40). Despite this he allows his mind to wonder—to ponder what it would be like to live with Sethe as a family man. He admits to himself that a life with her would be drastically different from how he lived before—moving from place to place, never staying in a "place for over two or three months" (40). To be with Sethe means to be static and content with life in a house with a family. That idea wasn't too bad as long as he "shut down a generous portion of his head, operating on the part that helped him walk, eat, sleep, sing" (41). Keeping his memories locked away is Paul D's strategy for survival. Kitts describes Paul D as a wanderer—traveling from place to place searching for work. Paul D "reaches the gunboat by walking to

Mobile, Alabama, where he discovers black soldiers rebuilding the tracks that they had destroyed during the war. He . . . had tried to join a black regiment—the 44th Colored Infantry Regiment of Tennessee" (2006, 501). He continues to sing, rethinks the order of the lyrics, and changes the order of the words. This is an extemporaneous endeavor. "He contented himself with mmmm-mmmm, throwing in one line if one occurred to him. . . . It was tempting to change the words (Gimme back my shoes; gimme back my hat)" (Morrison 1987, 40). "Paul D draws upon music's openness to the dialogic interplay of texts to reconcile the songs he learned in prison with the songs of yearning he learned at Sweet Home: a lesson that allows him to imagine a new relationship with Sethe" (Wolfe 2004, 265). This again emphasizes Paul D's relationship to language as being similar to Sixo's (dynamic and entrenched in the African American song tradition) but also as a strategic strategy of endurance.

In effect, Paul D contends with the impact that Sweet Home had on slaves' marriages and relationships. In *Beloved,* male slaves are unable to protect or provide for their families; instead, men live in fear for their lives as well as those of their loved ones. They understood having a family included taking the chance that one day they might not be able to protect their loved ones from abuse or death (a fact that Halle exhibits in his relationship with Sethe). Morrison not only demonstrates Paul D's subjectivity construction process against the other male slaves who succumb to racism and oppression, she also illustrates the dynamic process against his relationship with Sethe, a former slave from Sweet Home. The love and compassion that Paul D shows her (such as chasing the baby spirit away, trying to cheer up Denver by taking her to a carnival, and returning to care for Sethe at the end of the novel) has been read as Paul D's attempt to locate Sethe in paternalistic discourses. Specifically, he signifies on her ethics, morality, and parental love. After learning about Sethe's crime of infanticide, Paul D snidely reminds her that she is not an animal; he says to her, "you have two feet not four" (Morrison 1987, 165). In a single rhetorical move, Paul D becomes what he has been trying to avoid. He positions himself as a definer—a perpetuator of paternalism. This argument suggests that Paul D's subjectivity is dependent on Sethe's, as opposed to sharpened by her experiences. I believe that Paul D's masculine impulses demonstrate the extent to which he is inscribed in paternalism and that deinternalization like "de-colonization is always a violent event. At whatever level we study it . . . decolonization is quite simply the substitution of one 'species' of mankind by another. The substitution is un-conditional, absolute, total, and seamless" (Fanon 1963, 1). As Paul D deinternalizes, or realizes the difference between his slave and free self, he learns to listen to the voices of women. This is evident in his final interaction with Denver (he attempts to offer her his "opinion" of the baby ghost), who reminds him that "I don't . . . I have my own" (Morrison 1967, 267). Thus, Morrison suggests the critical role that black women play in black men's subjectivity construction process.

•

> Now, his coming is the reverse of his going.
>
> —TONI MORRISON, *BELOVED* (1987, 273)

Why does Paul D return to Bluestone Road? Andrew Schopp reads the conclusion of *Beloved* as an indication of how "Paul D's conception of manhood has radically changed" (2000, 222–23). Schopp believes that "from listening to Sethe's story, sharing his own, and sharing in their story that [Paul D] is able to return to Sethe because he has been able to 'ponder' over the wounds inflicted by Garner, schoolteacher, and white patriarchal culture" (222). This personal growth Schopp describes as a "process of negotiation":

> Paul D's process has been one of negotiating cultural narratives—master narratives—and learning to construct his own, to construct a position of potential agency in a world in which freedom from schoolteacher does not mean freedom from a master. (222–23)

Thus, Schopp's analysis questions the easy assessment of Paul D's motivations and behaviors by feminists who locate his subjectivity along the continuum of white patriarchy. This omission, I believe, is not deliberate but is the fallout of reading the desires of the women characters as self-fulfilling against the backdrop of the systemic conditions that in a general and unspecified way oppress them. The desires and motivations of black men are not simply to oppress, overwrite, and control. As I have argued, the historical experiences of African American men do not inculcate them in this ideology. Instead, these experiences demonstrate that black men have intimate knowledge of the sadistic and inhumane practices of white men.

Paul D's subjectivity construction is not at the expense of Sethe's expressive freedom, womanhood, or space. In choosing to give up his lifestyle as a wanderer who did not want to expose himself by sharing, he is not interested in just fulfilling his psychological needs, as Schopp states: "Of course, Paul D's reaction to Sethe's tree is informed by his own conception of what a tree should be, and this conception is informed by his attempts to heal a personal psychological wound, a rupture in his sense of self as a man" (2000, 221). Paul D sees his feelings for Sethe as different from any feelings that he has had for any other woman. Paul D had not believed that he could make a life with a woman for more than two or three months. In fact, he had come to accept the bare minimum from a relationship. After "Alfred he had shut down a generous portion of his head, operating on the part that helped him walk, eat, sleep, sing. If he could do those things—with a little work and a little sex thrown in—he asked for no more, for more requires him to dwell on Halle's face and Sixo's laughing" (Morrison 1987, 41). Only after Paul D leaves and returns to Sethe does he develop the strategies to have a deeper and more meaningful relationship with her.

Inspired by Sixo's love for Patsy (the Thirty-Mile Woman), Paul D returns to Sethe because he realizes that after seven years of "eating, walking, and sleeping, aimless wandering, his times with her was life as good as it got" (270). Again, Paul D uses Sixo's relationship as context for thinking about how to meet Sethe's needs. Lovalerie King states, "Paul D's memory of Sixo's attraction to Patsy helps him to summon up the courage to return to Sethe near the end of the novel" (1998, 281). Paul D adopts a definition of black masculinity that embraces women and family and eludes the determining aspects of racialized discourses.

At the end of the novel, Paul D is standing at Sethe's back door. After entering the house, he finds a grief-stricken Sethe lying in Baby Suggs's room. He remembers how Sixo used to describe how he felt about the Thirty-Mile Woman who gave him back the pieces that he was: "It's good, you know, when you got a woman who is a friend of your mind" (Morrison 1987, 273). He remembers this because he realizes that Sethe had left him his manhood. As a friend of her mind, Paul D tells her that he needs some kind of tomorrow with her. And instead of telling her that she was his, he tells her that "you are your best thing. Sethe You Are," giving her back her pieces as Thirty-Mile Woman did Sixo (273). Wyatt explains the significance and difference of "you are your best thing" and "you are mine":

> Paul D "wants to put his story next to hers"; the two stories may complement and complete each other (each person having lived out the missing fragment of the other's slave narrative) but they will lie "next to" each other—each whole. Circumscribed, with its own beginning, middle, and end. (2000, 273) Difference can emerge within the space of relationship; a dialogue between self and other can replace the circular mother-daughter dialectic between same and same. (276)

Paul D privileges Sethe's subjectivity because he recognizes the importance of listening to black women's pain. In the span of the novel, Paul D has come full circle. Paul D has redefined himself against Mr. Garner's emasculating discourses, Schoolteacher's dehumanizing discourses, and Brandywine and his men's sadistic advances to become Sethe's confidante and caregiver. Paul D learns through interacting with Beloved that he can't simply maintain silence and listen to women as a strategy because she is silent too. He has to have patience and talk to the woman he loves and wait for Beloved to speak, or accept her choice not to speak. In stressing Paul D's struggle to resist patriarchal tendencies, Morrison suggests that Paul D is aware that he must embrace a black male feminist stance in his relationships with the women at 124 Bluestone Road. Paul D demonstrates the complexity and sophistication of African American male subjectivity construction and, as such, Morrison reminds us of real black men's humanity. In a 1976 interview, Morrison talked about the dialectical relationship between black men and women as a dynamic process that is often mischaracterized for the purpose of fulfilling Moynihan discourses about domineering black women and emasculated Black men. Morrison criticizes the notion that black women compete with men for a patriarchal position and that women prevent men from being significant contributors to their families and communities. To disprove this pervasive belief about the relationship between black men and women, Morrison points to the autonomy that black men exercise, to the resiliency that black men exemplify in society, and to the historical relationship between black and white men (1994a, 234).

CHAPTER 2

"My Witness Is in Heaven and My Record Is on High"

Discoursing the Spiritual and the Secular in *Go Tell It on the Mountain*

> The church aided and abetted the Negro slave trade; the church was the bulwark of American slavery; and the church today is the strongest seat of racial and color prejudice.
>
> —W. E. B. DU BOIS, "THE CHURCH AND THE NEGRO"

POST-EMANCIPATION, the dominant culture supported a Christian theology that included the conviction that if African Americans remain patient, diligent, and law-abiding citizens that they will achieve their reward in heaven. The dominant culture willingly promoted this repressive function of Christianity as a means to distract African Americans from the multiple ways in which they suffered from racial persecution and to deter them from attempting to transform their material conditions through various strategies of resistance. In the above quote, W. E. B. Du Bois expresses a particular enmity toward biblical teachings that celebrates egalitarianism among humanity but authorizes teachings and practices that oppress people of African descent. Anticipating later African American scholars' preoccupation with the repressive function of Christian ideology, Du Bois offers an incisive critique of the Christian church: one the one hand, the Christian church proclaims to be a group of ordinary citizens who are victims of their own human weaknesses and prejudices and a religious group of individuals who are governed by the laws of God. On the other hand, the Christian church refuses to denounce the demeaning and dehumanizing discourses that characterize people of African descent as lacking the "requisite souls to be fully humanly receptacles for salvation" (Alexander 2011, 37). Du Bois is concerned with the rhetorical ways that the Christian church maintains the color line through the merging of national identity, biological conceptions of race, and theological explanations of human difference. Du Bois emphasizes that the church remained silent on scientific and philosophical discourses that denied people of African descent independence and freedom of choice in America, and it used biblical narratives to distort, conceal, and justify the oppression of people of African descent. Recognizing that this hypocrisy promotes white dominance at the expense of African American identity and cultural formation, Du Bois states that the church justified the oppression of people of African descent by preaching a theology that failed to address the material and psychological needs of African Americans.

Over the years, African American writers and scholars continued Du Bois's critique of the Christian church's feigned innocence of its teaching and practices. Besides emphasizing the role of the Christian church in racial oppression, they expanded their concerns to critique the function of Christianity as a global force that endorsed slavery and colonization. For example, James Cone contends "that white Christian clergy and missionaries promote Western culture not only through slavery and colonization, but also through the rejection of people of African descent's worldview, experiences, and their right to interrogate whiteness" (1997, 5). And Ishmael Reed states that "I'm opposing Christianity the same way that Black authors that preceded me opposed Christianity, from William Wells Brown, right on back. Because it was an insidious institution. It worked hand in hand with exploitation and imperialism. Everywhere they went everybody else was a heathen" (1995, 46). Indeed, Baldwin offers the most sustained and incisive critique of Christianity as an epic catastrophe that almost annihilated African people and culture. In a 1967 interview, Baldwin stated that "except insofar as the Negro transformed Christianity to meet the needs of his brutal situation, Christianity was a disaster. In no way whatever has it replaced, especially in Africa, what it destroyed" (1989, 63). Similar to other African American intellectuals, Baldwin expresses concern with the oppressive function of Christian teachings in African American families and churches. However, Baldwin restricts his critique to African American Pentecostal preachers who lived with racial oppression and wrestled with ideas of faith, salvation, or deliverance while using the prestige and authority of the clergy to personal gain. In his semi-autobiographical novel *Go Tell It on the Mountain,* Baldwin examines black male subjectivity construction between spiritual discourses about piety, redemption, and veneration and secular discourses about desire, self-actualization, and family and community responsibility. Drawing on his memories as a talented teenage minister and aspiring writer, Baldwin explores black male subjectivity by exploring the paradox. How do African American men use Pentecostalism to transform themselves from oppressed and disenfranchised to devout preachers and family men?

In this chapter, I argue that Baldwin's *Go Tell It on the Mountain* articulates a counter-history of Christian innocence—one that suggests that Pentecostalism since Emancipation has had a damaging impact on black male subjectivity formation. Whereas Pentecostalism imagines spiritual fulfillment via the construction of patriarchal domestic and political formations, Baldwin's novel stresses Pentecostalism's failure to create emancipatory potential in either domain. Gabriel is in the discursive divide of the secular and spiritual. Therefore, what Baldwin highlights is not his success or failure as a father and preacher but the processes by which he attempts to fulfill these roles. The discourses that Gabriel draws on to redefine and reposition himself speaks to his desire to fulfill what he imagines as God's favor to him: a family, an heir to his "throne," and pastor of his own church. For Gabriel, serving God means reconfiguring Christianity within an African American context—this means disconnecting it from its historical uses (if all possible), reaping the rewards of respect and salvation, and articulating one's struggle for empowerment and individuality on the terrain of Christianity. Gabriel uses Christianity not only to resist racial oppression but also to redefine his subjectivity. Unfortunately, Gabriel contributes to the reconstitution of a religious hierarchy that is predicated on African Americans' subjugation and religious marginality. An integral element of *Go Tell It on the Mountain* challenges Pentecostalism through the text's rigorous analysis of the failure of biblical teachings to generate emancipatory social arrangements publically or domestically.

Similar to Du Bois, Reed, and Cone, Baldwin condemns biblical teachings as a discourse of innocence that promotes a racial agenda and passes itself off as a natural way of seeing the world. In presenting Gabriel's struggle to reconcile Pentecostalism with his experiences as a black man in the South who confronts racism and emasculation at every turn, Baldwin demonstrates an understanding of the nuanced ways in which competing discourses about race, religion, and community shape African American subjectivity construction.

•

> Well, he is dead, he never saw you, and he had a terrible life; he was defeated long before he died because, at the bottom of his heart, he really believed what white people said about him.
>
> —JAMES BALDWIN, *THE FIRE NEXT TIME* (1995, 4)

In order to explore biblical teachings as an emancipatory discourse, Baldwin draws on his childhood and his experiences in the Pentecostal Church. At fourteen, Baldwin says he realized that he had to decide who he wanted to be and how he could realize his dreams. He wants to be a writer, but doesn't know how to achieve it. Also, he says from seeing his friends that he knew a real possibility for surviving was to become a hustler, drug addict (like many of his friends), or join the ministry. In an attempt to escape the apathy and alienation that was engulfing his friends, Baldwin writes, "The most devastating aspect of this is that black boys learn at an early age that they don't have any options in life and they see this playing out all around them. It was this last realization that terrified me and . . . helped to hurl me into the church. And, by an unforeseen paradox, it was my career in the church that turned out, precisely, to be my gimmick" (1998b, 301). Upon joining the ministry, Baldwin witnesses clergymen who preach against materialism while using church funds to purchase luxury items and lecture congregations on racial exploitation but not enough to uplift the community (providing resources or opportunities for people in their communities). Critical of the hypocrisy and exploitation in the church, Baldwin leaves it but not before learning that black male subjectivity construction is a complex and complicated process that can't be reduced and simply evaluated as a failure or success. However, sometimes black men can undermine their own effort to be self-actualizing or self-affirming. Black men can be self-abusive and self-annihilating.

Publications on *Go Tell It on the Mountain* demonstrate an understanding of the discursive dilemma in which Baldwin places Gabriel, but they fail to thoroughly explore how this predicament impacts his ability to imagine his own character and individuality. Concerned with the autobiographical elements of the novel, literary critics' pyscho-biographical readings examine *Go Tell It on the Mountain* as Baldwin's attempt to console who he once was: a young boy who suffered as a result of his father's (David Baldwin) religious zealotry and abusive and domineering behavior. These critics merged David Baldwin, the historically defeated black man, with Gabriel Grimes, the fictional tormented black man, and John Grimes, the ambitious and persecuted boy, with a young James Baldwin, dutiful, ambitious, and hopeful. Encouraged by Baldwin's descriptions of his father as locked up in his own terrors, hating and fearing every living soul including his children, James Campbell argues that *Go Tell It on the Mountain* "is informed by deep autobiographical feelings from which Baldwin had distanced himself during the writing of the novel and in the months immediately following its completion" (1991, 77). Similarly, focusing on John as the center of action in the novel, Shirley S. Allen argues that John's coming of age narrative bookends the greater family story about Gabriel as a descendant of slaves and part of the first generation to migrate north (1988, 167). Baldwin describes the malaise in the Grimes household as that of the feeling that all of the characters are trapped in their own way by their choices, as well as by their culture, a discursive move that posits each character as confronting separate struggles. Drawing comparisons between Baldwin's critique of his father's malevolent behavior toward his family with the depiction of African American women in Baldwin's fiction, Trudier Harris argues that Baldwin's African American female characters lack individual voices and serve to affirm the identity of the male characters. Harris contends that the women in the novel lack a voice of their own and in various ways function to reinforce Gabriel's masculinity (1985, 25). Harris takes issue with the lack of dimensionality given to the women and limitations that biblical teachings impose on female subjectivity formation. "Gabriel operates at a surface level with powers he thinks have been bestowed upon him by the supernatural; he seldom, if ever, operates at the level of conscience to respond to human needs in this world" (27). In her critique of Gabriel, Harris argues that he sees patrimony in terms of biblical inheritance and ignores the tension that this places on the women in his life (27). I argue that Baldwin's novel is an incisive critique of how difficult it is for black men to transform a historical oppressive ideology into a cultural emancipatory discourse.

In contrast, Baldwin understands his novel as not a denunciation of his father but more an attempt to understand his father and other black man who relocated from the South and struggled to protect and provide for their families in the North. In discussing the book, Baldwin writes, "I suppose that *Mountain* can be considered a kind of love song—a confession of love for that David Baldwin it took me so many years to understand" (Campbell 1991, 77). As a member of the first generation born in the North, Baldwin is sympathetic toward his father and other African American man who fled the South. Besides lacking language outside of racialized discourses to describe "what it meant to be black," these men resist being called black and in return suffer from the absence of another way to conceptualize their existence in the North that comforts them against the "humiliation and self-humiliation," which was not their burden. "It was the context in which we were born" (Baldwin 1989, 143). "My father's disaster and part of the danger which menaced the entire family was our relationship toward our own blackness, which was very painful" (143). I argue for a sympathetic reading of Gabriel as a confused fictional male character who is overwhelmed by his circumstances. Neither Baldwin nor his protagonist think about how complicated it would be to inscribe themselves in the Pentecostal discourse. In fact, both recognized the Pentecostal Church as not only a refuge from the Harlem streets, but as a way to construct themselves as prominent and positive people in their communities. Although they both recognize that racism is an immediate issue that affects theirs and others' daily lives, Baldwin and Gabriel are comfortable with hoping that their determination to live righteous lives will inspire the congregation and community members. This is the case of David Baldwin and Gabriel, who both struggle to reconcile or appropriate the multiple social, cultural, theological, and historical discourses about black men in the South and the North.

In *Negro Migration During the War*, historian Emmett J. Scott states that many African American men fled the South as if they were running for their lives or pursuing new lives. Pastors, seeing their flocks leaving, at first attempted to dissuade them from doing so but eventually "left as though they were fleeing some curse. They were willing to make almost any sacrifice to obtain a railroad ticket, and they left with the intention of staying" (1920, 44). While he escaped the wickedness of New Orleans or the "New World Sodom and Gomorrah," as David Baldwin referred to the southern city, he encountered a hostile New York that relegated African Americans to dilapidated ghettos and low-paying servant and factory jobs. Although he held a steady job at a "soft drink bottling factory," David Baldwin was still unable to feed his family and he would often send young Jimmy Baldwin out to purchase day-old discount bread, and watch his older sons leave to work as shoeshine boys and his wife to clean the homes of white women (Campbell 1991, 4). Searching for a better quality of life not only included living without the threat of violence and murder, but also acquiring higher-paying jobs and better working conditions. David Baldwin relocated from Louisiana to New York and settled in Harlem. Baldwin says that his father left Louisiana for two main reasons: he couldn't reconcile the sin of the New Orleans social scene with his desire to live by faith, and "lynching had become a national sport" (Campbell 1991, 4). David Baldwin learned that the narratives about how hospitable northerners were that were circulated in black institutions in the South were true in one sense but didn't get at the full story: while there were job opportunities besides agricultural work, Jim Crow segregation was in the North, too. While they brought many cultural practices with them to the North (cuisine, folklore, and religion), their faith gave them the most hope and hopelessness. The same religious practices that promised deliverance from evilness and irreverence couldn't save African American immigrants from racial hate and intolerance.

•

> The Christianity taught in the slave fields was not the same that was taught to the planter's son at the University of Virginia. The planter's son was taught to use his heaven on earth; we were taught to be miserable and wait for "habin."
>
> —ISHMAEL REED, *CONVERSATION WITH ISHMAEL REED* (1995, 82)

David Baldwin found solace in the biblical narratives and verses that encouraged people to have faith that God will save and deliver them from their present conditions and make them an example of His will and work. Inspired by the heteropatriarchal biblical narrative of Abraham, who faithfully and steadily travels from Schechem to Bethel and back to Bethel before traveling to Negeb with only the promise that one day he would found a great nation and be a blessing for others, David Baldwin (and Gabriel) represents the promise God made to Abraham: "I will bless those who bless you, and the one who curses you I will curse." Regrettably, the Pentecostal theology that provides David Baldwin a discourse to imagine himself as father, preacher, and black man also reaffirmed his feelings of alienation and dissociation. Not only does David Baldwin believe these principles to the detriment of himself and his family, as a result of his zealousness, Baldwin writes, his father's physical and psycho-spiritual abuse (he often quoted biblical scripture to admonish his children and wife and to refer to evil that whites represented in his life and the world) made it unpleasant to live in the house. Baldwin's childhood friend recalls visiting the Baldwin household and seeing David Baldwin in a bathrobe and slippers moving around the house like a dark cloud. Years later, Baldwin wrote about his father having an undiagnosed mental illness that manifested itself in unprovoked fits of anger. Unfortunately, during the time that he was a teenager living at home, Baldwin simply saw his father as a very unreasonable and mean-spirited man who wreaked havoc on the subjectivity of anyone who imagined a life outside the confines of his home and the Pentecostal Church.

David Baldwin's tyrannical behavior represents the extent to which the history of racism and oppression in Christianity grinds away at African American subjectivity construction. Each time David Baldwin draws on Christian teachings as an emancipatory discourse, he encounters a theology of innocence that on the one hand marks him as the "socially dead"; on the other hand, it signifies his immediate predicament. Sanctioning the development of Western civilization at the expense of Eastern cultures and peoples, Christian missionaries, colonizers, and slaveholders defended their projects with biblical verses and passages such as the Ten Commandments that notes sins as "coveting" property—"thy neighbor's house . . . manservant . . . maidservant"—as well as narratives about the God-fearing Paul who returns a runaway slave to the slave's master. In defense of slavery, theological scholars argued that although slavery was widespread throughout the Roman world, Jesus never spoke out against it. Other Old and New Testament verses and proverbs require slaves to obey, respect, and please their masters. Searching for values and beliefs that distinguish them from people without faith,

Christians chose biblical teachings as the foundation on which to base their identity. Using the Bible as a critical context, Christians constructed a spiritual identity and then ventured out into the world searching for peoples and cultures against whom they could reaffirm or establish an oppositional identity. In the case of Africa, Africans, and people of African descent, Christians casted them as savages that needed civilizing and sinners that needed saving. Baldwin argues that Christians scapegoated Others so that they didn't have to confront their own feelings of loss and absence. Blaming Others also provided Christians with a way to claim innocence for white and African American Pentecostal churches to practice a particular brand of innocence that, Baldwin argues, highlights their inability to recognize their own complicity in the oppression of African Americans. Baldwin says, "many of us, I think both long to see this happen and are terrified of it, for though this transformation contains the hope of liberation, it also imposes a necessity for great change" (1995, 44).

Since discourses of innocence are an integral aspect of Baldwin's writings, readers have the opportunity to envision the subtle but profound ways that Christian discourses impact African Americans. Baldwin argues that innocence provides Christians a way to avoid accepting responsibility for the legacy of racism or ignore sociopolitical oppression when they believe that their lifestyle or livelihood is threatened. While he acknowledges the political ground that African Americans made between 1930 and 1970, he understands these gains not as a reflection of white benevolence or Christian charity but as gains that reflect white Americans' struggle to maintain their sense of place in American society. For example, Christians joined the fight for separate but equal housing, education, and employment to keep African Americans out of middle-class or affluent communities, to block African Americans from attending the same educational institutions, or to relegate African Americans to low-paying jobs. Another way that Christian discourses impact the lives of African Americans is through a theology that combines Christianity with American capitalism. When African American preachers use offerings and tithes to supplement their lifestyle, as opposed to building strong institutions in African American communities, they are complicit in the oppression of African American people. American capitalism infiltrated African American churches in the form of "ministers acquiring houses and Cadillacs while the faithful congregation continue to scrub floors and drop their dimes and quarters and dollars into the plate" (Baldwin 1995, 309). Baldwin compares the African American preachers in his church to the street hustlers he saw standing on corners and huddled on the avenues very close to the Harlem church he attended:

> And it was the fact that I was the young Brother Baldwin increased my value with those same pimps and racketeers who had helped to stampede into the church in the first place. . . . They themselves did know the score, and they knew that the odds were in their favor. And, really, and they knew it too. I was even lonelier and more vulnerable than I had been before. And the blood of the Lamb had not cleansed me in any way whatever. I was just as black as I had been the day that I was born. (309)

If Christian teachings are part of the African American experience but are inadequate as an emancipatory discourse, then what do African American men do with the heteropatriarchal authority embedded in biblical narratives that are deeply ingrained in their consciousness? Twenty years after Baldwin published *The Fire Next Time,* James Cone and Gay L. Byron suggest Afrocentric theologies that meld Christianity with African and African American ways of feeling, knowing, and understanding subvert the biblical stories, but their progressive theologies fail to equip African American men with a critical lens for surviving their daily racism. Baldwin's main concern is with exploring how black men use religion as a liberating discourse to negotiate the secular and spiritual.

Baldwin's critique of the self-serving fashion in which preachers employ Christian values generates and prefigures his conflict with the Nation of Islam (NOI). That is, by tying the black Muslims' interpretation of African American history and nationalism to the larger ideology of the church, Baldwin unites community upliftment and personal responsibility. In a chapter dedicated to the NOI stance on religion as a liberating ideology, Baldwin proposes that the NOI's ideological failure is its lack of investment in encouraging young African American men to develop their intellectual potential. Baldwin writes that "Whenever Elijah spoke, a kind of chorus arose from the table saying 'Yes, that's right.' This began to set my teeth on edge. And Elijah himself had a further unnerving habit, which was to ricochet his questions and comments off someone else on their way to you. Now turning to the man on his right, he began to speak of the white devils with whom I had last appeared on TV: What had they made me feel? Elijah went on about the crimes of white people to this endless chorus of 'yes that right'" (1995, 79). Baldwin perceptively outlines the ideological underpinnings of the NOI. He suggests that the NOI's leader, the Honorable Elijah Muhammad, advances a fiction about black supremacy countering white hate, yet he never disrupts the racial binary to show an African American project beyond the black and white dialectic. The NOI philosophy functions like an ideology in that it promotes a fiction that masks a universal truth about black resistance that correlates directly with an

African American slavery past. For the followers of Islam, the negotiating purpose of these representations, the random correlation between sign and referent, resists scrutiny, for accepting the sign as real or actual inspires devotion. By expressing the philosophical purpose of the temple's beliefs and outlining the meaning of followers' material needs, Baldwin elucidates NOI dogma to show that the real relationship between NOI and Christianity is that they both exploit African American oppressive conditions. Therefore, neither NOI nor Christianity can serve as a liberating discourse for black men.

Baldwin doesn't encourage individuals to replace one ideology with another. Instead, he argues for a more complex understanding of black men—one that suggests that Pentecostalism has had a damaging impact on black male subjectivity formation. In *The Black Church in the African American Experience,* C. Eric Lincoln and Lawrence H. Mamiya provide a model for examining the structure and purpose of the black church in African American communities. Their dialectical model accounts for the series of tensions that shape black churches and to which black churches respond. Besides holding "polar opposites in tension, constantly shifting between the polarities in historical times," the dialectic model "leads to a more dynamic view of black churches along a continuum of dialectical tensions, struggle, and change" (2003, 16). Applying their paradigm to Baldwin's writings about black men, preachers, and Pentecostalism, I resist a single interpretation of black preachers that categorize or stereotype Gabriel as wholly saved, ungodly, or a hypocrite. Besides overlooking the historical dynamism of black preachers moving back and forth between the church and government and pulpit and classrooms, a dialectical model of black preachers offers methodological flexibility.

My decision to apply Lincoln's model to *Go Tell It on the Mountain* is encouraged by African American writers and intellectuals who suggest that nuance and complex understanding of the role of black preachers can be attained if we consider how difficult it is for them to engage and negotiate the secular and spiritual contexts. Du Bois writes in *The Souls of Black Folk*:

> The Preacher is the most unique personality developed by the Negro on American soil. A leader, a politician, an orator, a "boss," an intriguer, an idealist—all these he is, and ever too, the center of a group of men, now twenty, now a thousand in number. (1997, 126)

Highlighting the creativity of the preacher's imagination, Hurston thinks preachers' rhetorical dexterity is a God-given talent:

> Merely being a good man is not enough to hold an important charge. He must also be an artist. He must be both a poet and an actor of a very high order, and then he must have the voice and the figure. (Plant 2007, 108)

While Hurston is mesmerized with the voice and posture of the preacher, Adam Clayton Powell, a highly respected former preacher explains that his effectiveness as a preacher and congressman was a result of his ability to travel and communicate with people from various backgrounds:

> I preached my trial sermon. It was a strange crowd that listened—all the girls from the Cotton Club, others from the downtown nightclubs, girls of every color, bootleggers, gamblers, all the fantastic array of acquaintances I had accumulated through the years. (1971, 13)

Unless one understands that black preachers are involved in a dynamic series of dialectical tensions, a series of misunderstandings can occur because the usual tendency is to collapse the dialectic and assert on the side of the polarity, which often results in a simplistic view. The above polarities share the danger of oversimplification when certain insights about black preachers are made the predominant and defining quality. In *Go Tell It on the Mountain* the polarities that are put in play are male/female sexual politics, oppressor/oppressed, father/preacher, and secular man/spiritual man. The dialectical model of the black preacher is helpful in explaining the complex and dynamic position the black preacher represents in the black community. Given that black preachers have the potential to represent multiple black personal, social, and community identities, I recognize that black preachers are always a risk to a corrupt white Christian nation because they can (also) covertly reproduce or defend the oppressive conditions under which African Americans live.

As a preacher, there is a chance for Gabriel to be viewed as equal to a white male or get the same social opportunities. However, he struggles with the transformative power of biblical scriptures within the context of his everyday life as a man and father. In contrast to his spiritual life as a preacher, Gabriel is marginalized in society. He is only able to find employment as a yardman in Mississippi or a chauffeur or factory worker in New York. These jobs don't pay him enough to care for his family, nor empower him to feel like a man in society. Still, Gabriel believes that he is God's anointed son, God loves him unconditionally, and that God has a special place for him in heaven. In his reading of biblical scriptures, Gabriel encounters a paradox: while he is oppressed because of his race, biblical scriptures empower him to decide his eternal fate and save his soul.

•

> The day my dungeon shook and my chains fell off.
>
> —JAMES BALDWIN, *GO TELL IT ON THE MOUNTAIN* (1963, 105)

In *Go Tell It on the Mountain,* Gabriel vacillates between understanding life through his direct observations of events (secular) and how his everyday experiences coincide with the Bible or Christian teachings (spiritual). At times in the novel, Gabriel resists the limits established by the religious rules of the Ten Commandments and he wavers in achieving the faith in God demonstrated in the biblical narratives of Job, Moses, and Abraham. Other times, he gives in to carnal desires and his manly need to feel in control of his surroundings. Significantly, Baldwin draws Gabriel as a character who is imprisoned by lust or sexual desires. He is caught between respecting black womanhood and exploiting and disregarding black women in the manner in which the southern white men did during slavery and post-Emancipation. In the South, Gabriel spent a significant amount of time striving to change or adjust his predicament. In the North, he slowly gave in to his feelings of inferiority. Unable to gain respect as a preacher, Gabriel heads north with the hope of leaving behind the racist South and his lustful behavior. In the North, he encounters a more complex and pluralistic urban environment that, although providing African Americans with low-paying service or manual labor jobs, enforces segregation through unequal housing and education. Unlike down South where he was a young minister frequently engaging in elicit affairs, in the North he is married and a church pastor who feels the pain of racism in his inability to provide an adequate life for his family. Frequently, he expresses his disdain for whites by verbally and physically abusing his family. Gabriel's wife and step son John receive most of the abuse, for his dutiful wife's pregnancy out of wedlock reminds him of the women and harlots in the Bible that caused men to sin. His son (despite his obedience and righteousness) reminds him of "the heir to his throne" that he will never have, for Gabriel's biological son's engagement in secular behaviors harks back to secular Gabriel down South. By contextualizing Gabriel's narrative in the Great Migration, Baldwin makes clear that he shouldn't be read as simply a sexist, abusive, and overbearing man. Instead, he is a product of a particular era when black men struggled to define themselves and build a life for themselves and their families. Unfortunately for Gabriel he embraces an ambiguous discourse that places him in a discursive predicament—secular and spiritual.

Gabriel uses biblical teachings (when it is convenient) to explain or defend his faults and choices and to negotiate multiple contexts: the South, North, and family. In the South, Gabriel seeks refuge in Christian teachings as he struggles to grow spiritually and repress or restrain his sexual desires. As head of the Holy Temple Fire Baptized, Gabriel demands that his family follow a strict religious doctrine that is inherently sexist and patriarchal. Besides challenging the women in his family to prove their faith and devotion to God by humbling themselves and adopting traditional (read repressive) notions of womanhood and motherhood, Gabriel sees his son John's attempts to reconcile Pentecostalism with his academic aspirations as an example of how the devil works through whites to oppress Negroes. Gabriel prefers that John wrap himself in the biblical teachings and push against any notions that a Negro can be mentally, physically, and intellectually free in America. Gabriel sees the lack of opportunities and choices available to African Americans. As a parent, he is overprotective and overbearing. His rules are incomprehensible to the sons who in their lifetime have not seen the impetus to flee the horrifying conditions of the South. His extreme views seem harsh and unsubstantiated because they have been protected from the white world: "all white people were wicked, and that God was going to bring them low . . . white people were never to be trusted, and that they told nothing but lies, and that not one of them had ever loved a nigger" (Baldwin 1963, 36).

"Try as he might, Gabriel, who embodies the classic sermonic vision of the fall, cannot set his house in order until he confronts his past. Grounded in a rigid black puritanism, Gabriel is the rebellious angel, and the repercussions from his folly prove injurious to everyone who is dear to him—his mother, his sister, his two wives and especially his stepson John" (Hubbard 1994, 98). Unable to successfully separate the past from the present, he sees his experiences as the unchanging fate of the black man. In his own way, he wants to spare his sons some of the pain by having them accept their reality, seeking solace in being saved. Gabriel is on the discursive divide of North and South, past and present. What is highlighted is not success or failure but the processes by which identity is attempted to be constructed.

Gabriel is also a victim of racialized discourses as well as the inability of Christian teachings to bring about a change in his material conditions. Similar to Milkman in *Song of Solomon,* John is unaware of his father's life in the South. Unlike Milkman, John does not learn about his father or family history. It is the reader that must see the connection between the experiences of Gabriel and the other characters. For example, John (whom many critics read as the antagonist) has a powerful symbolic role, but his choice to be saved (instead of being a writer as suggested in the first chapter of the novel) is significant in the context of Gabriel's choices—to which the majority of the book is devoted—because Gabriel values biblical teachings over academic literacy. This Michel Fabre points out:

> On looking closer, however, the reader discovers that fewer than half of the three hundred odd pages of the novel express John's point of view, and these are found at the beginning and end of the tale, like the side panels of a triptych whose central panel (*The Prayer of the Saints*) relates the converging stories of Johnny's aunt, stepfather, and mother. These characters lean on their past in such a way that the figure of Gabriel . . . emerges a little like Christ between the Holy Women. (1974, 120)

As readers, however, we see the disarray and despair in the Grimes household. The choices, trials, and tribulations of Florence, Gabriel, and Esther disclose the greater historical and cultural context of the book. To read these stories as aspects of the family context alone would be to miss the focus on the larger cultural contexts and how these have impacted the lives of the characters.

The narrative structure of the novel reveals the impact of these choices on his family, whom he seeks to steer through the temptations of the secular world. More specifically, we see the effects and impact of Gabriel's profound belief in Christian teachings on all of the members in his family. His wives Deborah and Elizabeth are alienated but remain faithful and unconditionally support him. His young lover Esther suffers from shame after giving birth to an illegitimate son, but she is discrete about him (Royal). His sister Florence sees Gabriel as a hypocrite but does not cross him. He ignores his children but expects them to strictly follow Christian law. Through the lenses of the other characters, we are asked to answer the question that John asks his mother: "Is my father a good man?" (Baldwin 1963, 24). This question speaks to the spiritual/secular dilemma that is before John, but he is limited in his perspective about Gabriel. The answer is simple to some characters; for example, Florence sees Gabriel as a hypocrite, an abuser of his wife and children, but she too cannot speak to his struggles. However, this question of whether Gabriel is a good man is symptomatic of the text—because in answering the question it focuses not on the moral issue of Gabriel's character, but on the historical and cultural circumstances that construct his subjectivity and motivations. Why does Gabriel succumb to the pleasures of the flesh? Why does he choose Christianity as his personal and cultural salvation? Why does he migrate north? Why does he seek to define patriarchy with the context of

African American Christianity? How far does he succeed in these endeavors and at what personal costs? Besides centralizing Gabriel's subjectivity, these questions position him as the familiar archetype of the religiously saved man. Gabriel's personal transformation and salvation are depicted against the backdrop of his love for whiskey and women. His life is structured around the parable of "setting thine house in order" from Kings 1:20, which John recognizes as the piece of scripture that his father lives by (32). In retrospect, he comes to understand his time spent in bars and with prostitutes as giving in to temptations that kept him from his faith.

Baldwin further contextualizes Gabriel's narrative in a culture and family legacy of fear and intimidation. The stories his mother tells him are about how her eight children were sold to other plantations; how he and the other young African American boys would hide when white men rode through the town looking for a black male fitting the description of a man who allegedly raped a white woman. While these narratives affect how Gabriel perceives white men, they do not deter him from participating in sinful activities like drinking, gambling, and womanizing:

> On this plantation she had grown up as one of the field workers, for she was very tall and strong; and by and by she had married and raised children, all of whom had been taken from her, one by sickness and two by auction; and one, whom she had not been allowed to call her own had been raised in the master's house. (70)

Gabriel's mother encourages him to embrace Christian definitions of manhood and patriarchy. In Mississippi, the church represents Gabriel's salvation from a life that is rapidly spinning out of control.

As a young man, Gabriel frequently visits whorehouses and juke joints. One night while returning from a harlot's house, Gabriel feels an incredible amount of guilt. "Later, he said of that morning that his sin was on him, then he kn[e]w only that he carried a burden and that he longed to lay it down. This burden was heavier than the heaviest mountain and he carried it in his heart" (93). Saved, Gabriel's burden is lifted. In the section of the book entitled "Gabriel's Prayer," Gabriel's personal salvation is constructed as a memorial reconstruction that he presents to an audience: "I remember, he was later to say, the day my dungeon shook and my chains fell off" (95). In an episode reminiscent of Christ's struggle in the wilderness, "Gabriel cries 'Save me!' 'Save me!' And all creation rang, but did not answer. I couldn't hear nobody pray." He perceives his salvation as "the beginning of his life as a man" (97). Thus, through prayer as action, he spiritually invites a belief in an infallible faith, constructing his subjectivity and his identity with the performance of language from black spirituals (or, as Du Bois refers to them, "Sorrow Songs"). Putting all his faith in Pentecostal theology does not allow Gabriel to acknowledge his struggles and weakness in a public or intimate forum, except in terms of tests, trials, and tribulations. Belief in a personal Lord who will lead him through the wilderness is the performance of Christianized subjectivity. The historical and cultural function of Christian teachings in the African American context is Gabriel's urtext, the text in which he is resituated as an exemplary Christian whose personal narrative of salvation functions as a parable.

Gabriel's moment of personal salvation seems to be a sincere repentance for his lifestyle and a direct path to salvation because of the moral teachings of his mother: "Honey their mother was saying, Don't you let your old mother die without you look her in the eye and tell her she going to see you in glory. You hear me, boy?" (76). There is an identifiable social pressure, but Gabriel's conversion is presented as an intensely personal one. In retrospect, for Gabriel, salvation meant that God bestowed on him the subjectivity to negotiate secular temptations and circumstances. Thus, Pentecostalism becomes the critical lens through which Gabriel reconstructs his subjectivity. It is also the tool that he employs to pursue his middle-class ambitions of a family and life within the Harlem community.

Gabriel embraces the scripture, "the day my dungeon shook," as a parable of instruction for congregation members in the Temple of the Fire Baptized in Harlem. Besides marking his conversion, this scripture turns his personal epiphany into cultural cache and distinguishes him as a respectable elder of the community. To the congregation, he represents an example that personal dedication to the life of Christ enables African American men to thrive (Gabriel is a Christian man raising a Christian family) despite social and cultural oppression. However, the temptations are still visible and viable threats to his subjectivity. In Harlem, Gabriel combats these challenging circumstances socially and culturally. Walking to his storefront church in which he serves as a pastor on Sunday, Gabriel is surrounded by drunks and whores—the same conditions he negotiated as a youth in the South. The sinners are African American men who have become drunks because of the social despair that they face in Harlem: low wages, rundown living conditions (as depicted by the detailed descriptions of the Grimes' home), crime, and, increasingly, drugs. Craig Werner writes, "Economics exerts a more severe, if less direct, influence . . . on Gabriel, whose native cruelty and harshness are accentuated by the pressures of providing for his family. . . . His early idealism proves insufficient when confronted with the cynical economically motivated preachers at the revival meeting," and his demand for money after his adulterous affair. "These experiences engender the hypocritical cynicism which sets the tone for Gabriel's life and leads to the angry bitterness which he projects onto John" (1988, 82).

Besides biblical teachings, Gabriel's subjectivity is comprised of his memories and the guilt of those memories—the sight of a lynched soldier "face downward at the base of a tree, his fingernails digging into the scuffed earth. When he was turned over, his eyeballs stared upward in amazement and horror, his mouth was locked open wide: his trousers, soaked with blood, were torn open, and exposed to the cold, white air of morning the thick hairs of his groin, matted together, black and rust-red, and the wound that seem to be throbbing still" (Baldwin 1963, 142). His status as a preacher does not absolve him from experiencing the weight of racism. Still a victim of random acts of white violence, Gabriel struggles to maintain a belief in his conversion and that the white men who taunt him one night in town will also be converted:

> Now someone spat on the sidewalk at Gabriel's feet, and he walked on, his face not changing, and he heard it reprovingly whispered behind him that he was a good nigger, surely up to no trouble. (142)

Here the power of the phrase "good nigger" threatens to (re)name or (re) define his identity, a process that poses a particular problem for Gabriel's subjectivity construction process. In an effort to avoid reconfiguring his identity, Gabriel interprets the behavior of southern white racists as a problem of spirituality, not socialization. Interpreting their actions in this way keeps Gabriel from having to reconcile his position as God's messenger with the daily disrespect white men demonstrate toward him. Drawing on his experiences, Gabriel remembers his mother's advice "to pray for loving kindness" and "yet he dreams of the feel of the white man's forehead against his shoe; again and again until the head wobbled on the broken neck and his foot encountered nothing but the rushing blood" (142). These horrific scenes remind Gabriel about how African American men are expected to perform and the spaces that African American men can occupy in both the South and the North. It is important for this context (and my reading) that the complexity of Gabriel's positionality is acknowledged and that he is not reduced to a hypocritical and sadistic man.

The women characters do not acknowledge the social challenges to Gabriel's subjectivity. Gabriel's faith (equally important is hope and safety) demands that he acts on not his emotional needs and desires, but on the dictates of the Ten Commandments. His respectability has a very thin veneer supported as it is by the symbolic power of language alone. It is these conditions that Gabriel's sister and second wife, Florence and Elizabeth, do not see. Their relationship to Christian teachings and to their subjectivity as women is presumably what occupies them (as Harris points out), but Gabriel's struggles are only in part related to his struggles to create a devoted bond with a woman who can be a Christian wife (for this reason he chooses Deborah) (1985, 13). Notwithstanding, there are obvious benefits to being a black man, which are avoiding the social and cultural disadvantages of black women within the context of the African American community.

The women in his life, particularly his sister Florence, are critical of his choices and his heavy-handed manner with his children. Florence resents the male privileges given to Gabriel just because he is male: "With the birth of Gabriel, which occurred when she was five, her future was swallowed up. There was only one future in that house, and it was Gabriel's—to which since Gabriel was a man-child, all else must be sacrificed" (172). Thus, Florence functions throughout the novel as Gabriel's conscious, or mediator of his actions and behaviors, and she points out his patriarchal behavior at every turn. In many ways, to Florence, Gabriel represents a stereotypical man whose "thoughts rose no higher, and they lived only to gratify on the bodies of women their brutal and humiliating needs" (74). Gabriel does not condone his reckless actions, especially as he looks back on his earlier life. Instead, he believes he will have to answer for them—but only to God, as he tells Florence: "The Lord, he knows my life—he done forgive me a long time ago" (212). Florence isn't interested in Gabriel answering for his sins in the afterlife; she wants him to answer for his sins and transgressions now. However, Gabriel is a positive contrast to the other men in the book (Frank and Richard). He is not frivolous in his love, nor does he give in to the despair or tragedy in his own life as Richard does. He takes his responsibilities (although they are traditional patriarchal values) to his family seriously, which is very important given the fictional Harlem social context in which they operate. Nonetheless, Gabriel's relationship with the women in the novel is not inconsequential. In fact, it is important to see the nature of their intimacy with him. They criticize him, but they also support what he seeks to accomplish within his family and community. For example, Florence is angry because their mother privileges Gabriel's gender, but she does not tell his wife, Elizabeth, about the adulterous relationship he has had with Esther. In fact, the novel closes with Florence threatening to reveal Gabriel's illegitimate sinful life to Esther.

•

My witness is in heaven and my record is on high.

—JAMES BALDWIN, *GO TELL IT ON THE MOUNTAIN* (1963, 210)

Baldwin doesn't condone Gabriel's behavior; instead, he seeks to explore his choices and the consequences of his decisions. In fact, Baldwin centralizes the ambiguity of Gabriel's positionality (man of God and being black man in America) and illuminates the paradox that he encounters as a young preacher. The African American clergy subjected black women to a patriarchal order that required them to embrace God's will—which means submit to the men. They embrace a discourse of innocence that harkens to white innocence. They reinterpret religious texts to justify their active presence as leaders in black religious institutions. At different times in the novel, Gabriel changes his stance on the patriarchal pedestal: as a young preacher, Gabriel finds faults with clergymen's lack of empathy for Deborah after white men brutally rape her, leaving her infertile. He defends Deborah in a meeting with the preachers (no women were present). Admonishing them for making light of Deborah's rape, Gabriel demands that they "don't talk evil about nobody. The Bible tells me it ain't right to hold nobody up to scorn" (108). The African American clergy in Baldwin's novel advocate a relationship to language and meaning where contradictions are semantically recovered. African American preachers place black women on a "patriarchal pedestal (good, asexual women versus bad, sexual women)" in the church (Richards 2005, 138). They perceive black women's bodies as accessible to them as to the slave masters and his surrogates who raped and abused black women with impunity (Dyson 2001, 85–86).

While the white men's sexual assaults on Deborah reinforce the cult of true womanhood and project their own sexual lust and anxiety onto her body, the preachers' sexual harassment is a result of their refusal to critically engage historical discourses about black sexuality from the pulpit and their own situatedness in racist and exaggerated notions of black masculinity. Michael Eric Dyson writes, "For the most part, black sexuality was cloaked in white fantasy and fear. Black women were thought to be hot and ready to be bothered. Black men were believed to have big sexual desires and even bigger organs to realize their lust" (2004, 84–85). Dyson puts it this way: "during slavery and after emancipation, black both resisted and drank in sick white beliefs about black sexuality. Some black preachers sought to fulfill the myth of unquenchable black lust. The logic isn't hard to figure out: if white folk think I'm a sexual outlaw, some blacks perhaps thought, I'll prove it" (85). Again, this is another way that African American men are complicit in their own and the oppression of black women, but also a complex way for looking at black male subjugation. As a result of the history of black sexuality and patriarchal impulses, the African American church is a sexually contested space with sexual theology that plays out in relationships between black men and women.

Baldwin doesn't condone the behavior of Gabriel and the other minsters and preachers; instead, he seeks to explore their choices and the ramifications of their adultery and promiscuity. By placing Gabriel as defender and perpetrator of the patriarchal pedestal, Baldwin shows how black men benefit from ideologies and are complicit in theirs and black women's oppression. Richards argues that the absence of ethics of Baldwin's preachers "when absorbed into the minds and lives of blacks, imposes on any possibility of real relationship" (2005, 139). This ethical problem slowly and continuously erodes the fabric of African American communities. Baldwin writes, "like one of those floods that devastate counties, tearing everything down, tearing children from their parents and lovers from each other, and making everything an unrecognizable waste" (1995, 29).

Regardless of the clergymen's opinion about Deborah, Gabriel marries her, positioning himself as her savior and redeemer. He saves her from a spinster life and he validates her in the eyes of the black and white community (as white men raped her and the black men regarded her as worthless). However, once he realizes that she can't bare him a son, he resolves his predicament by embracing a strict interpretation of the biblical scripture. He loves Deborah because she prays and believes in him, but he wants the male heir that God has promised him. Unable to realize this promise with Deborah, he retains his faith in the transformative powers of God. Pursuing God's blessings is Gabriel's pretense for spending time with Esther at work (they both work for a white family) and after work (she attends church to listen to him preach). Gabriel's relationship with Esther leads to an adulterous affair and a son, who he ultimately refuses to claim.

When he conceives a child outside of his marriage, he believes that it is God's test, not his sin. He reasons that because Esther is a harlot, her baby boy cannot represent his "royal line." For this reason, he refuses a relationship with Esther and her "bastard" child. As a preacher, he asks himself, "where could [he] have gone with Esther?" (Baldwin 1963, 148). A relationship with Esther and Royal in Mississippi, or any other state, would be a sin before God. Gabriel finds comfort in his conviction that "the Lord held me back. . . . He put out His hand and held me back. I couldn't have done nothing else what could I have done?" (148). In his interpretation of the Bible, Gabriel is unable to distinguish between the spiritual and the physical world. In the Bible is written what God has promised Gabriel—that he will beget a son in wedlock "who would work until the day of the second coming to bring about His Father's Kingdom" (115). Esther dies while giving birth. She mocks Gabriel in naming his son Royal: "she remembered . . . what had perhaps been her last breath she had mocked him and his father with this name. She had died, then, hating him; she had carried into eternity a curse on him and his" (139). Gabriel's treatment of Esther is in sharp contrast to the chivalry he shows Deborah. It reflects the burden of his transformation, especially in the brutal death of his biological son. Gabriel's action, as Keith Clark points out, "is the historical desire for and abuse of black women by white men" (2002, 144). To repent for his immorality, Gabriel attempts to be a mentor to Royal. He plans to warn him about the path that he is on, but he hears that Royal has left to go north.

Gabriel defends his indiscretion with the Bible. Using it as a context, he defines patriarchy as receiving what God promised to those who faithfully serve Him. Believing that regardless of his sins and errant lifestyle he will reap God's blessings, Gabriel practices a theology that imagines a distinct difference between the secular and spiritual domains. On the one hand, he acknowledges that black women's material conditions are distinct from black men. However, he is inconsiderate of black women's experiences in the spiritual realm or context. Unable to empathize for black women in both domains, Gabriel egotistically accepts that he can simply pray away the contradictions of his secular and spiritual life.

By the time Gabriel migrates north, his memories include that his son's mother and his first-born son are dead and that his present wife Deborah died from grief and old age (she thought that believing in him as a "Reverend" was enough for him and for her). He embraces a theology that states that only God's grace in the form of Christian salvation and redemption can protect his family. His stepson John's perspective (with which the book opens) demonstrates the extent to which Gabriel has succeeded in implementing Christian family values. Regardless of the damage that Christian teachings do to his relationship with his son, John's memories demonstrate the success of what Gabriel is attempting to do with his family:

> His earliest memories—which were in a way, his only memories—were of the hurry and brightness of Sunday mornings. They all rose together on that day; his father, who did not have to go to work, and led them in prayer before breakfast. (Baldwin 1963, 11)

Here, Gabriel is successful at creating a family context and ritual. Whether Gabriel is admired for his attempts to separate his children from the drunken stupor and hopelessness of Harlem or not is not as crucial as recognizing the choices that he makes to counteract the hopelessness and cultural despair that surrounds his family in the North.

In the north, Gabriel embraces Pentecostalism as protection against the evil world. Thus, he embraces the Christian archetype: good vs. evil as subjectivity. Due to his experiences he considers all white people evil. And this structures his son's perspectives, although Roy agrees with him while John does not. A scuffle between Roy and his friends with some white boys across the city is "a warning from the Lord" about whites' contempt for "niggers" (48).

Gabriel, John, and Roy's differing commitments to church are the terrain of their differences. To Roy, church prevents him from experiencing the pleasures of adolescence. As was Gabriel as a young man, Roy is attracted to the street life. For Roy, manhood is aggression toward those who threaten his identity as a black boy (this is why he gets into a fight with white boys) and toward anyone (including Gabriel) who abuses his mother—for Roy, protecting his mother includes patricide. When Gabriel slaps Elizabeth, Roy intercedes on behalf of his mother. Roy calls Gabriel a "black bastard" and tells him "You slap her again . . . and I swear to God I'll kill you" (49). With secular language, Roy curses his father for hitting his mother. For Roy, manhood is justified aggression toward anyone who threatens his male identity (in this case white boys) and Gabriel's abusive nature. Because of his experiences in the South, Gabriel is aware of how quickly his life had spiraled out of control and thus he responds harshly to Roy's attraction to the streets. But Gabriel's personal narrative only underscores the direness of the situation facing African American men. He cannot protect Roy from himself any more than his own mother could protect him from his choices.

Roy's and John's interest in secular art, songs, motion pictures, and books challenges Gabriel's attempt to construct a Christian home that is free of worldly vices. This biblical interpretation is supposed to protect them from the distractions of the street. This works for John, who buries his ideas and feelings in books because it is a place where Gabriel cannot reach. From secular literacy, John constructs a subjectivity that distinguishes him from Gabriel. For John, academic literacy represents "power" and a space to hide "his intelligence from and hatred" from his father (21). As an avenue of middle-class hope, the movies give him an opportunity to imagine another world. The North also provides an opportunity to make distinctions between black communal identity and white society. These choices are not presented to Gabriel, nor does he have the avenue to explore them and what it represents in his life. To John, it is a choice between the secular world of language acts and the sacred but strict or harsh scriptural world of the church. The white world does not seem harsh to John. When he has a cold, for example, his kindly white teacher brings him castor oil. But this interpretation does not deliver Roy from the streets.

However, as a father, Gabriel has to try to use the tools that are available to him for a virtuous and respectable life. Outside of this context (and perhaps in spite of it) Gabriel is an unsympathetic character. His immorality can be seen as hypocrisy. This, I argue, is the significance of Baldwin's exploration of Gabriel's subjectivity—an outwardly unsympathetic man that is a victim of his own personal and cultural legacy. Thus, John, Roy, and Gabriel demonstrate how the oppressive use of patriarchy is constructed in response to particular and distinct sets of circumstances.

Thus, understanding Gabriel's subjectivity gives new significance to "The Threshing-Floor." Dolan Hubbard writes, "The Threshing Floor offers the power of redemptive love as the resolution to the impasse between father and son" (1994, 98). At the end of the novel, John is saved because he goes through the rituals of being saved. The ambivalent ending highlights how the performance of language is unable to contain the traces of intentionality, especially in the performance of being saved. The conversion leaves the course of the novel open-ended, allowing, simultaneously, for a reading of Gabriel's intentions and motivations. At the end of the book, Gabriel is skeptical of John's conversion because of his own experiences. The gulf between one's intentions and one's performance of those intentions is enormous. Gabriel appears to be indifferent toward John's conversion. Gabriel does not "move to touch him," "kiss him," nor "smile. They just stood before each other in silence while the saints rejoiced" (Baldwin 1963, 207). Elizabeth, Florence, and the congregation congratulate and praise God for choosing John as a faithful servant. Gabriel, on the other hand, is remote and unable to be enthusiastic about his son's conversion because he has experience with the relationship between language and intention. In response to John quoting the Bible passage "My witness is in heaven and my record is on high," Gabriel says, "It comes from your mouth. . . . I want to see you live it. It's more than a notion" (207). To Gabriel, being saved does not absolve one from their sins, nor does it intercept situations of temptations. Being saved will not make northern whites respect John any more than becoming a southern preacher made southern whites show deference to Gabriel. Gabriel's experience shows that being saved is a spiritual achievement that does not exclude one from worldly battles. John will have to face in the future his identity as a black man and his faith as a spiritual man. The differences in being "saved" demonstrate the focus on personal transformation and the burden of that transformation. While the beginning suggests that John is much like his father and will follow his footsteps, the ending demonstrates that being saved underscores their differences as old and new Negro, South and North, religious and secular patriarch, and fatherless son and son. Each saving is marked by historic and generational change and each "witnessing" underscores paradoxically the mysteries of personal transformation.

CHAPTER 3

"Look at the Nigger!"

Mimicry, the Black Male Artist, and *Tell Me How Long the Train's Been Gone*

> The day of aunties, uncles and mammies is equally gone, Uncle Tom and Sambo have passed on, and the Colonel and George play barn-storm roles from which they escape with relief when the public spot-light is off.
>
> —ALAINE LOCKE, *THE NEW NEGRO*

AT THE turn of the century, New Negro artists had a daunting task: to entertain white audiences without perpetuating stereotypes and to reaffirm African American identity and experiences without generating racial strife. While some African American artists kowtowed to public expectations, held chiefly by white benefactors, other African American artists confronted the race problem by expanding its social dimensions and broadening its widespread social implications. Alain Locke celebrates the "New Negro" artists who refused to perpetuate stereotypes in their art. Like many writers of the Harlem Renaissance, some of whom he mentored, Locke offers a countervailing master narrative: no longer subjected to stereotypes that fulfilled the desires of the largely white dominant culture, the New Negro artists resisted negative constructions of black identities (black characters speaking unintelligible language, violating the law, reveling in ignorance, etc.). Instead, they produced art that captured the nuances of African American cultural traditions and experiences and articulated the resiliency and determination of African American people. Through folktales and stories, artists related narratives about growing up in the South and about migrating to the North. In poems and plays, they remembered their African and Caribbean ancestral roots and honored the African American family and community as both a safe haven and a source of tension. In nonfiction and fiction, African American artists marked the process of writing an "authentic" fiction by highlighting the process itself, a process whose complex terrain is reflected in the struggles and consciousness of the protagonists.

Forty years after Locke publicly congratulated African American artists for introducing positive representations of African American culture and peoples, James Baldwin published *Tell Me How Long the Train's Been Gone,* a novel that highlights the second wave of intellectual thinking about representing the complexity of African American experiences within and without African American communities. While Locke highlighted issues of recovery and consolidation, Baldwin focused on the new orthodoxies of this solidarity, asking insightful questions about racial politics of representation. In Baldwin's novel, Leo Proudhammer eschews the pressures of the African American community of Harlem and explores how he can be true to himself on the stage and in his life. His struggles and developing consciousness reflect the very process of self-definition that many African American men undergo. In presenting a character who is conscious of how he is doubly defined (socially constructed and defined within and without African American contexts), Baldwin draws on his own experiences with turn-of-the-century African American literary and cultural discourses about the conditions of black subjectivity, namely W. E. B. Du Bois's double consciousness and Langston Hughes's concern with the relationship between the market place and "Negro" artists. Baldwin explores how many African American artists attempted to negotiate competing dominant discourses and demonstrates his understanding of the problematics articulated by his predecessors, particularly Du Bois and Hughes.[1]

In this chapter I argue that James Baldwin's novel *Tell Me How Long the Train's Been Gone* builds on and advances earlier writers' explorations of black subjectivity. By referencing early twentieth-century artists' scholarship on representation, I hope to contextualize Baldwin's novel within the larger discourses on black subjectivity construction and locate him within a canon of black writers (namely Locke, Hughes, and Du Bois) who discuss the responsibilities of African American writers and the complex rhetorical challenge of representing black subjectivity. Finally, I want to suggest that critical discussions about the representation of African American people and culture are not limited to African American literary studies, but extend to film and folklore studies. The nonfictional works of Du Bois and Langston Hughes provide a specific historical and literary context in which to locate Baldwin's understanding of the problematics articulated by his predecessors.

1. In *James Baldwin's Later Fiction: Witness to the Journey,* Lynn Orilla Scott supports my claim that there is "a relationship between Baldwin's point of view and those adopted by earlier African American writers" (2002, 26).

Continuing the cultural project articulated by such figures as W. E. B. Du Bois and Langston Hughes, Baldwin explores how many African American artists attempt to negotiate competing dominant discourses.[2] The protagonist of *Tell Me How Long the Train's Been Gone,* Leo Proudhammer, is a black artist who wrestles with the dialectics of black and white culture, white audiences, and black self-representations. The novel articulates the process of attempting to fulfill the cultural responsibility of black artists and the cultural function of art produced by African Americans about African American culture. Art, for Baldwin, should reflect artists' perspectives and experiences and illustrate the complexity of black subjectivity formation. In so doing, it may successfully critique (rather than promote) stereotypes. His understanding, in turn, sheds light on his own project of rhetorically recovering black subjectivity.

Unlike Du Bois and Hughes, who were primarily concerned with how dominant discourses over-determine black identities, Baldwin explores how Leo constructs a subjectivity beyond the black and white dialectic. Baldwin's story addresses the simplistic, but harmful, cultural politics that many African American artists encountered during and beyond the Harlem Renaissance—that in order to be successful African American artists and other professionals, they must "sell out" or remove themselves from the African American community. Baldwin presents this dilemma as a choice that African American artists make, as opposed to a consequence of their success. Importantly, Leo's

2. Although Du Bois is widely cited for naming the condition of black subjectivity after the issuance of the Emancipation Proclamation, he poses a question about a dilemma that impacted many African American artists at the turn of the century: How do black artists clearly and with certainty portray the beauty of African American culture to a dominant culture that has accepted negative stereotypes of African American people?

As observers of African American life, the task that African American artists face is one of interpretation and mediation. Artists interpret what is felt intrinsically to a non-African American audience, and they mediate public discourses about African American culture. In mediating public discourses, black artists attempt to present African American perspectives without offending white Americans. In addition, black artists make great personal and professional sacrifices to challenge public discourses about black identity

Besides posing the double consciousness of the black artists, Baldwin takes up a preoccupation of Harlem Renaissance writer Langston Hughes. In *The Big Sea,* Hughes focused on the decisions that artists made as opposed to the discourses that artists responded to. Hughes wrote that some African American artists created or performed two-dimensional characters to appease rich white patrons who visited popular Harlem nightclubs during the apex of the Harlem Renaissance. In *Tell Me How Long the Train's Been Gone,* Baldwin suggests that this predicament—caught between cultural and personal responsibilities—persisted in the production of art beyond the Harlem Renaissance. When Leo criticizes roles that perpetuate negative stereotypes about African Americans, Baldwin suggests that African American artists have a dual responsibility of actor and community activists. Leo walks a careful line: he satisfies the expectations of directors and white patrons and delivers inspirational speeches about community responsibility to the Harlem black community.

understanding of his situation suggests how well-versed Baldwin is in identity politics/politics of identity that plagued his predecessors, the African American literary tradition, and African American people in general. Leo occupies a space in his Harlem community that many young African American artists occupy.

Leo's efforts to be a successful actor are colored by his preoccupation with his desire to be a role model for the African American children in his Harlem community. Leo is not simply concerned with how he is defined by whites in the theater and social contexts; he is also concerned with how he is defined in African American cultural contexts: how his mother only sees him in opposition to his brother, who is a preacher, and how his older brother thinks his desire to be an actor is a way for him to live irresponsibly. Baldwin's concern with black subjectivity as represented by Leo is the subject of my analysis.

SUBJECTIVITY, THE BLACK ARTIST, AND *TELL ME HOW LONG THE TRAIN'S BEEN GONE*

In *Tell Me How Long the Train's Been Gone,* Baldwin presents a paradox as his central affirmation of community: one has to leave in order to understand how the community shapes one's subjectivity. Leo Proudhammer leaves Harlem to pursue a life as an actor, much as James Baldwin left Harlem to pursue a life as a writer. Neither Baldwin nor his protagonist intentionally set out to find community. In fact, both felt that they had to make a complete break with the poverty, despair, and hopelessness of Harlem. Although they remain critical of the sanctimonious idea that African Americans should stay for the sake of community, Baldwin and Leo return to Harlem having accepted that they have been shaped by its African American culture, and that they have a complex relationship with it. Ironically, the discourses that Baldwin and Leo were exposed to in Harlem enabled them to be successful, but not in the way that could be easily understood by white audiences:

> There, in that absolutely alabaster landscape armed with two Bessie Smith records and a typewriter, I began to try to re-create the life that I had first known as a child and from which I had spent so many years in flight. . . . The American writer, in Europe, is released, first of all, from the necessity of apologizing for himself. [When] he is released from the habit of flexing his muscles and proving that he is a regular guy . . . he realizes how crippling the habit has been. (1993b, 5–6)

It was in Europe that Baldwin came to understand the cultural experiences that produced Bessie Smith's talent, where he wrote *The Fire Next Time* and where he finished his first novel, *Go Tell It on the Mountain,* about growing up as the descendent of the Great Migration north to Harlem. In many ways, *Go Tell It on the Mountain* parodies Baldwin's religious experience to demonstrate the insidiousness of Christian discourses within the Grimes family. In traveling from America to Europe and north to south, Baldwin refined his talent as a writer and thinker about what it means to be a gay, black writer in America.

Baldwin's experience in America and abroad prepared him to create complex characters with sophisticated subjectivities. Unfortunately, book reviews indicate the difficulty that critics had in understanding the ways that *Tell Me How Long the Train's Been Gone* challenged uniform beliefs about African American experiences and narrow representations of black masculinity. For example, in the *New York Times,* Mario Puzo describes the novel as "a simple minded, one-dimensional novel with mostly cardboard characters, a polemical rather than narrative tone, weak invention and poor selection of incident."[3] But, as Lynn Orilla Scott argues in *James Baldwin's Later Fiction: Witness to the Journey,* Baldwin's "response to the events of the sixties and seventies was more complex than has been acknowledged" and that his "novel should be read not as evidence of either political capitulation or an artistic decline, but as evidence of the ways Baldwin creatively responded to a changing racial environment and discourses in an attempt to communicate the story he wanted to tell" (2002, 10). In short, Baldwin's position on the diverse subjectivities of black men, as opposed to the narrow politicized definitions reinforced by social movements, highlights the spaces that he chose for himself.

In Europe, he found himself outside the polemics of black and white and came to understand black subjectivity from a discursive space far removed from his Harlem community: "I realized that I had acquired so many affectations, had told myself so many lies, that I really had buried myself beneath a whole fantastic image of myself which wasn't mine, but white people's image of me" (1989, 4). Baldwin continually used this space to write about how African Americans define their subjectivity and to write about its relationship to the discourses of colonialism and their construction of the colonized (the larger sub-group to which African Americans belonged). In *No Name in the Street,* Baldwin notes how African Americans and French Algerians respond to racial

3. The several book reviews that focused on Baldwin's novel were not helpful to my analysis because the reviews primarily focused on how they thought the novel should have been written as opposed to Baldwin's artistic accomplishment. Scott strongly said, "The reception of *Train's* was not only marked by an outraged liberalism, but by a somewhat quieter, though not always subtle, homophobia" (2002, 22).

oppression. The Algerians in France, he states, "held something within them which they would never surrender to France. But on my side of the ocean, or it seemed to me then, we had surrendered everything, or had had everything taken away, and there was no place for us to go: we were home" (2007, 24).

Much like his character Leo Proudhammer, a bisexual black artist who performs the expected role of African Americans on the stage, Baldwin, the expatriate writer, reflected on African American identity, easily accepting his sexuality as an aspect of his subjectivity and masculinity. As Marlon B. Ross explains in "Some Glances at the Black Fag," "For the black homosexual, same sex desire was a matter of finding a way to reaffirm continuity, rather than a matter of breaking with a dominant culture in order to gain a new identity through an awakened consciousness shared with others of a similarly oppressed status. This is why Baldwin's refusal to identify as a homosexual is not necessarily a contradiction [as] it is often seen as being" (2000, 504–5). To consider Baldwin's and Leo's sexuality and masculinity as distinct is not only a mistake but falsely suggests that in the same context they are not *both* homosexual and masculine. For Baldwin and Leo, sexuality is an integral part of their subjectivity as African American men and artists, providing them with sophisticated perspectives on family and community.

Besides demonstrating how a bisexual African American man melds his sexuality with his identity as a black man, Baldwin demonstrates what Leo has learned about the performance of African Americans from the outside-in when he performs easily recognizable roles as an actor. Leo buries himself in a fantastic parodic and ironic image of himself on stage:

> And one learned, therefore, and long before one had learned anything else, the most abject reliance on the most shameful tricks, one learned before one learned anything else that contempt for the audience which is death to art. One was imitating an artifact, one might as well have been an icon, and one's performance depended not at all on what one saw—still less, God forbid, on what one felt—but on what the audience had come to see, had been trained to see. (1968, 343)

On stage, Leo is aware that he is not performing himself. He is employing what audiences expect to see. He is confirming their reality and what they believe about their reality. In fact, in front of most of these audiences, he performs stereotypes of African Americans while maintaining awareness that they are just that—performances. This discursive dissonance highlights the space of African American subjectivity. In terms of identity and subjectivity, acting has more to do with identity (public and outward), but there is a perceived and felt differentiation from an inner-self, which paradoxically the art depends on.

Presented from the viewpoint of Leo's self-consciousness, an actor playing a role of a socially viable black character for a primarily white audience, *Tell Me How Long the Train's Been Gone* provides a context in which to explore the self-conscious decisions that Leo employs to be a successful actor. By performing stereotypes as exaggerations, he exploits the limitations of dominant discourses. In the process of nuancing his performance with his understanding of stereotype, Leo displays an understanding of discourses and of his power to manipulate these discourses for the purposes of ironic presentation. This is the focus of his artfulness as an actor. By subtly maneuvering roles, he seeks to present the reality of his talent as an actor. While acting, Leo explores the limitations of white subjectivity and the power of black subjectivity in order to manipulate racialized discourses through performance.

Because theatrical performance is a part of novelistic discourse, the reader of *Tell Me How Long the Train's Been Gone* can see firsthand the distance between self and performance, the actor and the role. By presenting the performance of African American roles as the terrain of personal contestation and struggle, Leo represents both an awareness of discourses and a strategy for manipulating discourses. In his performance, Leo mimics these discourses to various degrees in order to construct a subjectivity as distinct from his socially constructed black identity. Leo even sees his own chosen path of being an actor as one of mimicry: one that stages a parodic performance of black identity to a white audience to reveal the extent to which social constructions of black identity are parodies of African Americans' lives. At specific times in the novel, I argue, Leo stands aside and apart from how he "performs himself" to critically engage the expectations of audiences and other characters:

> One had to change the beat: one had to find a rhythm, which arrested the rhythm. And the price for this was a sudden ruthless good humor, for the audience had, after all, placed themselves in your hands by lacking the courage to imagine about you what you knew too well about them. The people saw you showing your teeth: it escaped their notice that they were also showing theirs—and showing them, furthermore, on the key delivered by their Fool. (1968, 343)

In these observations, Leo demonstrates that he is aware of when he is performing his subjectivity and how others expect him to perform his identity. How Leo develops and utilizes this sophistication, and how Baldwin displays that characterizing idiom, is the focus of my inquiry.

It is important to look at how mimicry is understood in the colonial context to understand the power of representation. Mimicry marks the evidence of successful conversion and linguistic colonization; in the context of the African American performance of self, mimicry is neither affirmation nor denial, but rather a space of negotiation through uninflected performance, through irony and exaggeration, with the end result of creating a space for a differing self. In "Of Mimicry and Man: The Ambivalence of Colonial Discourse," Homi Bhabha describes mimicry as the presentation of the abject self, which represents an understanding of colonizing discourses, the performance that shields the performer from the panoptic gaze. For Bhabha, mimicry is not about individuals copying or parodying the behaviors of others; instead, mimicry articulates how oppressed people construct a subjectivity within the context of competing discourses about culture. Their subjectivity rearticulates dominant history through creating an alternative discourse that represents the significance of their culture and experience. Crucially, mimicry does not identify or define one's subjectivity. It is not just the doubled self of the mask or the veil; it identifies the processes of rhetorical performance. Removing the "mask" or the "veil" does not reveal the Self because that is a rhetorical impossibility. Rather because its material is discourse, Bhabha maintains, the self is revealed through the modalities of "irony, mimicry and repetition" (1984, 122). Mimicry is a discursive ambivalence that "continually produces its slippage, its excess, and its difference" (122). In a very real sense, then, for Leo the world is a stage. The awareness that Leo displays is consistent with Bhabha's mimicry, for Bhabha is most concerned with the performance of dominant discourses as a strategy to perform and, simultaneously, undermine social oppression.

Bhabha's powerful redefinition of mimicry as a cultural strategy, in a space where discourses are endlessly repeated, reveals the ways in which Leo's decision to be an actor allows him to utilize the rhetorical strategy of mimicry. As the terrain for subjectivity construction, mimicry distinguishes not between representation and reality, but between one representation and another. When Bhabha redefines mimicry in the colonial context, he explores the significance, for example, of whether bringing a Bible to a town gathering is an indication that the natives are truly converted. He describes a move beyond the impossibility of knowing intentionality (motivation). Let us assume, he argues, that mimicry is the differentiation between two performances—one of conversion and another of non-conversion. Each reflects on the other, each functions as the context for the other. And in the context of mimicry—irony, self-depreciation, and hypocrisy—the viewer is always made aware of the discourses that construct a particular performance. It is precisely this distinction that allows the reader to move away from the consensus that Leo does not know who he is to an appreciation of his self-knowledge regarding representation as reality and reality as representation. I argue that Leo's identity as an African American is literally played out, so that we are made aware of the choices that Leo makes and those with which he struggles. In performance after performance he comes to a deeper understanding of the discourses that seek to represent African American subjectivity. In recounting how these discourses function, he is able to name his negotiations.

•

I went to a masquerade / Disguised as Myself

—BOB KAUFMAN, "HEAVY WATER BLUES" (*GOLDEN SANDALS*, 1967)

At the beginning of the book, Baldwin introduces readers to Leo's self-reflections as a process of understanding African American male experiences. By forefronting Leo's thoughts about himself and his experiences, Baldwin focuses attention on Leo's subjectivity. From Leo, we learn how difficult it is to be a successful African American actor in the 1940s and 1950s. In the opening pages of the book, Leo is presented as narrator and interpreter of the events that shaped his life and the discourses that he negotiated to be a successful actor. Reflecting on how his past choices were conscious attempts at negotiating discourses within and beyond his community, Leo recounts and explicates the events that lead up to his heart attack, providing insights into his subjectivity. As readers, we are asked to differentiate between representations of Leo in society as the successful actor and Leo's representations of himself in society (the degree to which he identifies with and exerts control over dominant discourses on black identity). Moreover, in highlighting the differences between theatrical performance and novelistic discourses, the novel highlights the differences between one kind of representation and another. At the beginning of the novel, Leo is standing in the wing waiting to go on stage. Sweating, nauseous, and fatigued, Leo is having a heart attack. Out of breath, he walks on stage. Swallowing his vomit and wiping away sweat from his brow, he struggles to say his lines. Somehow, he manages to finish the act. When the curtain falls he collapses. Losing and regaining consciousness, Leo is carried off stage, placed in an ambulance, and admitted to a hospital. Staring at the ambulance ceiling, in a voice barely above a whisper, Leo asks his friend Pete to "wipe" the makeup from his face because "no one would recognize me where I was going! I would be lost" (1968, 11). Leo's makeup is removed, revealing the experiencer behind the performance. He thinks, "My life, that desperately treacherous labyrinth, seemed for a moment to be opening out behind me; a light seemed to fall where there had been no light before. I began to see myself in others" (8). Leo feels a sense of disintegration behind the mask he presents to his audiences, and we are privileged for a moment to experience dissonant representations.

In the novel, the metaphor of the mask has the same significance as it does in Paul Laurence Dunbar's poem "We Wear the Mask," which explores the self-conscious performance that early African Americans adopted to function in a society that was openly hostile to them and their experiences and that did not recognize them as American citizens. In response to the widely held belief in post-Reconstruction America that African Americans were content with working menial jobs for little or no pay, the metaphor of the mask suggests that African Americans unhappily took service-oriented jobs while maintaining a sense of self and performing outward signs of happiness such as showing a "grin" or a "smile." Dunbar's metaphor aptly illuminates the space between Leo's subjectivity and identity and highlights mimicry as a useful rhetorical strategy for negotiating social alienation and oppression. Before he was hospitalized from a massive heart attack, Leo accepted that changing social perceptions of African Americans required him to accept praises of white audiences and avoid revealing his feelings about performing stereotypical roles.

From his hospital bed, however, Leo's thoughts reflect his sense of disintegration. Decentering himself as an already fashioned subject, Leo searches for the sources of his tension, apprehension, and depression, and the reader is encouraged to assess and evaluate the choices that Leo made. At the crossroads of life and death, Leo evaluates the choices that he had made in his life. Did he compromise his integrity in choosing to negotiate his historical circumstances through performance and mimicry? Did he feel estranged because he had cut himself off from the experiences of other black men? Reflecting on the historical experience of black men and the tragic death of his friend, Leo's thoughts locate his experience within the historical and social experience of other African American men. Speculating on how he is connected to history and other black subjectivities, Leo's thoughts are about enslaved Africans who refused to die on American slave plantations and black men who were violently killed in the Deep South. Life had its own distinct struggles and rhythms, which Leo remembers as very different from how African Americans were constructed in theatrical fictions.

Leo recalls, for example, how while walking through affluent neighborhoods he manipulated his body to deflect social discourses about black identity. Aware of the performance that is expected of him, he delivers the performance on key. Mimicking the movements of what dominant society expects, his posture, eyes, and hands do not belong to him. On streets that are predominantly lined with businesses and sidewalks crowded with white men and women, Leo practices the strategies that he would later use in the theater as techniques to make African American characters believable. White gazes and presence are the discourses that Leo's body responds to as he walks down the street.[4] Leo tailors his body movements to communicate deference to whites:

> I kept my hand in my pockets [and so does his older brother Caleb] so I could not be accused of molesting any of the women who jostled past, and kept my eyes carefully expressionless so I could not be accused of lusting after the women, or desiring the death of the men. (1968, 225–26)

For he is not positioning his body or focusing his eyes for himself, but to reassure whites that he and Caleb are not a threat to them. Responding to dominant discourses in this manner is natural, for as Michel Foucault reminds us, "discipline produces subjected and practiced bodies, docile bodies" (1984, 182). Bodies are positioned to represent power, not the power of the individual, but the power and hegemony of white dominant discourses. Leo's automatic response reflects this. Refocusing attention from Caleb's body onto his body, Leo assumes a posture that reaffirms stereotypes, protecting both Caleb and himself from them and, in turn, negotiating the space between his subjectivity and performances and white subjectivity. In his struggle to be an actor, Leo encounters a superficial world of performance that depends on the discursive divide of black identity and white subjectivity. Because white directors are unable to see past his black skin, Leo is perceived as limited to and perfect for playing the part of porters, butlers, and waiters. He executes these roles not based on his prior experiences with being in servitude, but from his critical perspective and experience with white discourses that segregated his childhood world from that of metropolitan New York.

When Leo remembers his childhood experiences and feelings, he recalls how he believed that he had to choose between individuality and community. As an adult, this belief persists, but his choices are to remain in the African American community in Harlem or pursue membership in the community of actors, which are the communities he seeks both to belong to and to differentiate himself from. However, his choice is complicated by the discourses that maintain each community. In the African American community of actors, he uncovers a sense of hypocrisy. The community's politics present its members

4. For an exploration of representations of the city in James Baldwin's novels as well as other African American literary texts, see Joyce R. Durham's "The City in Recent American Fiction: Listening to Black Urban Voices" (1990).

as being above common prejudices, but their material conditions are steeped in racial politics. The African American community expects him to only represent its members positively and perform their achievements and disappointments while the white directors expect him to perform black male identity as they know it—insecure and ingratiating. He experiences his limited choices as intentionally "locking oneself behind mighty doors" and being trapped (Baldwin 1968, 99). In his self-reflection, he realizes that the objective of a unified self is not to combine or lessen the sense of self-division, but to be aware of the distinction and to explore what discourses are available to construct a subjectivity that defines him not simply as an African American man in American society but as a man and an African American actor.

•

> I am invisible, understand, simply because people refuse to see me
> —RALPH ELLISON, *INVISIBLE MAN*

In the theater, Leo uses acting to present the truths of life and embrace the contradictions of acting as truth:

> There is a truth in the theater and there is a truth in life—they meet, but they are not the same, for life, God help us, is the truth. And those disguises, which an artist wears, are his means, not of fleeing from the truth, but of attempting to approach it. (Baldwin 1968, 112)

Both contexts, real life and the theater, require one to perform a Self, but the anonymity of a costume enables one to pursue or perform truths about oneself that in life remain concealed: "disguises are designed to make the truth a quantity with which one can live—or from which one can hope, by the effort of living to be delivered" (113). Having the opportunities to explore his own humanity and experiences does not lead Leo to a truth about himself; instead, it takes him to the crossroads (where he is at the beginning of the novel) where philosophical questions plague him, such as: Who am I? Am I a credit to my race? Is my fame a testament to my talent or am I a victim of liberal white generosity? What will future generations of African American performers think about me? These questions are difficult, if not impossible, to answer and have different meanings for different readers of the novel. These questions are made poignant when Leo discovers that not only do social and community discourses deny him an individual subjectivity outside the theater, but they also deny him an individual subjectivity within it.

The problem is that the negative ideologies that affect him outside the theater are the same ones that his theatrical directors appropriate to communicate a character's values and beliefs. While audiences depend on these ideologies to engage African American culture and people, Leo experiences how difficult it is to convey positive perspectives of African American culture and introduce African American humanity to white audiences. As simple discourses that perpetuate unfounded beliefs about black subjectivity, stereotypes define African American subjectivity to fulfill white desires and fantasies. Representing subjectivity as flat or two-dimensional, these roles are not powerful or culturally grounded representations of his subjectivity. Performing these oppressive discourses is what Leo must agree to do to be successful:

> Well. It went on like that, and it got worse, and I don't think I'd have minded if I could have found a role which had some relation to the life I lived, the life I knew, some role which did not traduce entirely my own senses of life, of my own life. But I played waiters, butlers, porters, and clowns; since they had never existed in life, there was no conceivable way to play them. (343)

Aware that white audiences come to the theater to have their beliefs reaffirmed, Leo uses this information to his advantage. He remains aware of what the audience wants to see and knows what he represents to the subjectivity of different audience members. For whites, he is seen as exceptional, and to African Americans he represents how "one more of our boys have made it" (435). The audience presents an immediate context for Leo to rehearse the nuances of his subjectivity because they are at the mercy of his fictional manipulations. Aware of the limits of performance, Leo sees the impact of that performance. Now, the gaze that has been directed at him, in turn, has been directed outward from him. This places Leo in a unique position where acting, concretely, becomes a powerful metaphor for the performance of African American subjectivity. By using mimicry to perform how discourses function socially and culturally, Leo hopes to achieve his own artistry about the self, just as Baldwin sought to write beyond the limits of the social protest novel. Both artist and artist manqué reflect on how African American identity has been constructed within and outside of African American contexts.

When Leo, a struggling actor, joins Saul's workshop, his understandings of mimicry and performance contradict the renowned director and writer's received wisdom about unique talent versus African American limitations. Reflecting white perceptions that black performers are intuitively talented, Saul holds Paul Robeson up as a uniquely talented African American: "Paul Robeson was an actor who was made to play Othello. The instrument suggests it, the instrument, so to say demands it" (300). Saul's claim that black artistic abilities come from a magical and primitive source does not resonate with Leo. To Leo and to Baldwin, Robeson struggled to be an actor, struggled to bring attention to Negro spirituals, even as he was driven by the desire to perform African American hopes and to perfect his art (300). When Robeson performed Othello, the title character in a highly charged interracial relationship, he was threatened with lynching and with the death of his loved ones. Ironically, Robeson represents his construction as an African American actor who cannot (on pain of death) play a believable role as a black man in love with a white woman. Leo understands Robeson's performances concern assimilation and simultaneously cultural uniqueness. Drawing on Robeson's success in the theater, Leo wants to perform an African American cultural interpretation of *Othello* that (as many believed Robeson's did) would upstage Lawrence Olivier as the title character, a performance that Olivier himself says was more about exploring what he suspected was sexual tension between Othello and Iago (Olivier 1982, 105–6).

Leo faces stereotyping in the analysis of his acting abilities. Saul comments on Leo's ability to dance, calling it his "best moment": "There is nothing to indicate—ah—in our opinion—that you have any very striking theatrical ability. Except, perhaps, for that little dance at the very end of the scene. Then you seemed free, and, so to say, joyous and boyish. We found it your very best moment." In other words, Saul feels that Leo's talent is instinctive, not learned (300). For Saul, Leo's ability to dance is natural as opposed to, or based on, a learned skill, a stereotype of the African American performer. Still, Leo wants to be recognized for his ability to move in and out of characters, but his "authentic" contribution to the acting world is dancing. To his peers and Saul, dancing is his way to gain acceptance and credibility as a performer. As Bruce E. Johansen says in "Race, Ethnicity, and the Media," stereotypes are both barriers and entrances:

> Because no single person can directly observe more than a tiny fraction of events in the world, we rely on the reports of others and then fit them into our own perceptual framework. . . . We notice a trait which marks a well-known type, and fill in the rest of the picture by means of the stereotyping we carry around in our heads. A great deal of confusion arises when people decline to classify themselves as we have classified them. (1997, 514)

The negative ideologies that Leo employs to negotiate stereotypes are the same ones he needs to communicate a new message. Audiences depend on these ideologies to engage African American culture and people. Leo learns two important lessons: how difficult it is to convey positive perspectives of African American culture and introduce African American humanity to white audiences and what he has to sacrifice to be a successful actor. When Leo performs stereotypes, he is constructing an awareness of how he is perceived, rhetorically constructing a facsimile of an "authentic" cultural identity.

But years of working with directors who uncritically accept and adopt stereotypes has made Leo more intuitive about their expectations. He listens intently to what they say as well as what they do not say when they court him for a part in their plays. Depending on what they say, Leo can determine how much latitude he will have to perform his character. Leo observes the performances of directors to analyze his opportunities. When directors speak to him in a conspiratorial tone, they expect him to, without protest or suggestions, take roles that he believes are an "insult" to his "manhood." While acting, Leo's goal is to focus audiences' attention on culturally centered performances of black identity and the simultaneous conditions that mark his performance as authentic, on the one hand, and parodic, on the other. In this way, Leo maximizes the only available avenue to succeed as an actor.

By taking roles and performing them well, Leo demonstrates that he knows that there is nothing real about these roles—they are simply constructions that he can perform or use as tools for negotiating social racism and achieving success in theater. Playing these roles does not give Leo the opportunity to communicate African American sensibilities or dispel myths about African Americans, but they do compel him to search for a theatrical approach that communicates authentically concerning African American identity, experience, and ambition. In this sense, Leo takes steps to construct his subjectivity outside of social and community discourses.

•

> To expect the Negro artist to reject every role with which he is not ideologically in agreement is to expect the Negro artist under our present scheme of things to give up work entirely.
>
> —PAUL ROBESON (*AMSTERDAM NEWS*, 1935)

Despite the lack of positive roles for African Americans in the theater and in motion pictures, Leo discovers a way to construct himself as an actor. His focus turns to proving that African American actors can perform roles other than those of servants and butlers, which tend to reproduce the racial structure of society. Leo does this through employing a unique understanding of his position vis-à-vis white audiences. Positioned between black and white subjectivity, which he uses to his advantage, Leo takes the opportunity to explore the limitations of white subjectivity and the possibilities of African American subjectivity. Leo compares the humiliation that he feels on stage dressed as an "African savage" to the Native American stereotype of Tonto. Standing on stage, he thinks about the specific function of the African savage and Native American stereotype to white audience members: "Their bland dumpling exteriors concealed so much of fantasy, helpless, lonely, and vindictive I wore the regulation jockstrap, though this seemed silly to me. . . . But then I began to feel that the jockstrap actually functioned—and perhaps was meant to function—as a kind of incitement, both for them and me" (158). Leo's "Orientalizing" performance reveals the pastiche of discourses that construct the other and that deviate from any known reality. They exist in the realm of fantasy. Not only does Leo recognize this Orientalism as primitivism, but he sees it as the performances of white subjectivity, the by-product of secret fantasies: "I gave an awful performance, and I knew it. I couldn't find my way into the character at all, I didn't believe in his sorrows and I didn't believe in his joys and I found absolutely no way to play the scene in which the hero, having struck down a white man, loudly and sincerely repents. He sounded as though he had struck down the Son of God. The white man had beaten him with a whip: why was the nigger supposed to moan because he reacted—and, at that, belatedly—as the dueling codes of Europe assume a man should act?" (344). The irony and parodic humor highlights a crucial reason why these constructions cannot be psychologically "real."

On stage, Leo exploits the dialectic between performance and the audience's desires. Leo monitors the crowd's reactions. In control of how he wants to present these performances, Leo carefully appropriates the limitations and expectations of the primarily white, liberal audience members as he walks the metaphorical line between what they have been told about African Americans and what they believe about them:

> The play was put on as part of an educational drive: was this what we were supposed to learn? . . . Father forgive them because they know not what they are doing. . . . I knew what they were doing, and as long as they were doing it to me, I was going to do my best to give them a bloody instruction. (344)

Here, Leo is presented as a Christ figure who is prepared to give his life and sacrifice his career so that future African American actors will not have to unduly suffer. His willingness to give what is most precious to him establishes him as the prototype African American leader, even, perhaps, a redemptive savior. As those who died before him dedicated their lives to uplifting African

Americans, Leo decides to do the same. This belief that he can reconstruct the sensibilities of his white audience members represents deeply held religious and cultural beliefs and traditions among African Americans. In the theater, mimicry as performance enables Leo to stand aside and apart from how he performs himself and recognize the distance that lies between his subjectivity and the social construction of black identity.

Through acting, Leo discovers that the white characterizations lack depth because their constructions of African Americans do not compel them to think about the material experiences of African Americans or allow for insights into themselves:

> It was not pleasant to be forced to reflect that they operated in a vacuum even greater than mine, and knew even less about themselves than I. . . . Most of the roles played by white people could only be played by means of tricks, tricks which would never help one to come closer to life. . . . I was discovering what some American blacks must discover: that the people who destroyed my history had also destroyed their own. (346)

In underscoring the irony of white history, Leo's words function as a powerful social critique of the United States as a nation. Baldwin speaks through the character/narrator precisely because it mocks the ability of white subjectivity to be the model for black subjectivity: "What emerges between mimesis and mimicry is a writing, a mode of representation, that marginalizes the monumentality of history, quite simply mocks its power to be a model, that power which supposedly makes it imitable" (Bhabha 1984, 153).

At the conclusion of *Tell Me How Long the Train's Been Gone,* Leo is standing in the "wings again, waiting my cue" (484). This replays the beginning of the book. In these existential moments, he understands his limitations as his possibilities. He can perform the pain that he feels as well as the pain he believes many African Americans feel about their social condition. In acting, he is able to move closer to the truth about himself and being a black man:

> I played that scene for all that was in it, for all that was in me, and for all the colored kids in the audience—who held their breath, they really did, it was the unmistakable silence in which you and the audience re-create each other—and for the vanishing Little Leo, and for my mother and father, and all the hope and pain that were in me. (433)

In this space between outward contentment and inward discontentment, Leo understands himself in differential terms.

CHAPTER 4

"My Great-Granddaddy Could Fly!"

Negotiating Cultural History and Family Legacies in *Song of Solomon*

> At its best American folklore, drama, the novel, literature, have always been concerned with teaching Americans how to accept their goddamned fate and then to go on to overcome it. And if a writer doesn't want to help them do that, then he should go into politics! [Laughs.]
>
> —RALPH ELLISON, "RALPH ELLISON: TWENTY YEARS AFTER," 1971

AFRICAN AMERICAN writers demonstrate that written texts and spoken discourses play and have always played an important role in instructing African Americans on how to negotiate various contexts and conditions. In the above quote, Ralph Ellison applauds these writers for equipping individuals with strategies for outlasting the unpredictability of their society and community. These tactics include but are not limited to imbuing particular images, artifacts, or objects with historic and symbolic meaning and embedding cultural narratives (about gender and sexuality) that deepen the story and character understandings. Also, they represent indigenous religious practices such as conjuring as protection against potential threats, folksongs as a means to sustain confidence in adverse situations, and folktales to instruct individuals on advantageous methods for circumventing difficult or dangerous contexts. Besides using creative expressions as defense against cruel, malicious, and violent practices in America, writers demonstrate the ways that folklore in particular addresses dissociation from cultural and community contexts. In novels that explore African American subjectivity in the Great Migration, many characters romanticize the South as a cradle for African American culture and creative practices and expression. They draw on folk practices and expressions to address unfamiliar surroundings and to reconstruct their southern past in the North. Indeed, African American writers embed folklore in literary texts to provide readers with rituals, practices, and knowledge for simultaneously revisiting the historical past and addressing the immediate social conditions of the present.

Within the same decade that Ellison highlighted folklore's pedagogical function, Morrison published *Song of Solomon,* a novel that suggests how descendants of African American migrants embraced folklore as a response to what Blayden Jackson refers to as the "aftermath of the Great Migration" or the crisis of dissociation that migrants faced after relocating from the South to the North (1991, xvi). While Ellison incorporates isolated historical items of folklore materials such as jazz and blues (as a vehicle to communicate deep innermost feelings) in *Invisible Man,* Morrison appropriates and transforms traditional folklore expressions into her fiction without "compromising its original quality" (Harris 1991, 7). Trudier Harris argues that Morrison "effortlessly and seamlessly embeds folklore into her novels. She allows no dichotomy between form and substance, theme and character" (8). Harris writes that Morrison's "literary folklore" "begin[s] with a joke or superstition in its recognizable, traditional form, but she then takes fictional license in making the lore into something that has never circulated in any folk community. Or she takes the form of traditions within African American folk communities and gives them fictional substance, so that we recognize the outline of a story, or a joke, or a belief" (8). Throughout *Song of Solomon,* Morrison integrates folktales and songs to symbolize black subjectivity as unrestrained and liberated and fashioned in the intersection of the past and present, North and South, family legacy and cultural history.

In Morrison's novel, Macon (Milkman) Dead III represents the first generation of African Americans born in the North. His father, Macon Dead II, and his Aunt Pilate travel from the South to the North after a group of white men murdered their father and stole his land. After arriving in the North Macon pursues his middle-class ambitions: he marries Ruth, the daughter of a prominent doctor and works to become a wealthy landowner in the predominately black Southside community. While Macon symbolizes the values of Locke's ambitious and confident New Negro, Pilate represents the Old Negro: a backwards and spiritual person who embraces African American folk practices and expressions as subjectivity. Milkman symbolizes the first generation of southern migrants born in the North. Situated between Macon and Pilate's northern and southern value systems, Milkman leaves the comforts of his upper-middle-class lifestyle in the North to search for his family inheritance in the South. His willingness to travel from the North to the South to retrieve his birthright speaks to the importance he places on family duty and commitment and also his susceptibility to the influences of the discourses and the narratives that are instrumental to African American migrants' process of redefinition. In presenting a character who unknowingly undergoes a process of redefinition, Morrison draws on two sets of beliefs about turn of the century African American men: first, that unlike African American restrictions to search for meaning and identity in domestic spaces, African American men define themselves against notions of manliness in the intersections of society and community. Secondly, although a major impetus for the Great Migration was to achieve a better life, African American men consciously or unconsciously relied on folklore to survive the northern landscape.

By exploring the suggestion in *Song of Solomon* that folklore addresses the fragmentation that migrants experienced after relocating north, I contextualize Morrison's novel within the larger discourses on black male subjectivity construction and locate her within a canon of black writers (namely Richard Wright, Gayle Jones, and Langston Hughes) who represent characters who draw on folk traditions to negotiate racial hostility and economic disparity after relocating to northern cities such as Chicago, Harlem, and Boston. However, unlike her predecessors who draw black characters who suffer as a result of northern segregation and alienation, Morrison's protagonist attempts to address his feelings of dissociation with a folktale and song about resiliency and resistance. In the tradition of Hughes, Cullen, Hurston, Ellison, and Baldwin who articulate migrants' subjectivity through vernacular forms such as jazz, blues, spirituals, and biblical stories, Morrison represents the subjectivity of her protagonists in *Song of Solomon* through folklore forms such as tales, songs, and hoodoo. If *Tell Me How Long the Train's Been Gone* presents mimicry as a discursive strategy for negotiating the negative social discourses about black male identity, *Song of Solomon* depicts folklore as a rhetorical strategy for navigating the regional divide of the North and South. As bearers and practitioners of the folklore, the characters carry the South (in the form of folk practices) to the North (a region absent of African American cultural traditions).

The North and South exist in the imagination of the characters in *Song of Solomon* and functions as crucial contexts for the oral history of community construction. As Ralph Story points out, "Morrison's intuitive and experiential understanding of the urban, Northern Black community is strengthened and enhanced by her consciousness of Afro-American history and culture and the internal and external forces which have swirled within and without its citizenry" (1999, 91). The community of Southside uses the South as a common point of reference. The novel is a fascinating commentary on how African American males come to understand the relationship between their southern heritage and northern life.

In contrast to her predecessors' explorations of economic disparities and social injustices, Morrison represents folk practices as being significant to community building in the North. In this way, she harkens to the Harlem Renaissance debates about the old and new Negro or southern and northern African American identity. Morrison challenges the belief that northward migration represents unadulterated progress for the race. Morrison explores folklore as essential to subjectivity construction and the northern negro can't understand himself without knowing where he came from. Besides empathizing with migrants' feelings of cultural and psychological dislocation and dissociation and celebrating the cultural legacy rooted in the rural southern communities the migrants had left behind, Morrison emphasizes the role of black women as essential and custodians to black male subjectivity construction—thus another way Morrison intervenes in the critical concerns during the Harlem Renaissance and the Great Migration. In imagining the male protagonist for *Song of Solomon,* Morrison writes that she wanted to examine how males grow to become men. "Men have more to learn in certain areas than women do. . . . Well, I think women already know that surrender part, and can easily learn how to dominate. But what I wanted was a character who had everything to learn, who would start from zero, and had no reason to learn anything, because he comfortable, he doesn't need money, he's just flabby" (1994a, 75). For Morrison, male subjectivity construction is an inward/outward or dialectical process shaped internally from external stimuli as traveling, gender, and sexuality. While this is not the only novel in which Morrison explores folktales and male subjectivity within and without African American communities, *Song of Solomon* is the only novel in which Morrison investigates the relationship between folktales, migration, and male subjectivity construction.

•

I've seen them come dark / wondering / wide eyed / dreaming / out of Pennsylvania Station / but the trains are late / the gates open / but there're bars / at each gate.

—LANGSTON HUGHES, *SELECTED POEMS OF LANGSTON HUGHES* (1959, 269)

Morrison's experiences as a wife and mother prepared her to explore African American male ways of thinking and knowing about migration in relation to selfhood, family, and community. Traveling is so instrumental to black male subjectivity construction, Morrison contends, that when her sons were adolescents they often talked about traveling through flight to different places all the time—they were amazed when they found they couldn't fly. "They took it for granted that all they had to do was jump up and flap their arms" (1994a, 46). Also, she continues, to her ex-husband, an architect "every house is a hotel" (1994a, 46). African American men travel through cities and states in search of the conditions under which they can realize (or at least try to achieve) their potential. Morrison writes:

> Black men travel, they split, they get on trains, they walk, they move. I used to hear those old men talk about traveling—which is not getting from here to there, it's the process—they even named themselves after trains. It's a part of black life, a positive majestic thing, but there is a price to pay—the price is the children. The father may soar, they may triumph, they may leave, but the children know who they are: they remember, half in glory and half in accusation. That is one of the points of *Song of Solomon*: all the men have left someone, and it is the children who remember it, sing about it. Mythologize it, make it a part of their family history. (46)

Traveling or flying in search of a place to grow has its consequences, which is that the men father children away from their communities without introducing them to the folklore that binds the father and offspring to the same community, as happens to Milkman in *Song of Solomon*. Thus traveling and flight for Morison is not only the "the African sense of whirling dervishes and getting out of one's skin, but also in the majestic sense of a man who goes too far, whose adventures take him far away" (46). Characters searching for their places in families and communities are pervasive throughout Morrison's fiction. Not only are these characters present in the Morrison novels I examine in this book, but also her other novels represent female and male characters who travel or migrate from the South to the North and draw on folklore to help them define a place for themselves in their communities. Traveling in search of selfhood is a significant metaphor in migration narratives.

Constructing male subjectivity from cultural artifacts and materials is a significant theme in migration narratives where male characters draw on folklore to negotiate or navigate their new region or terrain. Previous studies fail to give the relationship between folklore and black male subjectivity construction substantive attention. For example, Susan Willis's (1987) concern with the impact of historical discourses within the migration on black women's identity formation, Hazel Carby's (1999) argument that blues women warned urban and rural women that "the city was not . . . the promised land" (14), Charles Scruggs's (1995) exploration of utopia and dystopia in migration narratives, and Lawrence Rodgers's (1997) study that identifies the literary moments that defined migration narratives are important and original contributions to understanding twentieth-century migration narratives. While my project benefited from the interrogations of gender and landscape of Willis, Carby, Scruggs, and Rodgers, my project is strengthened from incorporating Stepto's (1991) and Griffin's (1995) focused attention on the deep structures of south-to-north movement in migration narratives and informs my thinking about Milkman in the discursive divides of the North and South and cultural history and family legacies. *Song of Solomon* is a migration narrative.

Building on Robert Stepto's work on "narratives of ascent or immersion" as articulated in *Behind the Veil* (1991), Griffin (1995) identifies dominant themes in migration narratives, complexities of gender and sexuality, and the Great Migration narrative as a literary movement. Griffin delineates the four pivotal moments (which don't necessarily occur in a particular order) as "an event that propels the action northward, a detailed representation of the initial confrontation with the urban landscape, representation of the migrant's attempt to negotiate that landscape and his or her resistance to the negative effect of urbanization, and a vision of the possibilities or limitations of the Northern, Western, or Midwestern city and the South" (3). In Morrison's novel, these moments are represented from the time of the protagonist's birth and through his maturity in flashbacks that provide readers context for significant events and relationships that impact Milkman's self-actualization. In contrast to Baldwin's and Ellison's questing characters who travel to the "symbolic" North and learn to incorporate the vernacular as a critical lens to read the system of signs in order to navigate the oppressive northern social structure, Morrison's questing character retravels the Great Migration: he travels south and immerses himself in his roots and culture, then returns north with a folktale and folksong that enables him to negotiate the demands of family life, only to return again south "free in the sense that he has regained sufficient tribal literacy to assume the mantle of an articulate kinsman" who "is willing to forsake highly individualized mobility in the least oppressive social structure for a posture of relative stasis in the most oppressive environment, a loss that is only occasionally assuaged by the newfound balms of group identity" (Stepto 1991, 167). Besides fulfilling the criteria for migration narratives, Morrison's novel engages the North and South or rural and city dialectic introduced by earlier twentieth-century African American writers.

Morrison challenges the problematic notion that African American migrants must either embrace or repudiate folklore. Morrison highlights the significance of folk beliefs and practices to the subjectivity construction of the descendants of the migrants. In this way, Morrison's novel intervenes in early twentieth-century African American literary preoccupations with the role of folk culture as a means for migrants and their descendants to realize self-actualization or social and economic power in the North. For example, sitting in a soul food restaurant, Bigger feels more alienated from his blackness; after Ellison's protagonist travels from the South to the North, he achieves a self-awareness of "that heart of darkness across the Mason-Dixon line. . . . Sometimes I feel the need to reaffirm all of it, the whole unhappy territory, and all things loved and unloved in it, for all of it is part of me" (Ellison 1995a, 22). Similarly, Morrison highlights the folksong as a vehicle for transporting descendants from a physical to a spiritual world. Morrison's protagonist, at the end of his journey, sings a folksong to his aunt as she dies in his arms: "Milkman knew no songs, and had no singing voice that anybody would want to hear, but he couldn't ignore the urgency in her voice. Speaking the words without the least bit of a tune, he sang for the lady. Sugargirl don't leave me here" (1977, 542). Milkman sings to his aunt for three reasons: to send her comfortably to the spiritual world, to pay homage to her as a cultural ancestor, and to place his story next to hers as he achieves a sense of self. Now a conduit for the ancestors, Milkman's voice soothes Aunt Pilate and gives her peace as she slowly slips away to the spiritual world to take her rightful place next to the ancestors. Thus, the novel is a fascinating commentary on how folklore fosters intimacy between African American men and women.

•

> The griot symbolizes how all human ancestry goes back to some place, and some time where there was no writing. Then the memories and the mouths of ancient elders was the only way that early histories of government passed along . . . for all of us to know who we are.
>
> —ALEX HALEY, *ROOTS* (1976)

The exchange of folklore in a community fosters intimacy. In communities, folklore circulates between characters and from other characters to and through Milkman, connecting him to his family, extended family, and his ancestors who are no longer living in the physical world, such as his deep emotional response to his aunt Pilate and cousins singing a folksong while sitting around a table separating blackberries from their branches. His deep emotional response is described in mythical/romantic language: "Milkman could hardly breathe. Hagar's voice scooped up what little pieces of heart he had left to call his own. . . . He thought he was going to faint from the weight of what he was feeling" (Morrison 1977, 93). Folksongs connect Milkman to his African ancestors. Chimalum Nwankwo describes Morrison's use of the African past and expressions as traffic between the ancestors and Milkman collapse time, space, and history in the physical and spiritual worlds. He writes, "in her works that time, history, and space are collapsed, but that is part of a gesture that affirms the existence of the kind of traffic between humans and spirits prevalent in African culture" (1996, 173).

In "Rootedness: The Ancestor as Foundation," Morrison describes the ancestor as "timeless people whose relationship to the characters are benevolent, instructive, and protective, and they provide a certain kind of wisdom" (2008b, 62). The ancestor is significant for bridging the divide between the North and South. Thus, northern culture is merely a reflection of southern culture and vice versa. Since this is the case, they are aware that there isn't a single or ideal home for African Americans. Instead, for African Americans, home is wherever they decide to build a culture, and they thrive wherever they decide to live. While there are regional differences in terms of terrain and landscape, the ancestor speaks to the cultural similarities that unite African Americans regardless of class, gender, and sexuality. In this sense, the ancestor embodies a single culture composed of multiple rhetorical practices and represents the cultural practices that individuals carry with them as they travel throughout America and abroad. They understand that the products of culture and its capabilities (the capacity of folklore to transmit community values and beliefs) reign supreme in all instances and triumph the oppressive nature of the dominant culture.

The ancestor appears or has a presence in many forms in *Song of Solomon*. In *Who Set You Flowin'?*, Griffin writes that the ancestor is present in creative expressions such as song, "food, and performance" and "the oral tradition" (1995, 5). I want to emphasize that Morrison's definition of ancestor encompasses the advice, warnings, and knowledge that is passed along in traditional conversations as well as songs and folktales. The ancestor decides the most effective and meaningful vehicle to use to pass knowledge as he or she is aware that his or her physical presence is not as important as the wealth of knowledge that he or she imparts to an individual who is about to embark on his or her life's journey. "Pilate had a dozen years of close, nurturing relationships with two males—her father and her brother. And that intimacy and support was in her and made her fierce and loving because she had that experience" (Morrison 2008b, 63). For Karla Holloway, the ancestor and its presence serve "as a recursive touchtone" and "a posture of remembrance" (1987, 115). Figuratively and literally Pilate "save[s] Milkman's life" and guides him across the discursive divide (Morrison 1977, 236).

That the ancestor functions on multiple levels in women's novels is consistent with Houston Baker, who argues in his book *Workings of the Spirit: The Poetics of Afro-American Women's Writings* that the act of writing and mediating a story is the duty of ancestors. Baker states that a person possessed by a loa (a spiritual intermediary between human and supernatural) loses all control of the first-person and her/his personality to the possessing spirit (1991, 74). Here, Baker moves beyond contemplations of African influences on European and Western writers to theorize the role of African folk beliefs, values, or spiritual practices in African American women's invention process or literary production. In other words, Baker is concerned with African American women writers as conjurers who surrender their story to a supernatural being. Morrison's loa is her father. In the forward to *Song of Solomon,* Morrison refers to this process in regards to consulting her father, who had passed while she was writing the novel: "I think it was because I felt closer to him than to myself that, after his death. I deliberately sought his advice for writing the novel that continued to elude me. . . . What are the men you have known really like? he answered. . . . Whatever it is called—muse, insight, inspiration, 'the dark finger that guides,' 'bright angel'—it exists and, in many forms, I have trusted it ever since" (1977, 12). Morrison's novel, like conjuring during a voodoo rites ceremony, marks the presence of her male/father ancestor who gives voice and insight on male subjectivity—a perspective that primarily was taken up by African American male writers. Including a discussion on how she called on her recently passed away father for inspiration is an example of how Morrison incorporates southern ways of knowing into her invention process and literature.

Besides invoking the ancestor through directly appealing to her father, Morrison also displays the workings of the spirit through the voice of a narrator who describes how the immigrants in the fictional town mark, familiarize, and remember its layout and the names of the streets. The relationship between memory, the ancestor, and southern ways of knowing is the process by which individuals recall folk songs and sayings. Through rhetorical devices such as word play or play on words, individuals learn at a very young age to use rhythm to create a pattern that is easy to remember. In *Memory in Oral Traditions,* David C. Rubin states that rhythm and alliteration "work locally within lines and between nearby lines. Meaning and imagery also appear to function mostly in a local, serial fashion to limit choices and to increase the discriminability of items in memory. . . . Rhythm is the most effective globally because the specific rhythm being used in the line of stanza being sung is usually the same specific rhythm. . . . However, rhythm does combine with and accentuate other constraints to increase discriminability" (1995, 177). Southside's residents use rhythm to rename and understand their northern community. No longer a physical place, the south has come to inhabit their memories as a discourse that can be sentimentalized and recuperated in narratives. The southern migrants generated a new cartography and nomenclature of the North based on their folklore about the town:

> Town maps registered the street as Main Avenue, but the only colored doctor in the city had lived and died on that street, and when he moved there in 1896 his patients took to calling the street, which none of them lived in or near, Doctor Street. (Morrison 1977, 14)

When African Americans continued to move north and the postal service became a common means of communication, they received letters from Louisiana, Virginia, Alabama, and Georgia addressed to people who lived on Doctor Street. In response, the city government officially declared that the street was Not Doctor Street, an official denial that became its new name. By keeping the oral history of Dr. Foster alive, the rhetorical gesture of naming and renaming the street celebrates the success of the North and its potential for the subversion of the official white culture. Through Not Doctor Street, the residents forged a new relationship between north and south.

This rhetorical ways of reinscribing and renaming also mark the struggles of each resident of Southside and the function of African American folklore in the lives of the characters. Some, like the Dead family, are well established, while others have just made their journey north, looking for work, lodging, family, and happiness. With each succeeding generation, the struggles and challenges continue to be about personal meaningfulness, which is directly connected with the need to remember their past in a particular way: to acknowledge debts to family and culture so that children and grandchildren continue to have a sense of roots. Morrison explores how these generational issues affect Milkman Dead, who constructs his subjectivity after literarily retracing the Great Migration. Milkman retravels the Great Migration from Michigan to Pennsylvania, to Virginia, back to Michigan, and ultimately to Virginia. In so doing, he gains a theoretical and philosophical understanding of individual and community responsibility.

We see the ancestor embedded in the subjectivities of the New Negroes in the North. A few chapters into *Song of Solomon,* a "new Negro" remembers the old southern sights and sounds wafting through the poor African American community, but he resists locating his subjectivity in the South or folklore. "Surrendering to the sound, Macon moved closer. He wanted no conversation, no witness, only to listen and perhaps to see the three of them, the source of that music that made him think of fields and wild turkey and calico" (129). Alan Dundes explains African Americans' feelings of ambivalence toward folklore are a result of the "thorny" relationship between race pride and folklore. While some African Americans see folklore "as an indispensable means of promoting group solidarity," . . . others accept that "folklore is essentially a negative factor especially since it perpetuates racist notions such as white is pure and good and black is evil" (1973, 2). Dundes continues that these views together suggest that race pride can only succeed if folklore is fully eradicated. In other words, since folklore encourages group solidarity in the face of extreme racial oppression, African Americans question the purpose or function of folklore beyond slavery and the South. Morrison takes up the migrants' ambivalence toward southern culture. Some migrants left southern culture behind because they saw the creative expressions as slave culture and a reminder of the oppression they were under. Morrison explores the culture that migrants brought with them. They brought much of the culture they had in the South, including folktale and folksongs. Theodore Mason states that Morrison is an example of the novelist as conservator. She is a writer particularly interested in depicting, and thereby preserving and perpetuating, the cultural practices of black communities (1988, 565).

In life and death as an ancestor, Pilate influences Milkman's subjectivity formation in that she draws on her southern heritage and knowledge of her African ancestors to induce Milkman's birth and usher him into the spiritual world. Standing in the town square singing a folksong about flying away and "cutting across the sky," Pilate is a guardian or chaperon who embraces the subjectivity of African American migrants and represents the community's folk roots and its connection to an African belief system that speaks to but isn't limited by Western beliefs in the potential of the African American spirit. Morrison states, "If it means Icarus to some readers, fine; I want to take credit for that. But my meaning is specific: it is about black people who could fly. That was always part of the folklore of my life; flying was one of our gifts. I don't care how silly it may seem. It is everywhere—people used to talk about it, it's in the spirituals and gospels" (1994a, 122).

•

> Looks like everybody's going in the wrong direction but you, don't it?
>
> —TONI MORRISON, *SONG OF SOLOMON* (1977, 106)

The influence of southern cultural practices on the subjectivity construction of the characters in the North emerges in various ways throughout the novel and lends emotional force to what I argue is Morrison's cultural project, which is to explore how descendants of migrants negotiated the unawareness or unfamiliarity of African American folk culture. How does an African American man construct a subjectivity in the absence of their cultural history and family legacy? Morrison's depiction of characters content with or struggling with their ideological positionality, portraying the North and South as united by African American cultural practices and examining the role of African American folklore in addressing descendants' dissociation, creates a novel that addresses the debate about the role of the old Negro and his culture in the North. As readers learn, however, in intervening in this discussion, Morrison highlights the significance of folklore to the subjectivity construction of the migrants' descendants but also relegates them to a new discursive space. From drawing on folklore, Morrison deconstructs the ideological binary of the North and South on which many of the migrants' subjectivity rests—past/present, old Negro/new Negro, north/south—ideological binaries that finds its most conflicted expression in the characterization of Milkman, the conflicted embodiment of the novel's explicit interrogation of black male subjectivity construction.

The North and the South are presented to Milkman as the discursive divide of family heritage and the inheritance of traditions. The discursive divide of tradition is unbounded, existing in the present as a reinterpretation and narration of the past. The characters struggle to figure out what to do with the past in the present. For some characters the past manifests itself in the memories they acknowledge but refuse to adopt, for others the past is performed in practices, and for others that past is something to define themselves against to push against the evil and not let it happen again. But for all these characters they accept the past as it is. As Richard Handler and Jocelyn Linnekin argue in "Tradition, Genuine or Spurious," "there is not essential, bounded tradition; tradition is a model of the past and is inseparable from the interpretation of it in the present. Undeniably, traditional action may refer to the past, but to 'be about' or refer to is a symbolic rather than a natural relationship, and as such it is characterized by discontinuity as well as continuity" (1984, 276). Folk practices as well as public and private performances of events and traditions (re)constitute tradition as the link between the characters and their northern and southern roots.

African Americans reenact historical events (slavery, emancipation, and the Great Migration) in a variety of public and private discursive and rhetorical performances in their families and communities in a number of traditions: carnivals, festivals, Mardi Gras, Kawanza, and Juneteenth celebrations, and reenactments of the Selma to Montgomery March or March on Washington.

The songs, tales, and spiritual practices that Morrison interweaves in *Song of Solomon* connect the characters to their southern heritage and enable them to address the disassociation in the North. Through these folklore practices, Milkman inherits the feelings of disassociation that the migrants experienced after relocating to the North. He inherits the burden of tradition or the power of the past on the present. Milkman is caught between the past of his historical and family legacy (his past embodied symbolically in the folktale of the flying African) and his northern inheritance (his present suggested by his maternal grandfather's and father's wealth, success, and respect in their community). Milkman refuses to make a choice between the North or South, affluence or poverty, urban or rural. Instead, he strives to interpret his predicament in the discursive divide for himself. At the end, he begins to see that the past is continuous as well as discontinuous. His quest is not a physical or psychological progression as much as it is an understanding of the discursive divide of tradition. This transmigration is symbolically represented by his quest for gold (bounded tradition), which is revealed to be the bones either of his grandfather or of Pilate's murder victim (discontinuous and subjective tradition).

Through flashbacks, readers learn about Milkman's birth. His aunt Pilate conjures him into the physical world through a combination of hoodoo practices of herbs and art. First, she tells his mother Ruth to mix herbs into Macon's food so he would desire her. Pilate gives Ruth "some greenish-gray grassy-looking stuff to put in his food." Ruth states, "It worked too. Macon came to me for four days. He even came home from his office in the middle of the day to be with me. He looked puzzled, but he came. Then it was over. And two months later I was pregnant" (Morrison 1977, 215). After she conceives Milkman, she protects him from Macon, who attempts to abort him through his own version of folk practices. He forces Ruth to "drink a half-ounce of castor oil, then a hot pot recently emptied of scalding water on which she sat, then a soapy enema, a knitting needle, and finally he punched her stomach" (224). Again, Pilate intervenes by prescribing Ruth "cornstarch" to chew on and wrapped her up in a "homemade on-the-spot girdle" (224). Pilate "put a small doll on Macon's chair in his office. A male doll with a small painted chicken bone stuck between its legs and a round red circle painted on its belly" (225). Lastly, she induces Milkman's birth with a folksong that also announces the suicide of the migrant Mr. Smith, who sells life insurance policies to African Americans despite knowing that very few companies will honor contracts made between themselves and African American customers. Unable to reconcile exploiting African Americans with his personal ambition to make a living and empower the community members, Mr. Smith plans to "fly away" north to the "other side of Lake Superior," across the Canadian border to the Promised Land. The juxtaposition of Milkman's birth with Mr. Smith's suicide draws attention to the discursive predicament that Mr. Smith leaves and Milkman enters.

Morrison emphasizes the discursive divide between the North and the South in Milkman's life as a struggle about his rearing between his mother and father. To his mother, Milkman represents the last time Macon touched her and how it felt to be loved by someone other than herself. She nursed him until he was too old not to remember these "late afternoon sessions" as odd. When Freddie the handyman observes Milkman being breastfed as a young boy, he remembers it as an old southern practice, "I be damn, Miss Rufie. When the last time I seen that? I don't even know the last time I seen that. I mean ain't nothing wrong with it. I mean old folks swear by it. It's just you know, you don't see it up here much" (14). As a result of this incident, the community renames the protagonist, Macon Dead Jr. "Milkman"—a name that comes to signify his naiveté. Folklore is the "choral note" that resounds in two parts of town in *Song of Solomon*. From these afternoon breastfeeding sessions, Milkman is positioned outside the community. Macon thinks the name Milkman "certainly didn't sound like the honest job of a dairyman, or bring to his mind cold bright cans standing on the back porch, glittering like captains on guard. It sounded dirty, intimate, and hot" (16). Stigmatized by the family secrets of incest and unnatural affections, Milkman's earliest reading is of his mother's shame from the breast-feeding incident:

> There was this green room, a very small green room, and his mother was sitting in the green room and her breasts were uncovered and somebody was sucking them and the somebody was himself. . . . Then he heard something that he knew was related to the picture. Laughter. Somebody he couldn't see, in the room laughing . . . at him and at his mother, and his mother is ashamed. (77)

Milkman feels disassociated and disconnected because of the family secrets that threatened his very existence. It is only when Milkman takes on responsibilities as his father's property manager that he is able to separate himself from his mother. Besides distancing himself from the suffocating oedipal bonds of his family, Milkman's position as an apartment landlord allows him to freely visit the Southside neighborhood and interact with its residents. As a property manager, he is neither landlord nor Southside resident. Milkman is a northern resident and beneficiary of his father's accomplishments but is perceived as an outsider. Regarded simply as the owner's son by the Southside residents, Milkman wields power over their lives. However, Milkman accepts but doesn't acknowledge this inherited power. Positioned differently, Milkman lacks the firsthand knowledge about what it is like living as a slave or working as a sharecropper in the South. In addition, since Milkman is born into a wealthy family, he has a mildly strained relationship to hegemonic masculinity, for he lacks knowledge about what it is like to live poor in the black community.

On one hand, Morrison presents Milkman's inability to grasp the complexity of his positionality as a matter of maturity and an understanding that he achieves as he grows up and gains life experience. Until he comes of age, he is only able to define himself in opposition to his father in subtle, profound, but superficial ways—such as deciding which of his father's expectations he wants to meet. Similar to his father, Milkman fulfills the notion of "Victorian manliness" as, according to Martin Summers, "the consumer of goods one owned, the leisure practices one engaged in, and one's physical and sexual virility" (2004, 8). Using his father's wealth he deliberately fashions himself as his father's opposite in looks and taste: "Macon was clean-shaven; Milkman was desperate for a mustache. Macon wore bow ties; Milkman wore four-in-hands. Macon didn't part his hair; Milkman had a part shaved into his. Macon hated tobacco; Milkman tried to put a cigarette in his mouth every fifteen minutes. Macon hoarded his money; Milkman gave his away. But he couldn't help sharing with Macon his love of good shoes and fine thin socks" (Morrison 1977, 63). However, Milkman does not know about the past to draw on or push against. Therefore, he can't willingly emulate the life that Macon Sr. has chosen for himself not only because he senses the unhappiness and despair of "owning things and letting those things own other things. Then you'll own yourself and other people too." Milkman uses his father's wealth to vacation on "Honoré Island" with his girlfriends, his best friend, and other black bourgeois families (55, 133). In depicting Milkman as spoiled and superficial, Morrison shows him as a trivial and selfish young man positioned between his own desire to foster a broader and deeper understanding about himself and his father's upper middle-class ambitions. This positioning and reflection is seen when Milkman ruminates about a possible identity that would contextualize him in his maternal grandfather's legacy as opposed to his father's southern legacy as the son of a slave. Considering medicine as a profession like his maternal grandfather, Milkman thinks Foster would be a better last name because "if you were sick, would you go see a man named Dr. Dead?" (69).

On the other hand, Morrison represents Milkman as lacking a sense of family and inheritance. Milkman does not just rebel against his father in superficial ways, he differs in his desire to understand the family history and southern heritage that bond the community but that his aspirational father has rejected. Morrison depicts Milkman as a naive and culturally uninformed young man who lacks knowledge of his family legacy and cultural history. In Milkman's first interaction with his aunt, he is unaware that she conjured him from the spiritual to the physical world; Milkman sees her and her lifestyle as a stark contrast to his home and family. In his home, mistakes he made were met with a quiet understanding from his mother and his sisters, or indifference and criticism from his father. In Pilate's house, Milkman is accepted "without question and with all the ease in the world" (79). Milkman finds Aunt Pilate refreshing and drastically different from his father. He enjoys having conversations with her because she asks him questions, waits to hear his responses, and quarrels and laughs with him. He enjoys listening to her stories about growing up on a farm, how she and Macon eluded the white men who murdered her father, and how she ran away with a bag that now hangs in the middle of her living room, which she sentimentally calls her inheritance. Later these events surrounding Macon's father's death serve as a reminder of the forces that Milkman constructs his subjectivity against as he travels south in search of his family's inheritance and as he constructs a subjectivity that is distinct from his father and aunt. These stories will later become useful to Milkman's subjectivity construction when he retravels the Great Migration. While Macon eschews folklore as articulations for the afterlife, Pilate adopts folklore to address her feelings of loss and alienation and to respond to race and gender oppression.

Clearly, Morrison emphasizes that Milkman holds ambivalent feelings for his father. However, Morrison's representation of Milkman's uncertainty toward his father's wealth is further complicated by his inability to fully understand Aunt Pilate's decision to live impoverished in the Southside community. As I have demonstrated, Morrison associates Macon with wealth, especially as it symbolizes the promise of the North. In contrast, Morrison associates Pilate's poverty with the South during the Great Migration, when African Americans' primary job opportunities were as house servants and sharecropping. If we examine the instability of these oppositions—past/present, affluence/poverty, and North/South—we will be able to see how the novel deconstructs its own ideological project. In his interactions with Aunt Pilate, Milkman rejects the discursive divide of affluent and poor as he gets to know her as a humble person who lives a modest life and makes very little money. However, the respect that others in the community have for her and the love that she exhibits toward her family is more appealing and attractive than the lovelessness and coldness of his own home. Preferring to draw inspiration from family and cultural practices, Pilate lives in the community, but she is not of the community. Jan Furman describes her as "out of place in the big northern city" (1999, 30). Having spent most of her life in a community where women walk the road without purses, "bare legged" and with "unstraightened hair," Pilate has given up interest in manners and money but has acquired a deep concern for and about human relationships (Morrison 1977, 206). She accepts and appreciates her southern roots, and she operates a small illegal wine selling business out of her kitchen. The novel's underscore of Macon's wealth with the contrasting poverty of Pilate creates an unstable opposition between North and South because it underlines the text's own awareness that the North was not idyllic for everyone.

In representing the relationship between Milkman and Pilate, Morrison draws attention to the false binary of poor and affluent by informing readers of Milkman's surprise to learn that law enforcement doesn't afford Macon's wealth or class status a different consideration than Pilate's indigence and lower social status. Milkman feels ashamed and embarrassed when he sees Pilate (and his father) perform the identity of a poor and uneducated person in front of a policeman. Because Milkman does not have the maturity of experience to know that posturing was a rhetorical strategy that many African Americans used to outsmart white authority figures, he judges Pilate's actions as appalling and obsequious. This further demonstrates his lack of cultural moorings and that he does not appreciate the sacrifices that people made directly or indirectly for him:

> Then more shame at seeing his father with an accommodating 'we all understand how it is' smile—buckle before the policemen. But nothing was like the shame he felt as he watched and listened to Pilate. Not just her Aunt Jemima act, but the fact that she was both adept at it and willing to do it—for him. For the one who had just left her house carrying what he believed was her inheritance. (208)

After seeing this performance, Milkman appreciates Pilate's resourcefulness, but he's perplexed at how easy it is for her to access an old Negro servile performance of blackness. Not having the knowledge base for understanding mimicry as a strategy of resistance (she uses this strategy to survive her migration to Virginia and ultimately to Michigan), Milkman perceives this self-conscious construction as an inauthentic performance that is not much different than his father's class discourse. Instead of perceiving Pilate's performance as an opportunity to understand African American rhetorical performances of survival and as a critical moment to question notions of authenticity, Milkman dismisses her as dimwitted and easily fooled or easily exploited by someone (himself) who selfishly stole from her. Even so, Pilate is instrumental in Milkman's process of self-realization. Morrison foreshadows during a conversation between Ruth and Pilate: "Ain't nothing goin to kill him but his own ignorance, and won't no woman ever kill him. What's likelier is that it'll be a woman save his life" (140). Literally, Pilate saves Milkman's life, for while standing next to him at her father's gravesite, she is killed by a single gunshot that was intended for him.

Pilate's death signifies Milkman's rebirth. However, before Milkman is reborn in the South and into southern values and beliefs in the form of folklore, he struggles to come to terms with Guitar's investment in countering hate crimes against African Americans. Impatient with Milkman's insensitivity, dissociation, and complete indifference to the material experiences of Southside African Americans that are less fortunate, Guitar is no longer interested in accompanying Milkman to parties with the black bourgeois. Guitar adopts a culture of consciousness that privileges the quality of one's life over material possessions or spiritual understandings. Guitar states that "it's not about you living longer. It is about how you live and why. It's about whether your children can make other children. It's about trying to make a world where one day white people will think before they lynch" (160). Guitar echoes Kevin K. Gaines's response to the dominant culture's expression of ignorance or innocence of African Americans when they demand civil rights and access to fair housing and employment. Gaines emphatically states that it is easier to imagine African Americans having a single preoccupation as opposed to accepting that they want to share the material benefits in America (1996, 11). In promoting cultural consciousness, Guitar recognizes that, despite the location, the dynamics are fundamentally comparable in terms of the elements of basic structures. The majority (if not all) of city officers and managers are white men who ignore, instigate, or encourage oppressive acts against African Americans. By representing Milkman's childhood friend's transformation from a boy grieving over his father's death to a revolutionary murderer, Morrison introduces the failure of the Great Migration as not only the dashed dreams of the migrants, but also the seemingly hopelessness of the future for the descendants of the migrants.

•

> People pay for what they do, and, still more, for what they have allowed themselves to become. And they pay for it simply: by the lives they lead.
>
> —JAMES BALDWIN, *NO NAME IN THE STREET* (2007, 55)

Through Guitar, Morrison represents the mentality of an antiassimilationist who accepts the impossibility of eradicating racial inequality and racialized terror in urban cities and rural towns. Guitar joins the Seven Days, a secret society that avenges racial hate crimes against African Americans. The members of the Seven Days accept community solidarity over individual wealth. Guitar, "Railroad Tommy and the others in the Seven Days accept that they will never be millionaires nor will most of their people." They have, in essence, "rejected all racial upliftment strategies that preceded them, do not see evolutionary progress as meaningful," and "the integration of the individual as a beneficial approach to success for the black masses and instead adopted a more radical and extreme collective posture" (Story 1999, 91–92). For Guitar, the society offers agency against racism, oppression, and discrimination and an opportunity to be an actor rather than a victim. As the Sunday man, Guitar is responsible for revenging assaults or deaths that were committed against African Americans on Sunday. Accepting community consciousness over individual wealth or spiritual upliftment, he practices the society's goals of retribution or an-eye-for-an-eye justice: "If the Negro was hanged, they hang, if a Negro was burnt, they burn, raped and murdered, they were raped and murdered. If they can. If they can't do it precisely in the same manner, they do it any way they can, but they do it" (Morrison 1977, 154–55). Guitar insists that the Seven Days are an important and necessary organization within the African American community, a group that understands the "unnatural" part of the white psyche. But he has doubts about being in control of the outcome, partly because times have changed and groups of African Americans are frequently being killed. Guitar's membership in the Seven Days is an expression of the futility that other African American men might feel while defending their family members from white terror. Guitar's determination to use violence appears to be a rightful and justified response to black erasure or legalized Xing (as Houston Baker names it) because he believes that his actions are the only promising tactic for reversing the scapegoat for inadequacies of white masculinity that African Americans have come to symbolize in society. Guitar's love and passion for African American people and culture and his violent revolutionary stance functions as a counter-discourse to Milkman's aloofness and indifference toward his family and culture and his elitist and assimilationist perspective on society.

In regard to Guitar as an alternative expression of black male subjectivity, I am interested in his oppositional subjectivity as a subtext in Morrison's novel. More specifically, I wonder what this subtext suggests about a black man who ceases to be shaped by African American cultural values of respect and resiliency. In *Playing in the Dark,* Morrison proposes that black subjectivity has a similar function in society and literary texts. She argues that the symbolic meaning of blackness as denial and absence encompass the "entire range of views, assumptions, readings, and misreadings that accompany Eurocentric learning about" people of African descent (1992, 7). This symbolic meaning determines how we read, engage, erase, inscribe, or understand African Americans in relation to laws and social practices that define the status and limit the access of African Americans. Deeply embedded in American literary texts, this linguistic structure, Morrison argues, has several functions: "paradox, ambiguity; they strategize omission repetitions, disruptions, polarities, reifications, violence" (66). In Morrison's terms, "a writer's response to American Africanism often provides a subtext that either sabotages the surface text's expressed intentions or escapes them through a language that mystifies what it cannot bring itself to articulate but still attempts to register. Linguistic responses to Africanism serve the text by further problematizing its matter with resonances and luminations" (66).

With Morrison's ruminations in mind, what can one make of her decision to cast Guitar as revolutionary even though he confirms white stereotypes of black men? Guitar corroborates white stereotypes about the hyperviolent African American men, and he exacerbates white fears and anxieties toward African Americans in general. Guitar posits retribution as a vehement response to white Americans' belief that African Americans are inassimilable and a threat to the dominant culture (even though Guitar expresses in the novel that segregation is entirely the result of white Americans' feelings of inferiority). One could argue that it's counterintuitive for Guitar to then embrace violence as a real response to white aggression, for he is represented throughout the novel as being too smart to give in to base or simplistic definitions of black masculinity. Of course, it is intentional on Morrison's part to want readers to not simply see Guitar as an antagonist or anti-hero to Milkman who evolves throughout the narrative. Morrison states that it is sad to "see the decomposition of a beautiful idea go apart in Guitar" (1994a, 75). Guitar and the Seven Days' eye-for-an-eye biblical justice is an example of what Philip Brian Harper describes as "black masculine anxiety . . . largely intelligible, bespeaking a desperate urge to survival" (1996, 126). Provoked by white anxieties of blackness, Guitar is overcome with the desperate need to survive white Americans' "rhetoric of dread and desire" (Morrison 1992, 64). Thus, in struggling to outlast a rhetoric in which his fate is already sealed, Guitar desperately grasps a counter-ideology that reveals the extent to which his subjectivity is inscribed by American beliefs and values.

Guitar imagines that the Seven Days will bring about a place, terrain, or landscape where African Americans are free to live and indulge in the possibilities of life. If this is his romance, if he believes that violence will bring about an environment where he and other African American scan realize their identities, then he truly is an American. Thus, Guitar allows his fear (however legitimate) of black annihilation to motivate him to kill. Morrison writes, "Romance, an exploration of anxiety imported from the shadows of European culture, made possible the sometimes safe and other times risky embrace of quite specific, understandably human, fears: American fear of being outcast, of failing, of powerlessness, their fear of boundarylessness . . . fear of loneliness, of aggression both external and internal" (1992, 37). Guitar represents an American romantic notion that a new and innocent place can be cultivated on the backs of all the native and (non)inhabitants. Regrettably, Guitar holds a romantic notion of freedom that does not coincide with African American cultural values. Thus, I argue that Guitar's real ambition is to stop the violence against African Americans. However, the Seven Days project of retaliation only exacerbates whites' fear of blackness and black people, thus increasing white violence against black people. Without a doubt, each act of retaliation on whites will beget violence against blacks and in return violence against whites, and so on.

In this third space where black nationalism replaces assimilation as a more desirous sociopolitical positionality, Guitar conceals its repressiveness behind African American cultural discourses about empowerment and self-defense. Civil Rights leaders propose an assimilationist philosophy that African Americans show love and understanding but fearlessness and conviction to perpetrators of racial violence. In contrast, black nationalists (younger and comprised of educated and uneducated African Americans) demand that African Americans demonstrate love and compassion only to those who give it and return aggression to anyone who assaults their person. As Guitar challenges Milkman's assimilationist attitude for its lack of sincerity and seriousness, Guitar is exposed as an ideologue who is easily seduced by repressive ideologies that, although appear liberating, are in fact repressive and contradictory to African American cultural building (this concept is explored further later in this chapter). Guitar's idea about protecting African American people and communities from aggression is "beautiful" but his decision to devalue all humans (innocent or not) is heartbreaking.

Milkman responds to racial tension three ways: he ignores and dismissively attributes racial conflict to the "unnatural" whites, he retreats to the comfort of his middle-class home and his mother's and sister's unconditional love, and he spends more of his father's money on himself, girls, and his best friend Guitar. Milkman doesn't possess the power to easily navigate his social surroundings, as does Hurston's High John the Conqueror who is the embodiment of the quintessential function of humor as a shield and a weapon in the black folk tradition. With a laugh, High John casts off any suspicions that he couldn't cope with the daily toils of life in America. High John "was top-superior to the whole mess of sorrow. He could beat it all, and what made it so cool finish it off with a laugh" (Dundes 1973, 543). Unlike High John the Conqueror, Milkman doesn't know folk medicine nor is he versed in the trickster tradition. He is disconnected and lacks self and cultural awareness. He is uninterested in learning and is only interested in himself.

Appalled that Guitar perceives the Seven Days philosophy as a viable emancipatory discourse, Milkman contends that the group simply reproduces the actions of racist whites. Comparing the Seven Days to the hate-filled and regressive actions of the "Mafia" and "Nazis," Milkman suggests that retaliations against white violence do not curb white violence; they only reaffirm racist assumptions about the violent disposition of African Americans and exacerbate the tension between whites and Southside blacks. Besides expressing a common vehemence leveled toward domestic terrorist groups, Milkman's stance could be understood as representative of nonviolent discourse that was popularized during the civil rights struggle. These dominant cultural discourses are not an adequate response to oppression, genocide, and alienation that African Americans experience. In short, the Seven Days do not suggest a subjectivity that is not bound to white thinking and that challenges white discourses about blacks as being uncivilized. Because he has not experienced hardships first-hand, Milkman does not have the courage of conviction that Macon Sr. and Guitar have. The violence that African Americans faced in the South was in the North too and the events that happened in the South continued to impact them because they are black still, and being black is a universal condition that is about race not about region. Here again, the discursive divide of the North and South as opposite regions is challenged. Milkman believes that revenge is not an answer to the assault on African Americans; it is not an adequate response to the white men who killed Emmett Till and blew up four little girls in church.

Milkman points out that Guitar violates African American cultural values and the legacy of struggle. Privileging ethics and a sense of humanity, Milkman asks Guitar, "If they are as bad, as unnatural, as you say, why do you want to be like them? Don't you want to be better than they are?" which questions the Seven Days' eye-for-an-eye approach to revenge (Morrison 1977, 157). Milkman feels that Guitar's actions are an expression of the ultimate futility that African American men feel in their attempts to protect their loved ones from white violence—that they are an assault on African American humanity. This analysis is viewed as suspicious because Milkman does not speak from experience. To Milkman, Guitar was not less privileged than he was because neither of them lived in Alabama, and his viewpoints are the result of a cult-like indoctrination. Guitar stops viewing Milkman as the young boy of his childhood and begins to see him as the bourgeois enemy, while Milkman grows to love Guitar because of the past that they shared together. Thus, Milkman is twice removed from the experience of a majority of the migrants: he lacks knowledge about living oppressed in the South or poor in the North. The alienation that he eventually starts to profoundly feel is more that he lacks cultural moorings as opposed to feeling unwelcomed by his friend Guitar and other Southside residents. Unfortunately, Milkman mistakenly perceives his father's elitism, his best friends' violent nationalism, and his aunt's obsequious nature as character flaws and the source of his disconnection. Instead, before he can gain knowledge of his cultural legacy, Milkman must first learn that having character flaws is not the same as being a flawed character.

•

> Can't nobody fly with all that shit. Wanna fly, you got to give up the shit that weighs you down.
>
> —TONI MORRISON, *SONG OF SOLOMON* (1977, 179)

Spiritually dead and mentally enslaved, Milkman leaves Southside, Michigan. The reasons for Milkman's departure are numerous: it is the quest for gold, for his past, for an answer to questions about his identity. The gold that Pilate finds in a cave (and leaves) becomes his motivation. But as gold dematerializes into memories and stories, Milkman gets much more than gold. In leaving Southside for Shalimar, Virginia, Milkman thinks that he will have the opportunity to gain a perspective on himself and his southern and northern family roots. Milkman wants to construct a subjectivity different from the selfish womanizer that his sister says he is or the lazy and thoughtless man who prefers to go "wherever the party is" instead of busying himself with thinking about the implicit meanings of life (106). Upon reaching Shalimar, Milkman stands divested of his luggage, his money, his car, his watch, hunting with the sons of Solomon and learning the Song of Solomon. He is happier than he has ever been once he is rid of the middle-class entrapment that he sees as his future. Milkman finds himself in the context that created the legend of the dead men's bones, gold, and family origins. He discovers first hand that the legend is historical and supernatural. It is transmitted as family oral history and children's rhymes. After spending time in Shalimar, Milkman finds a community that loved and respected his grandfather, an old lady who took in his father and aunt and learns a story about his great-grandfather and Native American great-grandmother, Singing Byrd, who were slaves. Most importantly, Milkman collects information about his family history in the form of a folktale about an enslaved African man who, upon being fed up with his existence as an American slave, flew across the Atlantic Ocean to Africa. These are all elements of Milkman's growing ability to reinterpret the past in the present. This quest, paradoxically, leads him to an understanding of what is not passed down through the middle-class ambitions of his father.

The second time Milkman hears the flying African folktale, which turns out to be a children's rhyme about his family, he is sitting in Pilate's kitchen. Unlike the first time he is introduced to the folksong when he was born, Pilate's singing connects Milkman to communal consciousness. Upon hearing the song, Milkman goes into a trance. Unusually sensitive to his surroundings, he feels as if he is being asphyxiated. Hearing the song, Milkman feels as if he is being smothered in meaning, a meaning that is unspeakable—a meaning that he feels as intensely as his own heartbeat. The impact that the song has on his psyche draws him into its healing spell. Pilate's singing presents Milkman with an understanding of how communal and family subjectivity can offer him a key to his own. Pilate's singing signifies how communal and family identity is passed from generation to generation within the African American context. From Pilate, Milkman learns about his family history, African American powers of divination, and self-sufficiency. More importantly, this information links Milkman to his family history, the African American experience, and provides him with an alternative family history that is cultural and historical (about the Great Migration), as well as psychological.

The fact of the appearance of a tale in a novel is no proof that it originated among African or African American people because oral tales have been a very fruitful source of inspiration and imagination for African and African American authors. It thus happens that frequently the literary appearance of a folktale only represents one of many versions. Of course, more important is the history of the tale and the oral varieties in which it appears. Less important is whether the tale is primarily oral tradition, and frequently the problem of priority is quite unsolvable. But a very considerable number of tales appearing in literary collections show such a preponderance of oral appearance than would seem to be purely incidental. There can be little doubt that they are all essentially oral, both in origin and in history.

The flying African folktale is one of the most colorful and enduring tales in African American folklore. Also known as Ebos Landing, the folktale has been told and retold for over two hundred years in novels, movies, and children's stories. Based on an actual event that occurred in 1803 on St. Simons Island, this tale is a metaphor for African American resiliency, yearning, and principle. In the original story, slave traders purchased a group of Ebo Africans (properly known as Igbos from Nigeria) from a slave market. While being transported to the plantation, the slaves rebelled and overpowered the white crew, who abandoned the ship and drowned. The slaves escaped into the woods never to be seen again. This event served as folklore for white slave masters and African American slaves. Plantation owners tell this story and how important it is to bind and control slaves as to avoid losing expensive cargo, while slaves shared this tale as proof of their indomitable spirit and as an inspiration for themselves and their future generations.

In the late 1930s, the Federal Writers Project collected versions of the flying African folktale from various sources. In the interests of space, I included only two versions to give depth to Morrison's use and version of the folktale: the first is from the wonderful collection of Georgia folklore *Drums and Shadows* and the second is from Harold Courlander's *A Treasury of Afro-American Folklore.* The first is a reflection from Wallace Quarterman, a slave on a Georgia plantation:

> Well, at that time Mr. Blue he was the overseer and . . . Mr. Blue he go down one morning with a long whip for to whip them good. . . . Any way, he whipped them good and they got together and stuck that hoe in the field and then . . . rose up in the sky and turn themselves into buzzards and flew right back to Africa. . . . Everybody knows about them. (2010, 150)

The second version is from a slave named Shad Hall:

> Doze folks could fly too. Dey tell me deah's a lot ub um wut wuz bring heah an dey ain much good. Duh massuh was fixin tuh tie um up tuh whip um. Dey say, "Massa, yuh ain gwine lick me," an wid dat dey runs down tuh duh ribbuh. Duh obuhseeuh he sho tought he ketch um wen dey get tuh duh ribbuh. But fo he could git tuh um, dey riz up in duh eah an fly way. Dey fly right back tuh Africa. I tink dat happens on Butler Ilun. (2010, 139)

Through the sharing of folktales, African Americans transmit culture and shared knowledge, beliefs, values, and feelings of a group rather than those of any one individual and the wisdom of ancestors to current generations. John Roberts argues that folktales retain or reveal the continuity between African and African American cultures "when we approach both black culture-building and folklore creation as historically continuous Afro-centric activities" (2010, 11). Roberts continues, "we must approach African American culture and folklore as a reflection of the beliefs, concerns, and values of African Americans" (11). African American folktales connect communities to the African past while these communities evolve with the changing times. The folktales and traditions of African Americans reflect the philosophy, knowledge, and creative expressions of Africa while bending them to fit material experiences in the United States and other parts of North America.

The third time Milkman hears the folktale he learn its significance in the immediacy of the South. While waiting for his car to be repaired, Milkman overhears children singing and playing a game. The words sound familiar, so he listens intently. Upon realizing that the words they are singing are the same as those his aunt sang, Milkman relaxes, stares at the children playing, and allows the small voices to wash over him and penetrate his consciousness.

Many such games are played either in a ring or in a line. In the first, the children stand in a circle, often holding hands, and the leader is outside performing some action. In a line game, two lines are formed, with the leader at the head of one. While most line or ring games have formalized endings to them, others have some action that is carried through until all the children have participated. A play-party game, on the other hand, may go on indefinitely. Unlike games played by white children, African American children's games require more active participation by all players. The spirited children playing these games always accompany themselves with singing, skipping, clapping, or other movements to give a rhythm to their play. In each form, songs and tales are always in process and in a state of transformation, varying from time to time and even within one period from singer to singer (depending on the child leading the game and the region in which the games are played). Since children's games are shared between children or passed down from adults to children, the games are under constant revision and are full of nonsense words, complete words, words that tap into children's sense of rhythm, or words that are meaningless to the unacquainted listener. Morrison shares the flying African folktale in three forms: a folksong, folktale, and a children's ring game.

The folksongs mediate his memories about growing up poor on a farm and migrating to an urban city without acquiescing to an urban lifestyle (Morrison 1977, 49). He realizes that the song is about flying away and being at peace. Although he doesn't know it now, the songs connect him to his cultural history. Since the folk songs are typically understood to not have an author, only a cultural origin, the song connects all people of African descent to a single event or incident about a slave flying—escaping slavery. When Milkman learns that his grandfather was a flying African, a man who was capable of lifting his "big black butt in the air and flew back to Africa," he feels ecstatic. Fed up with "choking" on "cotton balls," Solomon "whirled about and touched the sun" flying across the Atlantic Ocean—"home" to Africa (1977, 322). Morrison uses the flight of the flying African as symbolic of cultural memory and as a metaphor to describe the process of subjectivity construction. Here, Morrison distinguishes between two kinds of flight—the flight from imminent danger from the South to the North and the flight to freedom of flying Africans, which is seen as the ultimate gesture of rebellion and self-possession. The journey from the North back to the South retraces family heritage and history. For Milkman, finding his roots, the words to the song, and the significance of the name Solomon becomes a matter of life and death on a psychological level and the key to his identity and subjectivity. In Shalimar, he hears the children sing about the flying African. He has heard the song in Michigan at Pilate's house, but here he hears it repeatedly in the context of the people who knew his family and the history of his grandmother. The information he gathers and the song the children sing tells him the answers to the questions that he is seeking, answers that are not apparent to anyone but himself:

> He almost shouted when he heard Heddy took him to a red man's house. Heddy was Susan Byrd's grandmother on her father's side, and therefore Sing's mother too. And "red man's house" must be a reference to the Byrd's as Indians. Of course, Sing was an Indian or part Indian and her name was Sing Byrd or, more likely, Sing Bird. No—Singing Bird. (Morrison 1977, 303–4)

Other parts of the song inform him that Jake's father was Solomon and that when Solomon "flew away" he left behind Ryna, the black lady that still cries in the gulch. The flying African conveys a sense of optimism and cultural pride because of the tragedy of enduring the harsh realities of slavery and the defiance of literally flying away. The community remembers not just archetypal African Americans, but Milkman's great-grandfather. Milkman learns that his grandfather exercised his subjectivity when he made a decision to resist oppression and fly away—presumably back to Africa. This tale, as community memory and history, throws individual and community in relief.

The meaning Milkman assigns to this legacy is a traditional folkloric process: the interpretation of the communal past by an individual in the present. Conversely, Milkman's experiences are the flying African folktale, which reconcile historical, social, and cultural discourses with specific experiences. Understanding the recursive meaning of the flying African is important to Milkman's subjectivity because how he thinks largely determines his ability to transcend oppressive situations. Milkman learns that the meaning of flying is not literal, but it is symbolic of how one thinks beyond the limitations of their present circumstances—"the shit that weighs you down" (Heyman 1995, 179). Performing the flying African may or may not involve literally flying, which is the significance of Mr. Smith at the beginning of the novel. When Milkman catches a glimpse of himself in the plate-glass window of the store, "he was grinning. His eyes were shining. He was as eager and happy as he had ever been in his life" (Morrison 1977, 304). The riddle of the flying African turns out to be the riddle to his psyche, the gold turns out to be the valuable treasure of his grandfather's bones, and Milkman becomes the oral historian of his family.

By translating the cultural values of his largely unknown family inheritance into personal meaningfulness, Milkman inherits the cultural paradox of constructing a sense of roots and belonging. Because this inheritance also takes the form of mythic gold, carried on the back of a magical, larger-than-life aunt, many critical readings see Milkman's journey as that of an archetypal hero like Sir Gawain, but this quest is squarely rooted in the capitalist angst of a new generation of northern-born African Americans. As Jan Furman points out, "Milkman is a contemporary black man lost to his community, family, and most important, lost to himself. His true quest is not for fortune or honor but for his humanity" (1996, 198). Thus far he had been told the bits and pieces of other people's past, and it was time to know his past on his own terms:

> He just wanted to beat a path away from his parents' past, which was also their present and which was threatening to become his present as well. He hated the acridness in his mother's and father's relationship, the conviction of righteousness they each held on to with both hands. And his efforts to ignore it, transcend it, seemed to work only when he spent his days looking for whatever was light-hearted and without grave consequences. (1977, 180)

These emotions make it acceptable to pursue something serious and significant and to escape from the life of meaninglessness that he had constructed for himself in the North.

In Shalimar, Virginia, Milkman gains an understanding of how he is connected from birth to the African American community. In the North, his name, the one word that defined him as different from the other men, locates him within the community of African American men. With his name, Milkman comes to belong, at least on the surface, to the group of African American men whose blues and jazz names are "Moon, Nero, Humpty-Dumpty, Blue Boy, Scandinavia, Quack-Quack, Jericho, Spoonbread, Ice Man, Dough Belly, Rocky River, Gray Eye, Cock a Doodle Doo, Cool Breeze, Muddy Waters, Pinetop, Jelly Roll, Fats, Leadbelly, Bo Diddley, Cat-Iron, Peg-Leg, Son, Shortstuff, Smoky Babe, Funny Papa, Bukka, Pink, Bull Moose, B. B., T-Bone, Black Ace, Lemon, Washboard, Gatemouth, Cleanhead, Tampa Red, Juke Boy,

Shine, Staggerlee, Jim the Devil, Fuck-Up, and Dat Nigger" (Morrison 1977, 331). Having accepted his northern heritage as incomplete, Milkman discovers that his names (Milkman and Macon Dead) connect him to his famiily history in the Southern community Shalimar. He, like the other men, had been given nicknames. These names not only speak to his personal experiences but also make his name significant. His name begins to acquire a community status, a cool grown-up sound. Milkman reconciles himself with his heritage in more ways than one. When he comes to the South, he is one of the sons of Solomon: "The superiority of the men in the South is indicated . . . by their names, the names of poets, kings, and the men of God: Omar, King Walker, Luther, Solomon, Calvin Breakstoned. They possess a pre-reflection awareness of the kind embodied by Pilate" (Peach 1999, 176). When he willingly gives up his worldly possessions, his bottles of Cutty Sark, his wristwatch, and his beige suit, which is hopelessly out of place, he dresses himself in camouflage and goes hunting for a bobcat. In this group of African American men, he challenges himself to find out his worth as a man and to earn their respect as a man who can live off the land. It is what is perceived as his unwillingness to connect with them that has thus far differentiated his class status. Milkman's actions in Virginia are class suicide, and it is a form of rebirth: "During the hunt, Milkman's class consciousness sharpens as well. Learning the insignificance of money and status when juxtaposed with a true communion with African people, Milkman commits class suicide. While it is true that the seeds of his decision to bond with the African masses instead of those having wealth and status are planted when he first meet Pilate, his conscious decision to do so germinates from his Shalimar experiences" (Mbalia 1999, 133). Class distinctions do not matter as much as the hunting and scouting skills of men in the company of other men. In Shalimar, soft clothes and shoes are woefully inadequate; what matters the most is the ability to see well and to shoot well.

The cultural function of the flying African folktale is that it conveys a sense of endurance and resiliency. As an indication of African American endurance, the flying African folktale articulates the possibility to name and utilize your own subjectivity. When hope wanes and despair sets in, a belief in the folktale is the power to imagine and to believe in the capabilities of African American subjectivity. It marks the precise moment where freedom can only be imagined as something that is truly amazing—like a person flying away from their captors, oppressors, or enslavers. The flying African folktale articulates resilience because it depicts black subjectivity as having the ability to be self-containing—capable of choosing to engage or disengage from the experiences of white oppression. From jumping off slave ships or removing shackles to participating in mutinies, African slaves embraced and believed in the mythic dimensions of lore like this, if only to strengthen their subjectivity. The folktale demonstrates African Americans' understanding that enslavement is temporary and that agency is possible despite their present condition. From it, Milkman makes sense of his motivations to value the community of the Bottoms in Michigan to pursue a different family legacy than the one that he is presented. For Milkman, the flying African folktale functions as the mythic dimension of his personal quest to find his self-worth as an African American man.

Collecting the flying African folktale dramatically changes how Milkman understands himself and his relationship to his family and community. After recovering the folktale, Milkman articulates the superficiality of his connection with his family, friends, and the Southside community. He expresses a profound understanding of what it means to be a member of an African American community that goes beyond his immediate town. He understands Guitar's concern with the "seriousness" about life and his sister's anger with his habit of "pee[ing] on people" (Morrison 1977, 214). Milkman realizes that his lifestyle and the majority of his past choices and decisions were self-serving.

At the end of the novel Milkman is poised to fly, willingly surrendering to Guitar's intense desire to kill him. Does Guitar kill Milkman or does Milkman succeed in being a flying African? The ending is deliberately ambiguous because it highlights our ability to understand Milkman's subjectivity. As Heyman argues, Milkman's quest is not a linear one. He writes, "Morrison, refusing to resolve the dilemma between the power of Milkman's logocentric claim to authority and the essentialist stance to which it leads, creates what I will call . . . a (w)hol(e)y black text, one that depicts empowerment while pointing to the holes, the gaps, the aporias in its own construction" (1995, 391). Milkman's linear quest for gold has long dissolved into the starburst of happiness when he is able to create meaningful relationships with Pilate, with Hagar (posthumously), and now with Guitar. But he has received an undesirable wealth. This is both progress and stasis. Can Milkman make a different life for himself now that he has a new understanding of the significance of his life, his past, and its importance to the future? This is the question that Morrison leaves us with, because whether an individual can make a difference in the cultural conditions that they find themselves in is the "koan" presented by the flying African:

> In *Song of Solomon* I really did not mean to suggest that they kill each other, but out of a commitment and love and selfness they are willing to risk the one thing that we have, life, and that's the positive nature of the action. I never really believed that those two men would kill each other. I thought they would, like antelopes, lock horns, but it is important that Guitar put his

> gun down and does not blow Milkman out of the air, as he could. It's important that he look at everything with his new eyes and say, "My man, my main man." It's important that the metaphor be in the killing of his brother, that the two men who love each other nevertheless have no area in which they can talk, so they exercise some dominion over and demolition of the other. I wanted the language to be placid enough to suggest he was suspended in the air in the leap towards this thing, both loved and despised, and that he was willing to die for that idea, but not necessarily to die. (Morrison 1994a, 111)

Thus, at the end of *Song of Solomon,* Morrison argues that the freedom that Milkman leaps to is not physical but a metaphorical death from which he could redefine or ground himself in notions of malehood that are not selfish and patriarchal, but thoughtful and productive for culture building and embracing family legacies. Thus, Milkman's leap into his brother's arms is the final scene in the novel, but the mark of the beginning of his journey toward an understanding of himself that is defined beyond ideologies about class, gender, and spirituality.

In closing, Morrison suggests that a viable discourse for black men is right in front of them: African American folklore (a combination of cultural beliefs and family values). Drawing on this discourse, Milkman develops the ability to define himself beyond dominant discourses but within a family legacy and cultural context that respect his ancestors, who strove to live under the harsh conditions of slavery. Milkman constructs his subjectivity from names, words, and stories about the past: "Shalimar left [his children], but it was the children who sang about it and kept the story of his leaving alive" (1977, 322). It is within the discursive divide of family legacy and cultural heritage that Milkman both flies and constructs a subjectivity.

CHAPTER 5

"Promontory of Despair"

Baldwin's Gay Sensibilities in *If Beale Street Could Talk*

> Once we reclaim the camp and crazy "carnivalesque" excesses of Little Richard—the original Queen of Rock n Roll—we can appreciate the way African American men . . . parodied the stereotype of African American masculinity to "theatricalize" and send up the charade of gender roles.
>
> —ISAAC JULIEN AND KOBENA MERCER, "TRUE CONFESSIONS: A DISCOURSE ON IMAGE OF AFRICAN AMERICAN MALE SEXUALITY," 2007

CONTEMPORARY AFRICAN American men face a discursive conundrum: they are expected to conform to traditional performances of masculinity and sexuality as well as meet the constricting, culturally specific requirements of the African American community. Overburdened with stereotypes (such as hypersexual, hyper-masculine, absent fathers, and dangerous criminals) and compulsive masculine practices (such as being the breadwinner with a secure job and being emotionally and physically sound), African American men are given very little space to build a life for themselves and their families in society and their communities. Thus, an integral part of black male subjectivity formation often includes attempts to counter these conflicting and impossible definitions of manhood. In the discursive divide, African American men challenge hyper-masculinity and compulsive heterosexuality and search for alternative performances of masculinity. In the above quote, Isaac Julien and Kobena Mercer lay bare the recovery project that African American gay male artists embark on when they explore African American male expression as an exaggerated performance of hegemonic masculinity. Like other late twentieth-century African American gay male writers who stress the significance of problematizing the notion of a universal African American masculinity, some of whom they mentored and published, Julien and Mercer demand recovery projects that consider the function of masculinity and sexuality in the minds of gay and heterosexual men. They focus on how the performance of black masculinity perpetuates or circumvents hegemonic masculinity, and how, through the performance of masculinity, in fiction and nonfiction, African American gay artists recall losing friends and family members, gaining new friends, and finding supportive communities after disclosing their sexuality. Also, African American gay artists relate narratives about growing up and engaging in, refusing to have, or knowing about illicit sexual relations between prominent married men. In films and plays, African American gay artists reenact scenes of gay men bravely suffering from AIDS, fighting for research and tolerance, and disclosing the multiple spaces where gay African American men gather and are welcomed in the African American community. Thus, African American gay writers unveil vulnerable masculinities that withstand verbal and physical abuse and endure under oppressive conditions.

Ten years before Julien and Mercer called for a rhetoric that makes "visible the positive ways black men have been involved in a political struggle around the meaning of masculinity" and demanded an interrogation of African American masculine performances as a site of struggle, Baldwin published *If Beale Street Could Talk,* a novel that explores how black men persist through individual and institutional racism that shape theirs and their families' lives. Julien and Mercer insist on a critical approach that exposes masculinity as a performance, and Baldwin represents the potential of black masculinity as a performative, fluid, and intentional practice in fiction. In *Beale Street,* Alfonso "Fonny" Hunt is racially profiled, falsely accused of rape, and imprisoned without collaborative evidence proving that he committed a crime. While he is in jail, he is emotionally and psychologically overwhelmed by the experience of confinement and angry and helpless that he is unable to care for and supports Tish, his pregnant fiancé. In presenting Fonny as powerless to change his circumstance, expressive about his sense of lost, passionate about his fiancé and family, and certain about his innocence, Baldwin explores black male subjectivity as a range of discourses and positions from which the black subject constantly adjusts and imagines himself and his relation to reality and people. Baldwin, like Julien and Mercer, is well-positioned to investigate compulsive black masculinity and sexuality because he is writing from a queer(ed) perspective, looking at a character like Fonny from both the inside, as an African American male subject to the same institutionalized racism (like criminal profiling), and from the outside, as a gay man. In Baldwin's words, "I think that I know something about the American masculinity which most men of my generation do not know because they have not been menaced by it in the way that I have been" (1998b, 170).

In this chapter, I argue that Baldwin's novel *If Beale Street Could Talk* advances earlier writers' explorations of larger conversations about modes of African American male expression. By referencing late twentieth-century writers' scholarship on manners of African American gay male expression, I contend that Baldwin's gay sensibilities are relayed through the insights of his female protagonist, Tish Rivers, who witnesses the carnivalesque and the shifting and competing subject positions that each character occupies at a given moment. Disassembling these moments through critical concepts that account for the turmoil that racial oppression engenders in African American families, I offer a queer reading of *Beale Street* that suggests the dynamics of black expression—the potential of black masculine performance as dynamic and honest expressions of characters' own emotional states. While Fonny expresses feelings of despair in jail, his family and in-laws feel vulnerable and powerless. Baldwin doesn't just simply introduce readers to these characters' trials and tribulations; he invites readers to witness their emotional turmoil and the chaos in their lives. Through an examination of the process by which he reveals his characters' interiority—their richness, complexity, multidimensionality—I argue that Baldwin demonstrates "a heightened awareness of certain human complications of feelings that spring from the fact of social oppression; in short a perception of the world which is colored, shaped, directed, and defined by the fact of [his] gayness" (Babuscio 1993, 19). I believe that Baldwin discloses a gay sensibility that is a consequence of intersectionality but nourished by his own unique take on gender performance as a reflection and resistance of dominant cultural values.

Besides utilizing theoretical concepts that African American gay and queer theorists have found useful for articulating gay sensibilities, I draw on black feminist discourse to argue that Baldwin's art and imagination engage intersectionality as the discursive divide where African American men and women are situated similarly but defined differently by competing discourses. While Barbara Christian (2000) coined the term "intersectionality" to illuminate the unique ways in which African American women are positioned outside the protections of the law, Baldwin demonstrates the paradox of intersectional oppression on African American families from the perspective of Tish, Fonny's pregnant fiancé. From Tish's perspective readers learn about the enormous responsibility that the African American male characters have to protect their families from (real and imagined) terror and physical threats; Tish's perspective provides readers an insight into the ways that the African American women characters disidentify (claim and disclaim) with patriarchal structures.

Through Tish's viewpoint, Baldwin raises a provocative question: How do African American families support falsely incarcerated African American men without putting aside their own immediate needs? This question has been explored in the edited collection *Impacts of Incarceration on the African American Family,* which challenges common perceptions of incarcerated African American men as loners, social misfits, or individuals who have been totally separated from the workings of society (Harris and Miller 2006, 5). In mapping the systemic causes of incarceration, this collection moves away from the preoccupation with the prison population as primarily composed of undereducated men who choose criminal activity over legal employment and racial practices that prevent African American men from securing gainful employment. Instead, the editors feature essays that are primarily concerned with the effects of incarceration on spouses, children, and extended families members. Besides producing emotional turmoil (such as distance between spouses and children), feelings of inadequacy, and clinical depression, this collection suggests that African American men believe that they fail to fulfill the patriarchal notion that men should be the head of their families or the primary breadwinner. In *If Beale Street Could Talk,* the African American male characters feel helpless, hopeless, and emasculated when they are unable to raise enough money to hire a lawyer to defend Fonny and hire a detective to locate the woman who can vouch for his whereabouts the day of the crime.

Baldwin directly takes up inequality and the American justice system in *The Evidence of Things Not Seen* (1986), an investigative nonfiction book about the Atlanta, Georgia, murder of twenty-eight African American children from 1979 to 1981, where Wayne Williams, an African American man, was tried and convicted. Although Baldwin is suspicious of Williams, who he describes as having the aura of someone "you'd just to love to burn," he also believes that the white politicians and African American clergy and leadership spent more time jockeying for media spotlight and social position and power than discussing the case. Baldwin suggests that although Williams was a suspicious character, the public will most likely never learn the truth about the circumstances surrounding the missing children since Williams, an unemployed struggling music producer, was unable to fund a strong defense against a case that was built on solely circumstantial evidence.[1]

Similar to other gay African American writers, Baldwin offers nuanced renderings of the variety of ways in which black men's sense of self is undermined within and without African American culture. Baldwin represents the nucleus of a tradition of gay African American writers who explicitly and implicitly challenged compulsory heterosexuality and hegemonic masculinity that function as a disciplinary formation seemingly emanating from every-

1. According to William G. Staples, the Innocence Project has used DNA testing to exonerate 186 African American men (2000, 151).

where and nowhere. Besides following a tradition of Harlem Renaissance writers and texts (Countee Cullen and Wallace Thurman) that covertly explore same-sex relationships, Baldwin writes literary naturalism with his contemporaries—Red Jordan Arobateau's "Suzie Q" and Samuel R. Delany's "Aye and Gomorrah"—to capture the inescapable forces that shape gay identities and subjectivities. Finally, Baldwin and *Beale Street* is in conversation with present writers who are more open about their sexuality and sexual identities (such as Melvin Dixon, Randall Kenan, Darieck Scott, and the late E. Lynn Harris's *Invisible Life*) and who wrote about down-low relationships, interracial sexual and romantic relationships, and the heaviness of family and community values. However, unlike many of the aforementioned authors and many of the writers featured in the collections *Brother to Brother: New Writings by Black Gay Men* and *Black Like Us: A Century of Lesbian, Gay, and Bisexual African American Fiction,* Baldwin rejects gay and queer as labels to describe his sexual identity. As Baldwin stated in an interview, the terms "homosexual, bisexual, heterosexual are 20th-century terms which, for me, really have very little meaning. I've never, myself, in watching myself and watching other people, watching life, been able to discern exactly where the barriers were" (1989, 55). Instead of labeling his sexual identity, Baldwin focuses on his inherent and natural need to feel love and to have various intimate and non-romantic connections or relationships with others regardless of their ethnicity, gender, or sexuality. In *Giovanni's Room,* "The Male Prison," and "Freaks and the American Ideal of Manhood," Baldwin focuses on achieving an idealized human connection as opposed to the gender of the subjects who are fostering the union. Transcending fixed understandings of difference, Baldwin upholds practices of same sex and hetero desire as a fundamental way to counter hegemony. Baldwin's contemplations coalesce in *Beale Street* where he challenges heteronormativity in all of its manifestations by arguing for a politic of love and family that questions the ability of men to achieve manhood without love and support from both men and women.

•

> It is perhaps more important to see that homosexuality is not merely a theme but comes to define a style, both as a lifestyle and as a mode of semiotic expression.
>
> —THOMAS E. YINGLING, *HART CRANE AND THE HOMOSEXUAL TEXT* (1990, 25)

I define African American gay sensibilities as an artistic and imaginative spiritness that is rooted in African American experiences and institutions but not confined to or defined by African American cultural values or beliefs about masculinity or sexuality (since masculinity and sexuality are usually influenced by hegemonic masculinity). African American gay sensibilities counter the hypocrisies and contradictions in African American institutions and recognize racism as harmful to African American people and communities. Not only do gay African American writers recognize what Frantz Fanon refers to as the "negating negativity" of dominant discourses, but also Essex Hemphill's "esthetic qualities and components," such as the soul in music, urban in fashion, and the vernacular of language that defy assigned categories and polarization. Gay African American writers notice the structures behind the patterns or hear and feel the beats and rhythms within African American creative arts and expressions and imagine the perfection of sounds and expressions. Since African American cultural expressions shape American culture, one could argue that African American gay sensibilities are a significant aspect of mainstream American culture (although white American gay and straight individuals might reject this notion, as their articulations of gayness and compulsory heterosexuality only considers expressions of African American masculinity in opposition to whiteness and masculinity). Baldwin's sensibilities shape his own perspective on his own sexuality. By this, I mean the fluidity or borderlessness in which Baldwin imagines his own sexuality stirring is key to understanding how he seamlessly interweaves the camp and carnivalesque into his narrative about how racial profiling and false accusation introduce chaos in the lives of African American families.

Baldwin's experiences growing up in Harlem equipped him with the insight to discern the complex ways that gender and sexuality position men and women in society. This ability to examine one's positionality and relationship to "activities, individuals, situations, and gayness," Jack Babuscio defines as camp sensibilities that are individually (and I add communally) based (1993, 20). Baldwin's gay sensibilities are exemplified in "Freaks and the American Ideal of Manhood," where he considers the several ways that discourses about hegemonic masculinity confine individuals to a fate that is physically and psychologically punitive. Labels are restricting and harmful. Baldwin writes, "once you have discerned the meaning of a label it may seem to define you for others, but does not have the power to define you to yourself" (1998b, 819). He continues that the homophobic words "faggot" and "pussy" individuals use to refer to gay men "had nothing to do with sexual preference. You were simply being told that you had no balls" (819). Learning at a young age the enormous emphasis that American society places on gender and sexuality prepared him to work as a server in a downtown restaurant where his insight into white subjectivity and sexuality were shaped in each interaction with lovers and customers. To lovers and customers, he was simply a phallic symbol to be feared and admired. Baldwin writes, "It is true, alas, that to be an American Negro male is also to be a kind of walking phallic symbol: which means that one pays, in one's own personality, for the sexual insecurity of others. The relationship, therefore, of a black boy to a white boy is a very complex thing" (270). Besides examining his gay sensibility in his treatment of black identity and sexuality, I argue that Baldwin's gay sensibilities are equally evident in his investigation of inherent privilege in white identity and sexuality. Baldwin predicts the critical issues and stances contemporary African American queer theorists have taken up in written and visual texts.

Baldwin's departure from Harlem to Europe provided him with an opportunity to denounce the restrictions involved in labels of sexual identity and to contemplate nonexclusive sexual attractions and behaviors. While living as an expatriate in France, Baldwin wrote personal reflections and semi-autobiographical and experimental narratives that critiqued racial and sexual oppression in America. In contrast to his freshman novel, *Go Tell It on the Mountain,* where he problematizes religion and sexuality and sexual behaviors such as masturbation and promiscuity, Baldwin's sophomore novel, *Giovanni's Room,* explores American masculinity as an ideal that depends on the denial of love, compassion, and racial and sexual difference. Although both novels illustrate Baldwin's insights into the inner workings of compulsory heterosexuality and hegemonic masculinity, *Giovanni's Room* questions the perpetuation of heteronormativity through perilous means and highlights the expressions required to maintain the status quo, as well as white American identity.

Baldwin's gay sensibilities in *Giovanni's Room* are noticeable in the obvious subject matter: a character's preoccupation with his sexual identity, compulsory heterosexuality, and hegemonic masculinity. Baldwin enters *Giovanni's Room* as David, an affluent white American male who is in love with an American white woman and a French man. Oscillating between heterosexuality in the form of Hella and same-sex desire in the form of Giovanni, David represents the radical potential of black queer theory to account for race colliding with class and gender and to reach beyond the borders of America to critique gay white male domination. As Baldwin's white mask, David "enables Baldwin to avoid presenting a narrative foregrounding the dominant culture's victimization of the disenfranchised, and instead to dramatize how normative notions of American white manhood (i.e., heteropatriarchy) injure not only America's Others, but those whose authority the norms appear to underwrite" (Charles 2013, 116). Mae G. Henderson points out the advantage of Baldwin's "literary performance of racial passing" as providing him "a position from which to cast his critical gaze on the Other, while creating a subject position that allowed him both to explore his own sexual variance or difference and to critique the dominant national construction of masculinity" (2005, 300). Arguing that Baldwin's rhetorical moves in *Giovanni's Room* anticipate Morrison's notions of Africanism in American literature, Henderson contends that Baldwin explores whiteness as a way to examine the "contours" of his own sexuality and identity as a gay African American man (300). Positioned in this novel as "the radical Other," Baldwin explores his own ambivalence toward heterosexuality, homoeroticism, American masculinity, identity, and his own sexuality.

Baldwin further delves into white identity and sexuality formation in "The Black Boy Looks at the White Boy" and "Stranger in the Village," where he describes white Americans as "being in the grip of a weird nostalgia" in which they are overwhelmed with thoughts of "a vanished state of security and order" (1998b, 270). For example, Norman Mailer, Baldwin contends, romanticized African American oppression and sexuality as liberating, therapeutic, and redemptive to the extent that he is unable to examine his own whiteness and accept the social structure that enables him to write and read about African Americans consumed with visions of an unbridled white masculinity. White males perpetuate stereotypes about African American people and culture without the fear of them writing back (or worse, even if African Americans write back, he is empowered to ignore their responses) and to act on them without having to worry about African Americans responding (or again worse, if African Americans reply with the same force or aggression the marketplace will penalize them). To be a white American male, then, symbolizes the privilege to not only define white identity and sexuality but also the power to restrict Others to a physical and imagined place in society. Equally importantly, it also means never having to reflect on the lies, myths, and narratives on which one constructs his or her own white identity and sexuality.

Baldwin argues that racial history doesn't provide queer African Americans with the luxury to disavow one's immediate family and completely repudiate the heterosexism ideologies in their communities. Queer African Americans rely on the African American family even though it is a contradictory space in which Christian notions of heterosexuality and material experiences with racism collide with the individual's pursuit of self-actualization, and they retreat to their families and communities for comfort, security, protection, and self-affirmation. In 1992, the "London Based Black Group argued that the call by gay activists to reject the heterosexist norms of the nuclear family was totally ethnocentric as it ignored the fact that black lesbians and gay men need our families, which offer us support and protection from the racism we experienced on the street, at school, from the police, and from the state" (Julien and Mercer 2007, 207). Baldwin's characters depend on their families to restore "in their minds and hearts despite poverty, hardship, and deprivation . . . the dignity denied" to them by "the outside in the public world" (1990, 42). Black queer sensibilities mean knowing that choosing one's kinship and family relations over formed, complex, or blended families and friendships is a detriment to the black subject. Black queer subjects maintain or reconcile various and competing relationships despite their opposing viewpoints or value systems.

Baldwin's choice of a female narrator queers the novel's protest elements. The protest narrative is by definition masculine, and Baldwin's placement of a female character at the center of this story about a man merely results in a simple gender permutation, creating a quasi-female, a hero in drag. Within Baldwin's gay sensibilities, being female does not relegate women to a subordinate position in society. Tish is not a gender stereotype, displaying quite a few traits normally associated with maleness. She is aggressive, very seldom emotional, caring but not to a fault, and vulnerable but not at her own peril, which definitely makes her a nonconventional protest heroine. Still, Tish, more complex and dynamic than Richard Wright and other protest protagonists, speaks to Baldwin's earlier disavowal of the protest novel as a gimmick that fails to realize black humanity. In its assessment of African Americans' black humanity, Baldwin's *Beale Street* represents their struggle against racial domination as not a matter of only striking out at the white power structure, but that one's humanity is developed within oneself and one's community "in the most private chamber of the African American man's heart always, he finds himself facing the terrible roster of the lost: the dead, African American junkie; the defeated, African American father; the unutterably weary, African American mother; the unutterably ruined African American girl" (Baldwin 1998b, 722). Besides advancing his earlier stance on the protest novel, Baldwin's novel forecasts current thinking in queer theory (which is heavily influenced by the transgender movement) by theorists such as J. Jack Halberstam and Judith Butler, who are now raising the same questions: what do gender categories really mean and do they do anything more than separate people unrealistically? Through a consideration of the critical issues and stances contemporary African American queer theorists take up in written and visual texts, I argue that Baldwin's gay sensibilities constitute the surface, thematic, and subterranean structure of his writings.

•

> Gender parody reveals that the original identity after which gender fashions itself is an imitation without an origin.
>
> —JUDITH BUTLER, "FROM INTERIORITY TO GENDER PERFORMATIVE" (1999, 364)

The highly influential second wave feminist theorist Elaine Showalter problematizes the practice of male authors authoring fictional texts from the perspective of female characters, for she questions if a male author can truly, with great objectivity, enter a woman's world and discern the interworking of oppressive ideologies and oppressive discourses. Can Baldwin explore African American male existence from the perspective of an African American female? What is the implication of Baldwin's feminine perspective in *Beale Street?* Showalter, for example, argues that this narrative strategy suggests a larger patriarchal practice of men speaking for women. Her concern is that this implies that men must teach women how to win their rights, or that cross-dressing in a novel is a way of promoting the notion of masculine power while masking it (1987, 122).[2] But in contrast, Judith Butler, writing from a later, queer studies perspective, believes that male writers cross-dressing or entering a text in drag highlights the performative nature of gender—"it reveals the distinctiveness of those aspects of gendered experience which are falsely naturalized as a unity through the regulatory fiction of heterosexual coherence" (1990, 137–38). Anticipating this perspective shift, Baldwin is neither patriarchal nor essentializing in his approach to viewing African American men from an African American woman's perspective. He seizes this narrative approach as an opportunity to explore the nuances of African American male subjectivity from the perspective of African American women. The men in his novel are exposed, defenseless, and in danger. They are socially vulnerable not as a consequence of their sexuality, but as a result of their race and gender. Pushing against hegemonic masculinity, Baldwin destabilizes or chal-

2. In *Gender Trouble: Feminism and the Subversion of Identity,* Judith Butler states that "gender is an act as it were, that is open to splitting, self-parody, self-criticism, and those hyperbolic exhibitions of the natural that, in their very exaggeration, reveal its fundamentally phantasmatic status" (1990, 187). In other words, gender is a performance that can be inspected and interrogated for how well it reifies social expectations of what it means to be a male or female. In a sense, I read Tish as Baldwin's ruminations of African American womanhood: who he believes them to be and what he believes are (or should be) their preoccupations with African American malehood.

lenges homophobia and stereotypes of African American masculinity propagated by writers/activists like Eldridge Cleaver, who embraced a narrow and stereotypical definition of African American masculinity and sexuality that fulfilled dominant forms of masculinity. Through Tish, Baldwin challenges hegemonic masculinity as an investment in male superiority and women's subjugation. When he depicts Tish observing Fonny socializing with other African American men, Baldwin queers black masculinity by highlighting the love, kindness, and sensitivity that men share. Tish watches expressive men who are just as imaginative as women. Baldwin writes, "This idea that women are more imaginative than men dreamed up by men, and it proves exactly the contrary . . . once you take seriously the notion that a man who is not afraid to trust his own imagination (which is all that men have ever trusted) is effeminate. It says a lot about this country, because, of course, if all you want to do is make money, the very last thing you need is imagination" (1974, 50). Tish notices the expansiveness of male expression that defies typical gender lines or expectations. Fonny articulates this performance of black masculinity when he describes himself as an artist who is content with nurturing his love for Tish, their unborn baby, and sculpting beautiful images from blocks of wood.

In *Camp and the Gay Sensibilities,* Jack Babuscio states that authors live vicariously through their characters by infusing them with their own intrinsic qualities, tensions, and anxieties. He writes that, in characters, the "artist finds a means of dealing with the tensions that plagued and defined him—tensions that reside in such dualities as flesh/spirit, promiscuity/pride, youth/(old) age" (1993, 33). In other words, when Baldwin writes, "She's a girl from the streets as I am a boy from the streets," he is not only figuratively placing himself in the text in Tish's place, but also seeing life as Tish and evaluating the predicaments he places her in through the eyes of a teenage African American female (1974, 109). Lynn Orilla Scott notes the physical similarities between Baldwin and his protagonist as primary evidence for arguing that he enters the novel through Tish. Scott says, "Tish is closely linked to her creator from her big eyes and small stature to her voice and sensibilities" (2002, 64). Not only does Baldwin acknowledge that he is in the novel, he doesn't limit his position to Tish. Baldwin shifts his perspective between characters. He writes, "The girl is telling the story. You can say I'm the girl, or the boy or the unborn child" (1989, 109). If we follow Baldwin's logic, he is an African American woman in love with an African American man, he is the African American man in love with himself as an African American woman, and he is the offspring of himself as an African American woman who is in love with an African American man. Multiple positionalities allow Baldwin to imagine what it is like to love and watch a African American man suffer, experience the hopelessness that

African American men feel when they can't provide for their families, and the loss that African American children feel when their fathers are absent.

Although Baldwin writes the story from multiple perspectives, he states that it had to be primarily told from a pregnant women's perspective for "she's the only one who can tell the story. The book ends with the birth of Tish and Fonny's baby. That's what the story is about, our responsibility to that baby" (1989, 109). If this is the message in the story and Tish gives birth to a male child, then Baldwin highlights the significance of women as bearers of men and that they share accountability in rearing and protecting them. As an example of the "contingency of sex and gender," Baldwin and Tish are engaged in a subtextual conversation about the conditions of African American male subjectivity (Butler 1990, 187). In casting Tish, Baldwin crosses the discursive divide to experiment with the feminine gaze that enables him to see the fractures in patriarchy and patriarchal structures.

Baldwin's cross-gendered storytelling engages fundamental questions about whether a man can (both in wisdom and possibility) portray a genuine woman—transcend gender and tell a story through the eyes of a young African American girl. In telling the story from Tish's point of view, Baldwin adopts an African American female perspective that is sensitive, deliberate, and convincing. To borrow from Zora Neal Hurston, Baldwin's "tongue is in" Tish's "mouf" (2006, 6). Instead of drawing on the qualities typically associated with African American men and identified as "African American rage" (frustration, vulnerability, and desperation), Tish's voice is urgent, honest, and sentimental. Tish talks about social injustice without diminishing Fonny's humanity or masculinity and she reminds him about how important he is to her and their unborn child. The opening lines of the novel forefront Baldwin's narrative strategy. Looking at himself in the mirror but seeing an image of Tish reflecting back to him, Baldwin writes, "I look at myself in the mirror. I know that I was christened Clementine, and so it would make sense if people called me Clem, or even come to think of it, Clementine, since that's my name: but they don't. . . . I'm tired, and I'm beginning to think that maybe everything that happens make sense" (1974, 3). Listing Tish's nicknames, Baldwin reminds readers how those who know him well shortened his name—often referring to him as Jimmy as opposed to James. Explaining (re)naming as an African American cultural practice, Melville Herskovits emphasizes naming as something that derives from Africa. He states, "a person's name may in so many instances change with time, a new designation being assumed on the occasion of some striking occurrence in his life" (1958, 191). The practice of naming has many purposes in African American culture. In Tish's case, Baldwin shows kinship, easiness, and endearment. In shortening Clementine to Clem, the speaker professes a familiarity with Clementine that transcends formalities. Also, Baldwin's use of naming discloses another reason he is exploring African American male subjectivity from the perspective of an African American female character: the intimacy of knowing someone well enough that one can confidently stand by an individual when he is accused of a terrible crime. Intimacy between African American men and women is an important aspect of Baldwin's cultural project. He writes: "African American men would not be here if African American women had not understood something about men" (1989, 196–97). In Baldwin's novel, intimacy includes sacrifice, support, heartache, selflessness, and possibilities.

Tish narrates the significant role that African American female characters have in African American male subjectivity construction in two fundamental ways: the ideal and real world. In the real world, where the weight of oppression overwhelms some African American men to the point that they lose hope, Baldwin's African American male characters love their wives and families but feel ashamed for not being able to provide for and protect them. Unlike the real world, the ideal world is that of fairytales and romance. This is the world where anything is possible—including two young African American teenagers having a baby out of wedlock and building a life together despite the high unemployment and disenfranchisement of African Americans. It is a world where raising a family very close to the line of poverty is acceptable as long it is intact and where the justice system that wrongly convicts African American men admits their mistakes and exonerates them. It is a world where an accuser, who identifies the wrong man, recants her story because she would rather have the right person jailed as opposed to the peace of mind that comes with believing that her assailant is in jail.

Tish speaks from multiple positions: a daughter, a sister, a girlfriend, and a pregnant teenager. While each of these are separate categories, Tish's race (the fact that she is African American) modifies or redefines each of these positions and shapes how she understands herself in these roles and how she understands how she is defined in society. The intersections of race, class, and gender relative to the dominant culture or to other social groups in society affect her view of the world and how she constructs and values knowledge.[3] Each category shapes her perspective of herself and the other characters in

3. Patricia Hill Collins describes African American feminist consciousness as having two main objectives: to foster an insightful and relentless critique of race, class, and gender as interlocking systems of oppression and to engage ongoing epistemological debates in feminist theory and in the sociology of knowledge concerning ways of assessing "truth." It also reveals new ways of knowing that allow subordinate groups to define their own reality with far greater implications.

the story. Baldwin selects Tish to narrate the story because she lends an enormous amount of sensitivity and objectivity to the African American male experience. This is better than Fonny telling his own story, for one can always question the objectivity of the person who experiences the traumatic event, especially since Fonny has a number of things working against him: he is in jail and incarcerated people always proclaim their innocence, and he is an African American male. Rhetorically, having Tish narrate the story circumvents the stereotype that the legal system falsely imprisons African American men. Thus, through Tish, Baldwin speaks for the nameless African American men who are in jail, demeaned, or left to wander directionless in society. It is through her persistence and perspective that she says to his family and the white man that Fonny shall not be forgotten and abandoned. She doesn't see him as handicapped or broken, but burdened with the trials of life as an African American man; she offers hope and redemption. For Fonny, Tish represents unconditional love and a consciousness that recognizes him as a human being and a significant member of the African American community.

As narrator of the events in the story, Tish's intersectional perspective interrogates male subjectivity. Although Baldwin doesn't employ womanism in his writings to describe Tish, she exhibits many of the "womanist" qualities as defined by Walker in *In Search of Our Mothers' Gardens.* According to Walker, womanism centers on African American women's experiences and suggests that African American women suffer a different, more complex, and more intense kind of oppression than white women. Unlike white feminism that privileges the upliftment of white middle-class women, womanism emphasizes the survival and the wholeness of African American men, women, and families and stresses the distinction between dominant definitions and African American women's material experiences. Womanist theory functions as a critical lens for viewing African American male subjectivity from an objective and fair position. The position that African American women occupy in African American men's lives (other than African American men) makes them the most fair and knowledgeable evaluators of African American men and their experiences. In evaluating African American men, African American women not only draw on their experiences in their families and communities, but also on their experiences in a racist and sexist society.

Narrating the story from Tish's perspective, Baldwin accesses African American female consciousness through the prism of his gay sensibilities. In *Sister Outsider,* Audre Lorde defines African American female consciousness as a rhetorical strategy that African American women adopt to survive race, class, and gender oppression in America. Lorde argues that African American women have a dual consciousness: "They are aware of their own positionality as African American women and become familiar with the language and manners of the oppressor, even sometimes adopting them for some illusion of protection" while concealing their intentions from the dominant group (2007, 97). African American female consciousness suggests an alternative discourse for understanding the pain that African American men internalize as a result of the dominant standards that are imposed on them. Mrs. Rivers reassures Tish that her anxiety about Fonny is a result of the emotional turmoil that comes with loving African American men, for they are often subjected to social persecution: "I know I can't help you very much right now—God knows what I wouldn't give if I could. But I know about suffering if that helps. I know that it ends. I ain't going to tell you no lies, like it always ends for the better. Sometimes it ends for the worse. You can suffer so bad that you can be driven to a place where you can't ever suffer again: and that worse" (Baldwin 1974, 98). Through Tish, Baldwin asks what African American women see when they witness African American men suffering. Thus, Baldwin explores the intrinsic qualities of African American men.

Placing Tish at the center of analysis opens up the possibilities for a conceptual stance, one in which African American men and women "possess varying amounts of penalty and privilege in one historical created system" (Collins 2000a, 246). African Americans benefit from a system of attitudes, biases, and discrimination in favor of opposite-sex sexuality and relationships. It can include the presumption that other people are heterosexual or that opposite-sex attractions and relationships are the only norm and therefore superior. According to Patricia Hill Collins, heterosexual African Americans are victims of race, class, and gender oppression but have some privilege in that they are able to benefit from their sexuality—i.e., exploit the fissures in patriarchal structures depending on the context. For example, "African American heterosexual women have been penalized by both race and gender yet privileged by their sexuality and citizenship status" (Collins 2000a, 246). In other words, society bestows heterosexual African American men and women such privileges as access to goods, services, and unquestioned access to institutions such as marriage, church, and military.[4]

Collins is accurate that heterosexuals are in many ways privileged above gays. However, she overlooks the fact that those who love, sympathize, or empathize with gay or heterosexual African American men endure feelings of sorrow and helplessness when they see them hurt or distressed. Empathizing

4. Although society is changing in regards to its view of gay men and women, I believe that the fact that this transformation is taking place through legislation as opposed to the population's change of heart reaffirms Baldwin's queer insight: anyone who loves African American men will suffer due to the man's powerless and persecuted position in American society.

with African American men who experience intersectional oppression transcends racial and gender lines. In responding to a draft of this chapter, my colleague Carol Siegel stated, "If we women—black or white—truly love them we suffer with them, just as the gay men who love them do. As a heterosexual woman seen as white I have lots of privileges, but that doesn't stop my heartbreak over the unfair treatment of my eldest godson, who I love very much, has suffered simply because he's African American!" In most cases, family and friends are aware of African American men's feelings of powerlessness and alienation, and they observe and are, sometimes, overwhelmed watching the disproportionate amount of psychic energy and attention that black men exude to building an elaborate defense system to navigate the discursive divide. They witness black men who are so preoccupied with honing rhetorical and discursive survival skills that they sometimes seem hypersensitive and emotionally unavailable and in such constant conflict within themselves that they struggle to love themselves and others.

The impact of African American men's suffering on family and friends is most evident in *Beale Street* and *Another Country*. In *Another Country*, Baldwin depicts Vivaldo, a white man who is in love with Ida, an African American woman. Both characters are grieving over the death of Rufus who, overcome with racial oppression, commits suicide. It is important to note that Rufus and Vivaldo are bisexual and lovers, and after Rufus commits suicide, Ida and Vivaldo assume a relationship, as it asserts Baldwin's commitment to conceptualizing sexuality on a continuum. As a result of Rufus's suicide, Ida, emboldened, maintains that there is a cause and effect relationship between racial oppression and black male suicide. Suffering too, Vivaldo looks at Ida while thinking, "I wanted so bad to take that girl in my arms and kiss that look off her face and make her know that I didn't do it, I wouldn't do it, whoever was doing it was doing it to me, too" (Baldwin 1993a, 113). Committed to racial justice, Vivaldo wishes that he could have done something to save Rufus.

Similarly, Tish reflects on the time when Fonny attempted to defend her from a young white boy's sexual advances at a bodega. Walking home after the incident, Tish recalls how she intervened on Fonny's behalf when a policeman allowed the white boy to leave the scene and threatened to arrest Fonny for disturbing the peace. Fonny experiences what Morrison and bell hooks refer to as white terror, which is traumatic grief and suffering that lingers as a result of white racial domination. Baldwin's "White Man's Guilt," Ralph Ellison's "A Party Down at the Square," Claude McKay's "The Lynching," and other African American writers' poems and short stories explore the devastation and turmoil that white terror engenders in the African American psyche and in African American communities and families. Tish remembers not giving into her fear. "I held my head against Fonny's chest, held both his wrists between my two hands, and looked up into the face of this cop" (Baldwin 1974, 114). However, her actions remind Fonny about his lack of power as a black man. Vulnerable Fonny states:

> "Don't ever try to protect me again. Don't do that."
>
> "I know I'm saying the wrong thing: But you were trying to protect me."
>
> "It's not," he says, with the same terrifying quietness, "the same thing, Tish."
>
> And suddenly takes the bag of tomatoes and smashes them against the nearest wall. (1974, 116)

By articulating the spectacle-spectator dynamic through Tish, Baldwin implies that such witnessing is a specific kind of emasculation. Adding the underscore of black vulnerability alludes to the experience of oppression or powerlessness; in defining power along lines of race and gender, the text reveals the ways in which black men are profiled and policed, resulting in anguish and a scathed sense of self. *Beale Street* steadily critiques the status of black masculinity, elevating black femininity as formidable enough to save African American men from white supremacy. The critique reminds readers of weakened African American men unable to realize their potential and walk safely hand in hand with the women they love. The novel, thus, articulates African American men and women as victimized along gender lines: the former indebted to protection by the latter.

She believes that every day that Fonny spends in a jail, he risks his ambition and creativity being extinguished. While Fonny can physically withstand the anguish of incarceration, Tish hopes that jail doesn't change him from the loving and caring man with whom she fell in love. Tish says:

> You can tell by the way he's taken all this shit that he's a man. Sometimes, I admit, I'm scared—because nobody can take the shit they throw on us forever. But then, you just have to somehow fix your mind to get from one day to the next. If you think too far ahead, if you even try to think too far ahead, you'll never make it. (7)

African American male subjectivity is resilient but exposed, rigid but sophisticated, and direct but compassionate. She perceives her unborn child as an extension of their love and hope for a future beyond the reality of social injustice. She states, "I had found someone to love and I was loved and he was released and verified. That child in my belly was also after all, his child, too. . . .

That baby was our baby, it was on its way . . . in spite of all that hung above our heads, that was promised safety. Love had sent it, spinning out of us, to us. Where it might take us, no one knew" (41). Although Fonny's race, gender, and sexuality (Fonny says repeatedly that the white world has black men by the genitals) places him outside the role of a family provider, Tish appreciates his desire to love and provide for her and their baby. By visiting him every day, she performs the fidelity and commitment that will be necessary in rearing their child and hopefully in maintaining their extended families.

Baldwin entreats the reader to consider the experience of African American male subjectivity as a story of pain, love, redemption, and survival in the urban cities of America. For Fonny and Tish, their relationship faces many great hardships that potentially could lead them down a road of destruction, but they emerge together. Tish narrates the significant role and influence that African American women have in African American male subjectivity construction by showing herself to be sensitive to his plight, trustworthy, and resilient—for she offers him hope. She does not see him the same as mainstream America. As she ushers him toward redemption, she reveals him to be a sensitive, responsible, and strong man that loves his family. In her she carries their unborn child, who represents the promise of their dreams and future together. It is the complexity of an African American woman's love, familiarity, and intimate knowledge of his struggle that places her in a unique position to shape and encourage him. *Beale Street* concludes with Tish giving birth to a male child and Fonny in jail. Although some critics argue that Fonny remains in jail and others believe he gets his freedom, I am certain that is not as much an issue as the persecution that he endured throughout the novel. In jail, his only escape is his imagination or daydreaming about fulfilling the promises that he made to Tish.

•

> Just as disidentification is a source of strength . . . it is also a strategy of empowerment.
>
> —FAEDRA CHATARD CARPENTER, *ROBERT O'HARA'S INSURRECTION* (2005, 335)

The subterranean structure of *Beale Street* provides a counter-history of black male and female relationships—one that suggests that official documents such as the *Moynihan Report*, as it is popularly known, only served to reinforce negative dominant discourses about African American men, women, and families. Published in 1965, the *Moynihan Report* addressed black urban poverty and the rising number of female-headed households. Patrick Moynihan argued that at the heart of the weakening of the fabric of Negro society or communities was the decline of the Negro family. He attributed the disproportionate number of black single-parent families, which he called a "tangle of pathology," to the matriarchal black family structure. A long history of slavery, exploitation, racism, and unemployment has led to a rise in the divorce rate, a large number of illegitimate children, male desertion, and a rapid growth in government subsidy–dependent families.

In *Beale Street,* Baldwin challenges the accusation that African American women distrust African American men as significant members of African American families and communities. Baldwin argues that while there is a certain amount of vehemence between African American men and women, women's "terrible dilemma was to treat a man as a man and protect him from being lynched" (1974, 196). Although men have a double responsibility (be a man and be an African American man in society), women have equal expectations (be a woman and an African American woman in society). Tish addresses these double expectations when she pursues Fonny's freedom, maintains a sense of self, and manages the gender dynamics between her and his families. In addition, Tish safeguards Fonny's feelings. At times, she notices that he is despondent in prison, so she doesn't tell him adverse news until the next visit. This does not mean she is submissive or accommodating at the expense of her own emotional needs; instead, it demonstrates the insight that Baldwin believes that women have about African American men and the sophisticated strategies African American women employ to navigate the patriarchal institutions within and without African American communities.

In *African American Women in Fiction of James Baldwin,* Trudier Harris postulates that Baldwin imagines female agency and resistance within patriarchal institutions and structures. She pays particular attention to the positionality of Baldwin's female characters and their relationship to patriarchy and to patriarchal institutions and reflects on Baldwin's male characters' identification with masculinity by exploring their relationship to women. Harris argues that within the small spaces that masculine domination permits, Baldwin's female characters acquiescence to African American cultural and gender politics and illuminates the extent to which Baldwin remains conflicted about his own "role as a man" (1985, 28). Harris suggests that Baldwin's discreetness about his masculinity and critical stance on institutional oppression influence how he represents his African American female characters. She writes that the portraits of the women are a result of Baldwin "wanting to strike out at what has oppressed him and the masculine identification with the perpetrator of that oppression, and the portraits of the women get caught in this tension"

(29). Harris concludes that although the African American women characters in *Beale Street* are divorced from the restrictions of the fundamentalist church, they still are defined in relation to Christian teachings as good or bad. In her view, Baldwin's female characters are guilty, unhappy scapegoats who, as a result of their gender, have very little space to define counter-subjectivities.[5] While Harris perceives the women in *Beale Street* as Baldwin's failure to construct African American female characters that are distinct from those in his other novels, I am more interested in how Baldwin draws on his sensibilities as a gay man to imagine the ways that African American women (dis)identify with patriarchal institutions and function to purposefully align themselves with or accept the perspective of men to not only advance their political goals and achieve ulterior motives that might not be in line with the dominant culture but also to live as comfortably as possible betwixt and between two worlds without one's intentions being detected.

In "Identity Trouble," Jose Medina's theoretical frameworks come from an understanding of how gay men and women critique but participate in the dominant sphere. Medina explains how disidentification works on multiple levels:

> Disidentification is a way of identifying with someone without losing sight of one's difference from them or counteridentifying with the members of other families while seeing one's similarities with them. However, it would be wrong to construe disidentification as a mere special case of identification and counter-identification. This construal would miss what is most characteristic about the relation of disidentification, namely, that it brings both similarities and differences simultaneously to bear on one's identity. (2003, 92)

Also (dis)identification is a widely accepted survival strategy for the oppressed minority because it allows them to be a part of the public sphere while critiquing it. It is a critique from the inside that highlights the inability of institutional discourses to completely overwrite the subjectivity of the characters. At times, the characters verbally oppose the family, the church, and the criminal justice system; on other occasions, the characters conform to the institutions and hope to survive patriarchy and white supremacy. In both cases, disidentification is a "survival strategy" deep in the structure of Baldwin's novel (5).

Through the act of (dis)identifying, the characters practice a strategy that minorities embrace in order to survive. Within the framework that Bald-

5. See Trudier Harris, *African American Women in the Fiction of James Baldwin* for an extensive examination of the representation of African American women.

win places his female characters in, it is impossible to ignore the way that he problematizes the roles of the female characters in the lives of the men. They push against institutional ideas and reflect on the immediate social threat to black male subjectivity construction. The female characters support the African American male characters, accept their plight as their own, and, at other times, dismiss the men as the source of their own troubles and deserving of the social oppression that befalls them. To illustrate, the Hunt women see the novel's African American males characters as unrepentant sinners, stubborn men who are content with struggling and living in a sinful world. They see suffering as African American men's burden to bear. In contrast, the Rivers women see African American men in the novel as hopeful but incensed and frustrated by the oppressive conditions under which they live. Their intimate knowledge of the men in their family, and the men that are family friends, reminds them that the African American male characters are not responsible for their oppression. Unlike the Hunt women who believe that deliverance from racial domination can only be gained through God, the Rivers women believe the only way to combat the threat to their families is to challenge social injustice and place the African American family at the center of male and female resistance. The Rivers women are self-defined and self-aware and deliberate in their evaluation of male subjectivity. They fight relentlessly against social injustice, and they believe that racism diminishes African American men's self-hood. Baldwin does not relegate the Rivers women to only a supporting role, for they work outside the home, meet with Fonny's lawyer, and use part of their earnings as a legal fund. Thus, while the Hunt women disregard, reject, and alienate men, the Rivers women support, affirm, and celebrate them. Although it is impossible to "evacuate" totally the grounding of cultural identity in spatial metaphor, we might be able to disrupt this spatialing tendency, at least temporarily, by thinking of cultural identification as a temporal process that enables and constrains subjectivity by offering up resources for affiliating with, while also disaffiliating against, particular social groupings

I compare the confusion and disorder that Fonny's arrest creates in Baldwin's fictional families in *Beale Street* to the chaos and upheaval Mikhail Bakhtin's carnivalesque performances, which interrupt the oppressive thoughts of the dominant culture with beliefs and values that come from the marginalized or lower class. Bakhtin points to its de-hierarchicalizing influence, the ability of the people during carnival both to parody and challenge the immutable codes and ordinances of official power. As Bakhtin puts it, "While carnival lasts, there is not other life outside it. During carnival time life is subject to its own laws, that is, the laws of its own freedom" (Eagleton

1981, 148). Bakhtin describes this moment of upheaval as the carnivalesque or the subversion and liberation of the assumption of the dominant style or atmosphere through humor and chaos. He defines the carnivalesque within the context of Rabelais's fiction as a "temporary suspension, both ideal and real, of hierarchical rank created during carnival time a special type of communication impossible in everyday life" (1984b, 10). Bakhtin argues that carnival is a special event that leads "to the creation of special forms of marketplace speech and gesture, frank and free, permitting no distance between those who came in contact with each other and liberating from norms of etiquette and decency imposed at other times" (10) and is concerned with the intermingling of binaries (rich and poor, comedy and tragedy, absurdity and reason) that occur therein.

Similar to Bakhtin, who explores how Rabelais depicts the carnivalesque through folk humor, I am interested in how Baldwin captures the camp in carnivalesque through "exaggeration, artifice, extremity" and cultural tensions (Bergman 1993, 5). Not only was carnival liberating because, for a limited period, the church and state didn't enforce laws—as Terry Eagleton argues, "Carnival . . . after all is a licensed affair in every sense, a permissible rupture of hegemony, a contained popular blow off as disturbing and relatively ineffectual as an evolutionary work of art"—but also because people are permitted to ridicule rules, beliefs, and values, which "cleared the ground" for new ideas to enter into public discourse (1981, 148). In the novel, Baldwin plays out how false incarceration engenders in African American families a lack of agency, feelings of helplessness, and a drive to do whatever it takes to free their loved ones. The upheaval that legalized oppression causes in Baldwin's African American families is akin to the social disorder that Bahktin identifies as the carnivalesque. I am not suggesting a traditional understanding of the carnivalesque as carnivals or fairs temporarily releasing individuals from their lives. Rather, I believe that Baldwin represents the carnivalesque in the binary relationship between the white and African American worlds, which is similar to the dominant and subordinate relationships in Latin America; his treatment of the African American family as grotesque and nontraditional in opposition to the dominant discourse of the white family as beautiful and traditional; and the grotesque stereotypes that govern the fictional world in which the characters inhabit, which harkens to the grotesque stereotypes of Africans that the Zulu parade in New Orleans Mardi Gras counters through African American men wearing traditional blackface. In the books *Darkest America: Black Minstrelsy from Slavery to Hip Hop* (Taylor and Austen 2012) and *Critical Theory and Performance* (Reinelt and Roach 2007), scholars discuss black face in Mardi Gras as an original example of an extreme parody of racism that is meant to shock the dominant culture.

As a property of the deep structure of *Beale Street,* the carnivalesque disrupts the patterns that Baldwin's fictional family and community relies on to function day to day. In other words, to function at all within Baldwin's fictional American society, the Hunts and the Rivers have to act most of the time as if they believe that laws and the justice system have meaning and that if they behave as the system dictates they will achieve the American dream. Therefore, they attend church, hold low-paying jobs, and require their children to graduate from high school and learn a trade. Unfortunately, when Fonny is unjustly jailed, the family and the community are forced to face the fact that law and justice don't apply to them. They embrace the imposition on them of the idea that their families are "grotesque and nontraditional" and discover nontraditional strategies to survive, such as traveling to Puerto Rico to search for the woman who accuses Fonny of rape.

In *The Politics and Poetics of Transgression,* Peter Stallybrass and Allon White state that the distance between the dominant and subordinate cultures provides a space for the subordinate culture to transgress the dominant culture's established laws and values. Within this space, where subordinate cultures mock the moral codes surrounding decency, gender roles, and sexuality, individuals ridicule and undermine dominant ideas and practices and the ideological structures that support them. Always rich in mimicry, pretense, imitation, and disguise, carnivals function as a jovial formalization of dissent. The events are highly politicized "by the very attempts made on the part of local authorities to eliminate them. The dialectic of antagonism frequently turned rituals into resistance at the moment of intervention by the higher power, even when no overt oppositional element had been present before" (Stallybrass and White 1986, 16). To be clear, I don't mean to overstate the transformative potential of the carnivalesque in fiction, for it is written to package and sell novels. The upheaval that occurs in Baldwin's novel can be transformative for readers depending on their ability to empathize with characters and their feelings about the family as a unit and the American justice system.

Protesting racial profiling and false incarceration are transgressive acts that break, infringe, trespass, and violate dominant ideologies about African American men. By refusing to accept domination as a boundary to self-actualization, the transgressor repeatedly broaches the racial borders of the white world through bodily activity and verbal conduct. Encroaching on the dominant cultural values through language and physical aggression is thoroughly improper but tolerated as a temporary indiscretion because the dominant culture possesses the repressive apparatuses to restore preferred order.

In *Beale Street,* the suspension of conventional norms and the transgression of established borders and boundaries occur after Fonny is falsely accused and arrested for rape. Before Fonny is arrested, the Hunts and Rivers are two working-class Christian families in Harlem, New York. The parents are small business owners, laborers on a shipping yard, and secretaries in downtown offices. Their comfortable lives include dinner with friends, socializing in their parlors, and talking about their grandchildren's future. After Fonny is accused and arrested, the characters take up positions and make judgments about each other and his circumstances. The Hunt and Rivers families primarily meet to discuss the progress in Fonny's case and to ponder ways to alleviate Tish's stress during pregnancy and incessantly argue about who is responsible for his imprisonment: is it Tish, since Fonny was trying to protect her when he was arrested or the city for hiring racist police officers to patrol African American neighborhoods? In jail, Fonny enters and tries out a new established symbolic order, where notions of freedom are determined by accepting that one can be physically imprisoned but mentally free, and that since he is innocent he will be exonerated in time to see the birth of his child. As with all carnivals, the upheaval subsides. At the novel's conclusion, everyone makes peace with the reality that exonerating Fonny is ongoing and everyone is expected to return to the normal or real world outside, the normality of which has been confirmed and affirmed by the safe experience of briefly escaping to a marginalized world. Still, we may take something from the carnivalesque in Baldwin's novel—such as a vision of a more equitable and humane world or empathy for those who transgress the norms of the white world. Baldwin's grammar generates an amusing spectacle where meaning is subverted and, of course, boundaries between the secular and profane are transcended.

Similar to camp, the carnivalesque is a sensibility and a language that follows from an expression akin to Bakhtin's grammatical jocose—whereby grammatical order is transgressed to reveal erotic and obscene or merely materially satisfying counter-meaning. Bakhtin states language usage, such as punning, transgresses or trespasses borders and boundaries. It provokes laughter, but, in substituting the standard discursive pattern with a new order of words and images, it also "reveal(s) erotic and obscene or merely materially satisfying counter meaning" (Stallybrass and White 1986, 10–11). Thus, the relationship between camp and the carnivalesque is observed in the codes that Baldwin uses in *Beale Street.* In his seminal research on the performance of gender and sexuality, Thomas E. Yingling argues for a reading of the codes in gay male writing that uncover the "system of culturally determined codes that gay men have historically had access to by virtue of their biological identities yet have been unable to employ as they might because those codes denied validity to their experience as homosexuals. Thus, gay writers seem often to have found literature less a matter of self-expression and more a matter of coding" (1990, 25). While, as Yingling points out, African American gay activist Joseph Beam made himself from "scratch," which means fostering "style . . . as an attitude, a reaction to oppression, a way of being perceived as less oppressed, a way of feeling attractive when we are deemed unattractive," Baldwin's code is the style in which he writes to get a reaction not only to the stated action or completed task, but to the utterance (336). By "making these 'culturally determined codes' self-conscious and conspicuous, gay writers destabilize them and open them to analysis and criticism" (Bergman 1993, 94). For example, when the narrator switches from standard English to dialect that is exaggerated and littered with profanity, the reader is forced to take note.

Similar to the blackface African Americans on the Zulu float, Baldwin's style "is the buffer between the private erotic world and the public civil world" (1993, 94). At times the language is crass and vulgar and intended to humiliate and emasculate. These absurd linguistic games produce suspense and hilarious repercussions as readers (or audiences) react to, and sometimes participate in, the character's performance. Some of the narratives in the novel are highly provocative. In one scene, for example, the narrator contextualizes Fonny's spitting assault on Tish (when they were gradeschool age) in non-judgmental language that he is simply displaying his crush on her. In another scene, Baldwin depicts love making between Fonny's parents in playful sadomasochist (a contradiction in terms) language that broaches on blasphemy. During sex, Mrs. Hunt cries, "'Oh Frank, let me bring you to the Lord,' Mr. Hunt responds, 'Shit woman, I'm the going to bring the Lord to you. I'm the Lord.' And she'd start to crying, 'Lord, help me, help this man. You give him to me. I can't do nothing about it. Oh Lord, help me.' And he'd say, 'The Lord's going to help you, sugar, just as soon as you get to be a little child again, naked, like a little child'" (Baldwin 1974, 14). The grammar in Baldwin's novel generates an amusing spectacle where meaning is subverted and, of course, transcends boundaries between the secular and profane, poking fun at the distinctions between them. In *Problems of Dostoevsky's Poetics,* Bakhtin claims that the parodying of religious structure and language and the implicit critiques of religion actually strengthens the law of the church by providing individuals an outlet to voice their discontent. After their parodic performances, Mrs. Hunt returns to behaving according to the laws of the church by reading the Bible and attending religious services, and Fonny and Tish return to daydreaming about their future together.

Baldwin advances traditional performances of black masculinity within and without black culture. It is in this critique that the carnivalesque occurs through language practices. Similar to *Tar Baby*'s concern with how racialized discourses create a discursive chasm between African American men and women, *Beale Street* is concerned with the role that African American female characters play in African American male subjectivity construction. The African American female characters decide if and to what extent they want to support or include the African American male characters in their lives. Two factors govern their decisions—the significance of the family and the church to their happiness and how they experience social oppression. The major critical problem in assessing women's role in male subjectivity construction in this novel (and it is one that permeates most of his fiction) is that regardless of how often Baldwin criticizes patriarchal institutions, he continues to revisit the African American family and church as a site where men and women struggle for self-definition and strive to coexist and work toward common goals. Although Baldwin recognizes the flaws in both institutions, the family and the church provide a context for readers to examine how men rely on women for emotional support. While Baldwin's women characters are aware of the privilege and authority men possess in families and churches (men who are suffering are their family members), some of the women refuse to suffer as a consequence of patriarchal oppression. While some of Baldwin's African American female characters seek salvation as defense against racial oppression, others perceive the family unit as protection for black male subjectivity constriction. Regardless of where they search for refuge, they adopt a critical stance that is both conscious and political.

•

> Given the black church's typical stance on homosexuality, some might view this avowal of Christianity as an instance of false consciousness. I argue, however, that these black gay[s] and lesbians are employing disidentification insofar as they value the cultural rituals of the black worship service yet resist the fundamentalism of its message.
>
> —E. PATRICK JOHNSON, "'QUARE STUDIES,' OR (ALMOST) EVERYTHING I KNOW ABOUT QUEER STUDIES" (2005, 144)

Although *Beale Street* doesn't have any gay characters, Baldwin's gay sensibility is evident from his use of disidentification as a strategy to highlight the complex relationships that characters maintain with patriarchal institutions, such as the family and fundamentalist church, and his employment of the carnivalesque to emphasize the upheaval that racial oppression introduces in African American families. The circus that Fonny's arrest produces is most evident in his own home. Here, readers see Baldwin's camp sensibilities in how Fonny's mother responds to his incarceration in over-the-top religious exaltations. His mother's and sisters' response to his innocence is a combination of indifference and skepticism to the point of disbelief. Instead of confronting the upheaval that Fonny's arrest introduces in their family and supporting Tish's campaign to prove his innocence, the Hunt women become more insolent and withdrawn. They believe that Fonny's incarceration is a result of his sinful ways as opposed to racism in New York, for God protects the righteous even in an unjust society. They choose to disidentify with the widely held belief that African Americans are racially profiled and falsely imprisoned because it doesn't match their deeply held religious beliefs that God protects those who believe in Him and the biblical word. They rationalize that God imprisoned Fonny in an attempt to save his soul and force him to repent for fathering a child with Tish. Mrs. Hunt refers to Tish and her family as sinners for having a child out of wedlock and warns Tish that she will never consider her as a daughter-in-law—even if she marries Fonny. Selfish and wrapped up in the rules and routine of the church, she does not tend to the needs of her family. Mrs. Hunt's lack of compassion for Fonny is only rivaled by his sisters who discover ways to demean and blame him for his predicament and the turmoil in their family. While he is in jail, they stoke each other's discontent for him because he refuses to regularly attend church services. Like their mother, they pray that God will strengthen them and, whether Fonny is released or not, end the circus of Fonny's imprisonment. Because they take their Christian faith literally, they are divorced from reality. Prideful, self-righteous, and self-important—much like the Pharisees that deny Jesus as the Messiah—they are more interested in keeping the laws of the Old Testament than serving or helping those in need as Jesus did.[6]

In Baldwin's carnivalesque fictional society, the women identify with the fundamentalist church but forgo Christian values whenever they don't meet their present needs or desires. Harris contends that for these women "Questions of morality are no longer simplistically two-sided; for these women, more complexity develops, and there is ample room for extenuating circumstances" (1985, 130). When Mr. Hunt's language transgresses the father/daughter boundary—"If you was any kind of women you'd be peddling pussy on the block to get your brother out of jail instead of giving it away for free to

6. Although he recognizes the influence and significance of Christian teachings to African Americans and African American culture building, Baldwin criticizes their oppressive uses historically (in American slavery), in his life (see *The Fire Next Time*), and in the African American community (see his novel *The Amen Corner* where the church members embrace negative logic in regard to who is a sinner and who is righteous).

all them half-assed faggots who come sniffing around you with a book under their arm"—Baldwin shows how carnivalesque language (riddled with racial and misogynistic codes) determines the body, making it accessible. However, how readers interpret carnivalesque language our own positionality determines how we see "age" and "ugliness" as undesirable attributes through our eyes, more than through his. By extension, then, my readings interpret the language as imbued with fear, loathing, and feelings of disgust and horror.

Also, Baldwin's gay sensibility is evident in the specific attention he gives to male language use that bonds men and invites women to experience homosocial behavior as an activity and performance that doesn't exclude women or encourage misogyny. Laughing and speaking fluent English and Spanish to the waiters, Fonny speaks a male language that isn't dominant or oppressive but open and welcoming to men and women who want to relish with him in ethnic diversity and life as an adventure to discover a self that is individual but connected and reaches across gender lines. The African American self that Fonny's language reveals isn't a parody of masculinity that simply reaffirms white anxieties or fulfills white fantasies about the African American self. In addition, the African American masculine language that Baldwin presents with Fonny contests Luce Irigary's second wave feminist theory of a hegemonic male language as "rigid, clarity, univocity, and non-contradiction" that all men use to expresses specifically male or masculine values (male body, male sexuality, and male unconscious). Through Tish's reflection on watching Fonny interacting with other men, Baldwin responds to Irigary's notion that male language represses, denies, and covers up the values that define women's sexuality and their unconscious: "many women—perhaps most women, feel, in this warmth and energy, a threat. They think they feel locked out. The truth is that they sense themselves in the presence, so to speak, of a language which they cannot decipher and therefore . . . so far from being locked out, are appalled by the apprehension that they are in fact, forever locked in" (Baldwin 1974, 49). Masculine discourse reminds Tish that she is in the presence of the man she loves and the man who loves her. She hears the masculine discourse (because she loves Fonny), but she can't decipher it because it is only intelligible to men, for it is intended to unite them.

To further highlight the upheaval that false incarceration introduces into African American families, Baldwin depicts the Rivers family as loving, hardworking, respectful, and politically active. Mr. Rivers works on the docks in the garment district, loading and unloading merchandise and running errands for his boss. Mrs. Rivers is the nucleus of the family and is socially and politically active, and her daughters are equally aware of the oppressive conditions under which African American people live. Although the Rivers family doesn't attend church regularly, they exhibit Christian values when they agree to help Fonny pay for a lawyer to fight the charges against him—suggesting a definition of Christianity that includes an idea of family that extends beyond bloodlines: adoptions, in-laws, neighbors, and the fellow men and women one comes into contact with every day. Unlike the Hunts, who regard the social constraints of family as a hindrance to spiritual salvation, the Rivers are ambivalent toward the fundamentalist church as a vehicle for salvation, and they turn to the family unit for protection. As Tish fights for Fonny's release from jail, the Rivers remind her about doctor appointments, help her locate witnesses, and encourage her to remember his virtues. Symbolically, the use of their name can be representative of rebirth or baptism. Fonny was once lost, but the Rivers family found and accepted him. While the Rivers family is not perfect (they instigate a couple of arguments with the Hunts over Fonny's imprisonment) they do represent a utopian ideal of an African American family. They continuously and tirelessly work together to meet each other's needs and fight for Fonny's freedom. About the Rivers family, Trudier Harris writes that "theirs is a morality of action, which demands that the individual does what he or she can to further the case of a loved one and to see the will of God manifested on earth; there is no philosophy of sitting around waiting for the Lord's will to be done" (1985, 130).

Baldwin casts the Hunt family as foils to the Rivers family. Unlike the Hunt women who want to leave Fonny in the wilderness of the prison system, the Rivers family notices the redemptive qualities in him and is willing to fight for his release. In particular, Earnestine Rivers, a brave, insightful activist, accepts the difficult task of exonerating Fonny and keeping Tish grounded and realistic. Baldwin depicts Earnestine as a flawed but venerable character with a commitment to social justice. She is also vulgar, however, when she feels attacked or witnesses her loved ones being attacked and will lash out with vile words. Baldwin equips Earnestine with a double consciousness that is informed by the African American tradition of social activism and the dominant culture's practices of patriarchal oppression. On the one hand, she discovers the damning information that the white officer who arrested Fonny also killed a twelve-year-old African American boy, and she constantly reminds Tish to consider the possibility that the fight for Fonny's freedom might fail. On the other hand, Earnestine's vulgar language thickens the novel's carnivalesque atmosphere. After Mrs. Hunt insults Tish, an angry and pained Earnestine calls her a "sick, filthy, dried-up cunt" and demands that she and her daughters immediately leave the Rivers' residence (Baldwin 1974, 90). These misogynistic words are horrible coming from a man, but from a woman they not only violate the shared understanding that women hold about how deeply sexism hurts, but they also verbally transgress and disfigure the female body. Besides enforcing patriarchal authority, Earnestine locates herself within a masculine discourse that devalues women and womanhood and ascribes women's mistakes or shortcomings to the absence of a penis. Earnestine's vulgarity is carnivalesque in that Baldwin uses it to elucidate how even an admirable activist has a double consciousness informed by the dominant culture's patriarchy.

•

> In prison, the black heterosexual male is often transformed into a vulnerable or victimizing gay man, at least in provisional, situational terms, his body marked by ad hoc homoeroticism.
>
> —MICHAEL ERIC DYSON, "HOMOTEXTUALITIES: THE BIBLE SEXUAL ETHICS" (2004, 379)

Baldwin explores innocence as institutional practices that violate African American men's civil rights and that lead to the high incarceration rate of African American men (Baldwin 1989, 119). In a 1972 interview, Baldwin stated that the disproportionate number of incarcerated African American men not only speaks to the persistence of racism in America but undermines the high ideas that America was founded on—liberty, justice, and democracy. As an effective tool of systematic racism, the penal system continues to alienate African American men from their families and remove them from their rightful place within their families and communities.[7] He writes that "African Americans are the people in prison. What do you think is happening in prisons all over America? Why do you think it's happening?" (119). Baldwin's condemnation of the justice system addresses the open-ended conclusion to *Beale Street.* In response to the question, "Is [Fonny] in prison for a limited term or is it one of those indefinite things?" Baldwin says, "Ask the American people that, don't ask me" (109). The unfairness and inadequacy of the justice system is at the core (or is the core) of the often plausible but roughly plotted *Beale Street.* Crucial to Baldwin's elucidation of these often discussed but not thoroughly explored social issues (racial profiling and false imprisonment) is the toll that social oppression takes on African American male subjectivity and the enormous burden it places on African American women. Baldwin conveys this with quotes like "They got us in a trick bag, baby. It's hard, but

7. *The New Jim Crow: Mass Incarceration in the Age of Colorblindness* by Michelle Alexander and *Against the Wall: Poor, Young, Black, and Male* edited by Elijah Anderson cite government and academic studies that prove that the incarceration rate of African Americans has increased significantly since 1972.

I just want for you to bear in mind that they can make us lose each other by making you try to protect me from it. You see what I mean" (118). Internalized racism turns into a consuming anger that engulfs African American men and women. African American men's high incarceration rates don't simply prevent them from reaching their goals and taking care of their families, it also reshapes how they eventually learn to see themselves.

Throughout the novel, Baldwin presents readers with scenes of African American men interacting with and confiding in other men or suffering alone in silence. In the scenes, the male characters paint pictures or are contextualized in heart-wrenching narratives about being victimized, feeling unworthy, being alienated from mainstream American society, and being persecuted by white authority figures. Tish looks on as Fonny's childhood friend Daniel Carthy tells about the night that the police falsely accused him of stealing a car. As a result of being wrongly convicted, Daniel is sentenced to prison, where he is repeatedly physically and sexually assaulted. As Daniel describes the incident to Fonny, he articulates the distress and hopelessness he felt when the police arrested him. "They said I stole a car. Man, I can't even drive a car, and I tried to make my lawyer—but he was really their lawyer, dig, he worked for the city—prove that" (Baldwin 1974, 85). "Got me off the stoop" and "searched me" and "nailed me on the car—that car I ain't even seen yet" (89–91). Repeatedly, Daniel tells Fonny that his thoughts were on his mother; here again Baldwin highlights African American male subjectivity as being concerned with African American women "because she couldn't do nothing for herself and she'd start to worry about me, and wouldn't nobody know where I was!" (89). Listening intently and patiently, Fonny empathizes with Daniel with the words "I don't know" and nodding his head, "his face still, his eyes very dark" (89). Although Fonny is younger than Daniel, he has been homeless and slept in parks and is more aware of life on the streets. As Daniel's friend and confidante, Fonny wants to reassure him that they will outlast, but Fonny (Baldwin says this in an interview) knows that "the police in this country" have great "authority over the lives of black people and poor people" (1989, 94). Baldwin's purpose isn't to explore the possibilities of hope for African American men to radically transform their social conditions through activism, violence, or the legal system. The likelihood that African American men can transform their material conditions through institutions established by dominant culture is optimistic, but it overlooks the "fact of blackness" in the discursive divide where black male identity is always subjected to hegemonic discourses. During this event, black men are always under the threat of erasure.

Baldwin gives readers the opportunity to reflect on the black male body as a grotesque embodiment of the liminal space between the black and white worlds. Because the grotesque black male body is utterly transgressive, it is completely liminal. It is the border and margin of the white and black world. The grotesque black male body is never individual, for it transgresses every isolating boundary:

> Contrary to modern canons, the grotesque body is not separated from the rest of the world. It is not a closed, completed unity; it is unfinished, outgrows itself, and transgresses its own limits. The stress is laid on those parts of the body that are open to the outside world, that is, the parts through which the world enters the body or emerge from it, or through which the body itself goes out to meet the world. This means that the emphasis is on the apertures or the convexities, or on various ramifications and offshoots, the open mouth, the genital organs, the breast, the phallus, the potbelly, the nose. (Taylor 2012, 79)

The grotesque black male body cannot be figured in proper language.

The characters' carnivalesque language is not structured by the rules of logic, nor does it conform to generally accepted norms of expression. Incorrigibly transgressive in words as well as deeds, the characters' discourse tends toward scandalous and eccentric language that is obnoxious and offensive to the dominant culture. This linguistic peculiarity is revealed in the indecency, vulgarity, and uncertainty of the characters' verbal conduct. The characters speak against racial oppression and white privilege in the presence of the dominant culture in the form of chants, picketing, verbal abuse, and insults, and they employ oppressive oppositions to bring about the release of repressed emotions. The double edge of abusive and insulting words suggests that such language is inevitably both destructive and creative. In addition, the occasion of carnivalesque discourses appears in its irresponsible profanity. Language is neither proper nor clean; it is improper and dirty. Its words seem to be indecent, indiscreet, impure, and strained. Such soiled language is usually quite earthy and tends to be sexual and scatological. Like the grotesque body that utters it, this language seems foul and is out of bounds. Filthy words inevitably dissolve restrictive limits and break down constrictive boundaries. Though undeniably destructive, such violation is also productive. By discharging what previously had been repressed, transgressive discourse release creative energy.

Baldwin captures the carnivalesque as African American men expressing frustration with oppressive institutions and ideologies. The oppressed black male body is supposed to instantiate for readers the conditions of black male subjectivity in all its functions. Baldwin's African American male characters cry for themselves and their loved ones, shout curse words at the system, sweat from physical exertion, and vomit racism. This catharsis doesn't change anything, but it does give readers a chance to understand the frustration. Hank M. Levin and Clive R. Belfield explain that although the notion of providing for one's family is "genderless, except for their deliberate usurpation and control by a chauvinistic power structure," African American men still measure their own self-worth against social standards that are designed to exclude them (2005, 220). African American fathers expect the "material and social psychological manifestations of capital to be their special domain and responsibility" (220). Since they only have minimum wage jobs, it is difficult to provide for their families and afford Fonny's legal fees.

The white power structure oppresses Frank and Joseph in primarily two interrelated ways: they are subjected to social oppression, and they can't afford legal services. Inasmuch as they imagine being part of American society, they are not. "It is thus that in much of our humor lies a strain of irony that is strongly flavored with hostility for society, as well as for ourselves" (Bergman 1993, 27). In an attempt to ameliorate their feelings of helplessness, they joke about their financial instability and about committing crimes to pay Fonny's lawyer's fees and bail bond. Similar to the laughter that Morrison's Sweet Home men share over their absurd positionality as slaves, Frank and Joseph use humor as a safe way to deal with their sense of emasculation. In statements of anger followed by jokes underlined with empathy, Mr. Hunt and Mr. Rivers express how they lack money to hire a committed and compassionate attorney for Fonny.

At times in the novel, the manner in which the men communicate with each other is so outrageous and ridiculous that one questions Baldwin's motivations for representing them as less than reflective and regretful for Fonny's predicament. Their communication highlights the arbitrariness of cultural conventions—for what are appropriate ways to respond to racial oppression? At one point in the novel, Fonny's father succumbs to his emotions and Tish's father jokingly reminds him that his feelings aren't the issue; Fonny's freedom is the focus. "Tears drop onto the table, trickling down from the palms with which he has covered his face. Joseph watches: the tears drip from the palm, onto the wristbone, to splash—with a light, light, intolerable sound—on the table. Joseph does not know what to say—yet." Joseph responds, "This ain't no time for crying, man" (Baldwin 1974, 160). The language has a dual function: black compulsory heterosexuality and patriarchy is reaffirmed as the mechanism through which they are compelled to address the reality of their predicament, and Fonny's incarceration heavily weighs on them. Fonny's father commits suicide, a terrible incident that Baldwin employs in this novel and *Another Country* to communicate the extreme reaction to and consequence of African American male oppression. Their influence and authority is further weakened by their inability to lead the family; thus, everyday life in the streets reminds them of the reality of the shackles of racial oppression. Baldwin doesn't suggest any possibilities or hope for the characters to transform their social conditions. Instead, readers learn how men feel guilty for not being able to provide for their families and how hopelessness drives them to commit crimes that they probably wouldn't under different circumstances. In a desperate attempt to raise money for Fonny's bail and legal fees, "Joseph is coldly, systematically, stealing from the docks, and Frank is stealing from the garment center and they sell the hot goods in Harlem, or in Brooklyn" (107). Unlike his and Tish's fathers, Fonny refuses to search for his self-worth in compulsory hegemonic masculinity or in the American dream.

Baldwin instructs readers to notice that the white gaze and homosocial behaviors extend behind the prison walls by briefly submerging readers in Fonny's experiences while incarcerated with domination and subordination. Concurrent with the most recent research on prison, masculinity, and sexuality, Baldwin suggests that compulsory heterosexuality emerges in prisoners' attempts to meld the prison to reflect social institutions beyond its walls. In "Rape and the Prison Code," Terry A. Kupers states that prisoners engage in sexual activities for a variety of reasons that include protection from predatory inmates, to experience affection from another human being, and to prove their manhood to others. While the first two reasons typically involve some form of consent (whether it is as a response to an immediate or perceived threat or gay men fostering relationships behind bars), the final reason emphasizes hegemonic masculinity expressed as violence and sexual domination. In this performance of hegemonic masculinity male prisoners recreate gender roles through imagining that their masculinity can only be realized in relation to the idea of the feminine as weaker and subordinate. The sexual crime of prison rape itself is undoubtedly bound to the establishment of intermale authority within the wider practices of homosocial relations, and it reflects and reproduces men's domination of women in the heterosocial world behind prison walls. Fonny is assaulted but he isn't raped: "He is placed in solitary for refusing to be raped. He loses a tooth, again, and almost loses an eye. Something hardens in him, something changes forever, his tears freeze in his belly. But he has leaped from the promontory of despair" (Baldwin 1974, 162). In a word, while incarcerated Fonny is as vulnerable as any black male—whether gay or heterosexual. Maybe the men who attempt to rape Fonny think of themselves as straight and him as weak or feminine, which reveals the confusing pliability of constructions of masculinity and sexuality in the service of hegemony. Fonny fights them—defends himself and maybe even his sexuality—but he doesn't judge them because he sees himself in them and his plight in their condition.

Baldwin still allows readers to imagine sexual desire, but he wants them to imagine same-sex desire as self-love. Although Tish's absence from the scene causes readers to question her narration of the events, readers are pulled into decoding the scene of Fonny masturbating while trying to recall the number of days he's been in solitary confinement. Neither the prison guards who escort Fonny to the shower nor the other black men who suffer with him in silence spark his arousal. Instead guards and prisoners serve as a backdrop to a larger issue that Fonny contemplates, which is that individuals are positioned in a discursive divide or nexus of discourses that further situate us in characteristics as differences (race, class, gender, and sexualities) as opposed to similarities.

The challenge, then, for African American men and women is to discover a discourse that enables them to cross the discursive divide without losing their sense of self. Finally, Fonny crosses this discursive divide through a sexual act of self-love that mentally transports him beyond the world of the prison. "Sex is a powerful mediator in transgressive contexts, since sexual encounters invoke uneasy tensions between consent, demand, resistance, and reciprocity, in which elements of domination, vulnerability, risk and safety all play a part" (Donnan and Magowan 2012, 3). Typically scholars identify transgressive acts as behavior that challenges social morals and expectations about what constitutes public and private behavior—for example sexual encounters in the streets during fairs and carnivals. I suggest that Fonny's masturbation scene is a transgressive act that pushes against the social beliefs that African American men are unlovable and are incapable of loving themselves. As he masturbates, Fonny's thoughts suggest that he believes that he is performing transgressive behavior: "He pauses, but his hand will not be still—cannot be still. He catches his lower lip in his teeth, wishing—but the hand will not be still. . . . It tightens, it tightens, moving faster, and Fonny sinks and rises" (Baldwin 1974, 151).

Throughout his transgressive sexual act, Fonny is overwhelmed with feelings of dissonance. "He wonders what the whole world, his world, is doing without him, why he has been left alone to die. . . . He cannot muster his defenses because he can't give himself no reason for being here" (151). Refusing to lose himself in the arbitrary discourses of innocence and romance that placed him in prison, Fonny steadies himself in his own sense of self. He reaches for himself. Lying on his back, stroking his penis with a cigarette in his mouth, Fonny loves himself. His position and the positioning of the obvious phallic symbols in this scene (one in his mouth and the other in his hand) suggest that Fonny is not only loving himself but metaphorically loving other men. His climax releases him from his feelings of disconnection for he "pretends that human arms are holding him" (152). Since we are told early in the scene that Fonny pushes Tish out of his mind and are given the placement of the phallic symbols, readers are free to consider Fonny as loving himself and other black men. Maybe Baldwin is suggesting here that African American men can only be free when they learn to do what Darieck Scott describes as "Black men loving black men"—literally or metaphorically. After this scene during a visit with Tish, Fonny states: "I'm beginning to see things I never saw before. I don't have any words for those things, and I'm scared" (152). He's "scared" but resolved with the thought that regardless of the outcome of his trial, his progeny will live on.

Similar to when carnival ends and the festive atmosphere that has animated the city for several months dies down, the novel ends with Fonny calm and resolute that he and the other Latino and African American men are not in prison for anything they have done (Baldwin 1974, 61). Fonny is as determined as Morrison's Sixo, who burns while thinking of his Thirty Mile woman and yelling, "Seven O!" Fonny tells Tish, "Baby. Baby. Baby. I love you. And I'm going to build us a table and a whole lot of folks going to be eating off it for a long, long time to come" (163). The image of the welcoming table emphasizes the different positions and roles of Leo Proudhammar and Fonny Hunt as African American artists/artisans vis-à-vis their communities. Fonny's commitment to build a welcoming table suggests the possibility of a new and sustaining relationship between the artist and the community (Scott 2002, 65). An appropriated image from Baldwin's *Tell Me How Long the Train's Been Gone,* the welcoming table leaves readers with the image of a dinner table where African American men and women come together to eat and feast.

CHAPTER 6

"Stop Loving Your Ignorance—It Isn't Lovable"

Tar Baby and the Rhetoric of Responsibility

> Now, it doesn't take any particular expertise to observe that one of the most characteristic features of our community is the antagonism between our men and women.
>
> —TONI CADE BAMBARA, "ON THE ISSUES OF ROLES," 2010

THE DOMINANT culture prescribes different work, clothing, rituals, language, and human nature for men and for women, thereby creating, enlarging, and making more salient various aspects of male-female difference. Because gender is visible, individuals invest and remember information through the prevailing gender schema. In fiction and nonfiction, African American writers engage gender performances in an attempt to explore how men and women's contrasting gender expectations create acrimony and resentment that is complex and not easily resolvable. For example, Toni Cade Bambara contends that while racist practices and ideologies destabilize African American institutions and communities and are a source of strife between African Americans, African American men and women should be more responsible for how they make each other feel and should always reciprocate the need to be loved and protected. In addition, Bambara argues that contrasting sociopolitical agendas and competing views on gender roles undermine their mutual desire to build strong families and viable communities that keep social and economic pace with the dominant culture and immigrant neighborhoods. Lastly, Bambara believes that African American men and women accuse each other of using sexist language that denies each other's experiences and reinscribes historical stereotypes about African American male and female identity and sexuality. After arguing that men and women have contributed to the instability in African American communities by embracing individualism and capitalism over liberation and community solidarity, Bambara proposes a solution that includes rejecting European models of family and community and reclaiming friendships between African American men and women. Bambara compares her emancipatory discourse to Father Divine's liberatory theology that centralizes notions of selfhood and "Blackhood" (2010, 109). She states that only when African American men and women get their "house in order" can they fight the real revolution against cultural genocide (109). Indeed, the discursive divide between African American men and women is substantial but reconcilable.

Close to ten years after Bambara described the gender conflict between African American men and women as a lack of comradery, Toni Morrison published *Tar Baby,* a novel that suggests that the strife between African American men and women is a result of their refusal to recognize that their lives are intertwined and their individual survival depends on their collective accountability. While Bambara proposes a nationalist ideology (class, community, or cultural solidarity) without gender oppression as a solution to the acrimony between African American men and women, Morrison advocates a gender neutral rhetoric of responsibility (which doesn't alleviate accountability or promote gender bias) that not only contends that men and women are equally culpable for the failure of their relationships, but that they also must be conscientious about the extent to which they charge each other with race and gender entitlement as a means to construct their own race, class, and gender identities. In *Tar Baby,* Son and Jadine are in love, however, they hold competing views on gender responsibility and community accountability. Most of their conflicting viewpoints are a result of contrasting backgrounds. Whereas Jadine grew up in an affluent family and attended prestigious colleges, Son comes from a working-poor community, joined the armed forces as a teenager, and traveled around the country working odd jobs whenever possible. Their contrasting perspectives reflect the various experiences by which their class and gender differences shape their subjectivity. In presenting characters who are aware of how they are positioned in society (uneducated black man v. educated black woman), Morrison's narrative suggests the discursive divide as Son's and Jadine's choice between internalizing dominant discourses and totally surrendering their autonomy, or resisting oppressive discourses and retaining their independence.

In an interview, Morrison represents the quandary in this way: Son "is determined to live in that briar patch, even though he has the option to stay with her and live comfortably, securely, without magic, without touching the borders of his life" (1994a, 47). Literally, briar patches are wild blackberry thickets with hard green knots that soften to light red before turning dark purple, sweet, and juicy. The delicious fruit is the reward for braving the sharp thorns. As a metaphor for the thorny paradox of the discursive divide, the briar patch represents the catchy and prickly ideologies that influence Son's conclusions about gender and community responsibility. Despite that he has the potential to travel through the brambles of life to realize his goals with few scratches and abrasions, Son embraces ideologies that reinforce manhood at the expense of womanhood. While he may deliver the incisive critique of society of the Black Panther Party, he enables a nationalist agenda by serving as both the blunt and protective African American man and unbending and hyper-masculine black man. The reward for navigating the sexist ideologies that surround Son is a loving relationship. Morrison states Jadine's dilemma: "will she go in that briar patch with him?" (1994a, 47). Staying in the briar patch includes accepting Son's worldview that hegemonic discourses about race and racism are elusive and persistent and impact every aspect of African American lives—including romantic relationships. On the other hand, for Son to leave the briar patch he must submit to hegemonic discourses, forgoing his sense of community, and embracing Jadine's upper-class lifestyle (which includes materialism).

In this chapter, I argue that Morrison builds on and advances earlier preoccupations with black subjectivity formation in relationships between African American men and women. By referencing fiction and critical essays that highlight the problems between African American men and women in romantic relationships, I contextualize Morrison's novel within larger conversations about subjectivity as a gender "performance of repetitious behavior within the limits of discursive gender requirements—in this case a performance of binary and univocal sex/gender within the framework of compulsory heterosexuality/romantic relationships between men and women" (Strozier 2002, 87). "Gender performance, in turn, creates the impression of a given or interior nature, a natural sexual disposition, which, like a textualized intention, is thought to be expressed in and by the performance" (87). Son and Jadine continuously locate each other within a strict gender discourse about expectations for men and women while refusing each other's attempts to locate them in a gender role and performance. While she envisages herself as more a career woman than a housewife, Jadine thinks Son should define himself in corporate America and embrace the role as provider and supportive husband. In contrast, Son perceives himself as a progressive antiestablishment activist as opposed to an aspiring industrialist or entrepreneur and believes that Jadine should embrace her socially defined position as a supportive wife and mother to their future children. In presenting Son's and Jadine's contrasting views on gender performances, Morrison highlights the extent to which Son and Jadine rely on traditional conceptions of gender roles. Son and Jadine repudiate gender roles for themselves, locate each other in gender roles, and blame each other for not fulfilling them. They believe that if African American men and women accept their roles as provider or caregiver, then African American communities will flourish, particularly in terms of economic stability and educational advancement. Thus, I argue that Morrison's experiences as an artist and woman prepared her to propose a rhetoric of responsibility that advocates African American men and women taking responsibility for how they make each other feel and how their behaviors shape African American culture and community.

Unlike Ntozake Shange's *For Colored Girls Who Have Considered Suicide When the Rainbow Is Enuf* and Michelle Wallace's *Black Macho and the Myth of the Superwoman,* which are primarily (but not only) concerned with exposing the patriarchal traditions and institutions that reproduce the material (physical) and economic conditions of oppression (for example, patriarchal beliefs about the difference between men and women and the laws and customs that govern marriage and motherhood), Morrison represents how men and women draw on gender and sexual politics to gain leverage in relationships and absolve themselves of having culpability in broken families and troubled communities. Morrison implies that the success of relationships depends on African American men and women taking responsibility and embracing the idea that they are each other's "ship and harbor."

GENDERED SUBJECTIVITIES

In *Tar Baby,* the discursive divide is Morrison's suggestion about the strife within African American relationships: African American men and women locate each other in gender roles and then blame each other for fulfilling them. Son's and Jadine's different backgrounds enormously shape their worldviews, and their interactions confirm their profound ideological differences. Son is an uneducated, unemployed, ex-sailor with dreadlocks who is wanted for murder. He prefers to work just enough to afford necessities and enjoy life in a small community as opposed to living in a large city and working for a large corporation. In contrast, Jadine is educated, an actress, a successful fashion model, and an aspiring businesswoman. Son criticizes Jadine for not understanding that oppression is created and sustained in a complex system of domination and subordination and for not recognizing that the consequences and severity of oppression and discrimination are different for individuals according to race, class, and gender. In contrast, Jadine believes that Son uses racial oppression as an excuse to not evaluate how he is complicit in his own oppression and that slavery is the past and African Americans have many options and opportunities in contemporary America.

Neither Son nor Jadine represent Morrison's own personal views on gender roles in relationships. This is evident in statements such as the "nuclear family is a paradigm that just doesn't work. It doesn't work for white people or black people. Why we are hanging on to it, I don't know. It isolates people into little units—people need a larger unit" (which I believe is community) (1994a, 260). Morrison advocates men and women replacing the notion of gender roles with responsibilities that privilege each individual's strengths not biological make up. Morrison states that

> It seems to me there were more excesses in women and men, and people accepted them as they don't now. In the black community where I grew up there eccentricity and freedom, less conformity in individual habits—but close conformity in terms of the survival of the village, of the tribe. Before sociological microscopes were placed on us, people did anything and nobody was run out of town. (125)

Judith Butler's scholarship on the individual's performance of gender supports Morrison's belief in its fluidity. Traditional gender performances don't convey a sense of a real or coherent gendered self, for Butler explains that such demands are artificial constructions that represent dominant expectations as opposed to authentic expressions of selfhood. Butler continues it is not that people are knowingly complicit in these performances—both actors and audience "come to believe and perform in the mode of belief" (1990, 141). However, as Butler notes, since performances are fluid and extemporaneous, individuals have the space to transform, subvert, or liberate themselves. Gender performance is transformative, subversive, and liberating. In particular to my argument, Butler posits gender performance as a transgression that can knowingly destabilize the "reality" of gender. In other words, subverting traditional gender roles by performing activities that cross restrictive race and gender boundaries expands one's sense of self. In contrast to gender bias language that assigns domestic roles to women and community roles to men, Morrison's gender-neutral rhetoric subverts gender roles by insisting on a perspective that isn't narrowly defined or performative or produced through acts and bodily performances of people as social actors.

Recent scholarship on the characters Son and Jadine represent my central concern with them as recognizable cultural archetypes and gendered subjects.

Sheila Radford-Hill argues that, traditionally, men have been the protectors or guardians of the community and women have been "cultural bearers and community builders" (2000, xx). For example, Karla Holloway describes Son as "representing natural truth" (1987, 126) and Jadine as "sacrific[ing] [her] feminine as well as racial self" (119). Doreatha Mbalia argues that Jadine expresses "hatred of Africa and all that is associated with it," while Son signifies a "people-class mentality" and a "sincere love for living things" (1991, 72, 76). Finally, James Coleman believes that Jadine represents "the antithesis of Black folk and community values" and Son is "a sensitive, warm man who possesses definite folk values and qualities" (1987, 65). While these scholars are equally critical of Son's and Jadine's defensive posturing and self-righteousness, I believe that more can be said about how and why Morrison equips Son and Jadine with uncritical and unreflective gender politics, nationalist rhetoric about community upliftment, and responsibility. Also, I believe that critics miss an opportunity to speak against violence and domination as a means to control black womanhood. Scenes where Son refuses to acknowledge Jadine as his equal (and equip her to offer support and camaraderie in the relationship) recognize the value of Jadine's educational achievements, critiquing patriarchy as a fragile discourse that depends on women's submission for vitality and longevity. In presenting Son as overbearing, well-intentioned, and verbally and physically aggressive toward Jadine, Morrison problematizes Son, who says, "I know all about women, you have to jack them up every once and a while. Make them act nice, like they're supposed to," (2006, 218). This is much like Hurston's Tea Cake, whose ego and sense of masculinity was so delicate that he resorted to physical violence "Not because her behavior justified his jealousy, but it relieved that awful fear inside him. Being able to whip her reassured him in possession. No brutal beating at all. He just slapped her around a bit to show he was the boss" (2006, 218). Morrison opposes Hurston's apparent attitude that we must accept such behavior; in her work men and women have equal responsibility in eradicating systems of domination and acquiescence.

Morrison's experiences as a woman/mother/writer prepared her to present the potential of African American men and women to defy historically, socially, and culturally situated categories of gender. Bravely, Morrison admits that she regrets some of the tough choices that she made while writing and "trying to keep career and family intact." "It was very difficult writing and rearing children because they deserve all your time, and you don't have it. . . . It's easy to overestimate and underestimate your ability to do both. I regret having had to work alone and raise children. But the other choices were unacceptable to me. I had to see if it was possible to be on my own" (1994a, 279). Morrison plays out her dilemma in *Tar Baby* through Jadine, who refuses any definition of feminism that embraces family and community responsibility. In exploring her dilemma, Morrison enters into the larger conversations about the function of feminism in the lives of contemporary black women. How do African American women continue the fight for family and community without disregarding the social, cultural, political, and ideological work of their foremothers? How do contemporary women "create a language and culture that signifies more than a lifestyle but also a political stance worthy of definition" (Springer 2002, 1067)?

These questions come to the surface in *Tar Baby* in the ease with which Jadine dissects definitions of daughter/mother—redefining it until it fits her purposes. This is reminiscent of the issue that Beverly Guy-Sheftall takes with Joan Morgan's willingness to avert her feminist gaze when it concerns chivalry. Guy-Sheftall writes, "What bother me about Morgan's statements, however, is an explicit rejection of fundamental feminist principles that I believe are cross-generational and still relevant" (2002, 1094). While Morrison figures out how to reconcile both career and domestic spheres, Jadine is unwilling to be the kind of woman who is "good enough for a child; good enough for a man—good enough even for the respect of other women" (Morrison 2004b, 281). For Jadine, a woman who regards motherhood and career as the same sphere or simply as ways of living as opposed to patriarchal conditionings, accepts being reduced to man's Other (de Beauvoir 2011, 163).

Much like her character Son, Morrison blames the dissention between African American men and women on the legacy of slavery. However, unlike Son, she resists any notion that it fixed African American men and women in eternal acrimony. Countering arguments from scholars such as Calvin Hernton, who argues that the "sexual alienation and conflict between black men and women" are a result of the illicit relationship between white slaveholders and black women (1971, 50), and Orlando Patterson, who contends that slave women "were doubly burden[ed] with the task of being both reproducer and worker" but slave men suffered an emasculation that persisted from their birth to their death (1982, 33), Morrison suggests that men and women experience a gender struggle that, at times, overlaps. In fiction and interviews, Morrison shows that "black men were emasculated by white men. . . . And black women didn't take any part in that" (1994a, 17). In *Beloved,* male and female slaves are raped, and in *A Mercy* Florens and the blacksmith are seen only as a labor force and contemplate the reality of suffering oppression for the rest of their lives. While Morrison outright rejects historians' implications that men had it rougher than women, or the reverse, she agrees that the legacy of slavery remains present in our thinking. However, we have agency: we decide the extent to which it governs our decisions in our own lives and the extent to which we will try to fit our family community structure in a Freudian paradigm that doesn't work. Morrison doesn't attribute her characters' lack of awareness of how they undermine their own relationships to the transcultural and transhistorical unconscious posited by Freudian psychoanalytic theory, but to the circumstances of the characters' lives as African Americans living in specific places and times.

As in real life, men and women aren't always aware of when their actions undermine their relationships. In some cases, class and regional differences complicate identity construction, as evident in scenes when Son and Jadine promote their own class values as the answer to their strife. Son and Jadine's major mistakes are their refusal to take responsibility for their failure, to see their responsibility in perpetuating ideologies about class and regional differences, and their failure to promote values and beliefs that cut across class, region, and gender differences. Morrison seizes these common occurrences in relationships to explore the possibility that men and women are so inscribed in their own gender reality that they are unaware that they perpetuate gender oppression. For instance, Jadine is correct to suggest that historically the lack of opportunities for African Americans restricted them to constructing a life around their communities. On the other hand, Son is correct to assert that being part of a community includes having pride in one's ancestry and not measuring one's self-worth by outside standards of beauty. This is the case with Jadine, who questions the sincerity of her Parisian boyfriend: Does he love her for who she is (accomplished woman) or what she represents in Paris (the exotic untamable Other)? Does marrying outside of her race make her culturally irresponsible?

Significantly, Morrison's *Tar Baby* comments on contemporary intellectual debates on issues such as gender equality and performance, ideas about community responsibility, the effects of the legacy of slavery on identity and subjectivity formation, gender roles in African American families, and the absence of African American men in workplaces. Also, *Tar Baby* engages critical discussions about lifestyle choices that exclude men and women from each other: professional career over family and community, singlehood or single parenting over marriage, and interracial dating and marriage. Besides critically evaluating the effects of lifestyles choices in African American relationships, *Tar Baby* implies that the strained relations between men and women are a result of their refusal to concede to their own responsibilities in the fragmentation of African American communities. Positioned along gender lines, *Tar Baby*'s main characters accuse each other of not having a firm commitment to the African American community.

•

> The writer who seeks to function within his race as a purposeful agent has a serious responsibility.
>
> —RICHARD WRIGHT, "BLUE PRINT FOR NEGRO WRITING" (1997, 102)

Community accountability is an important concept for Morrison. In an interview, she contended that artists have a responsibility to represent their communities' achievements and shortcomings, speak the secrets, and accept the right to make mistakes and evolve as an individual and a community. Through this process of airing dirty laundry, as Ismael Reed refers to this activity of public discussion, Morrison believes that the community will heal from the wounds caused by historical experiences and pain inflicted from within the community.

> An artist, for me, a black artist for me, is not a solitary person who has no responsibility to the community. It's a totally communal experience where I would feel unhappy if there was no controversy or no debate or no anything—no passion that accompanied the experience of the work. I want somebody to say amen! (1994a, 231)

In this role, the artist confirms and disavows community. As a provocateur, Morrison is an agent of social and cultural change. Her primary aspiration is to promote community solidarity and culture building across gender and sexuality lines by addressing debates and problems within communities and between classes and demonstrate that responsibility is meaningful to and of high importance for cultural survival. Morrison envisions a grammar of responsibility from multiple angles: being responsible, holding someone responsible, taking responsibility, to have responsibility, and being a responsible person. She creates a historical connection with people whereby community members can see their own lives and the lives of their ancestors reflected in the pages. She accomplishes this by drawing similarities between historical and contemporary lives. By showing how issues of individual identity, community formation, and cultural politics are reflective of the lives of African Americans in the United States, Morrison reveals a social consciousness that serves the community on a personal basis. Shouldering the responsibility to serve a community can be a difficult task.

As I will show below, Anders Nordgren's "social model of responsibility" and Morrison's rhetoric of responsibility are similar in their concern with the body as being naturally inscribed in social discourses. As a geneticist,

Nordgren examines the nature of and the extent of moral responsibility in genetics. More specifically, he is concerned with the ethics of human genetics research, and he problematizes scientists as engaged in a pure pursuit of knowledge, the social and ethical consequences of which are not theirs to contemplate, attempt to influence, or assume responsibility for. In his *Responsible Genetics: The Moral Responsibility of Geneticists for the Consequences of Human Genetics Research,* Nordgren argues that science communities share his perspective, and many accept that their obligations extend beyond technically sound science to morally good science. Besides revisiting theoretical discussions on the rhetoric of responsibility, Nordgren proposes a rhetoric of social responsibility that accounts for the relationship between individuals' ethics and their scientific research.

In recounting Nordgren's intricate and detailed models of responsibility, I pay particular attention to the aspects of the models that influence my argument that Morrison's rhetoric of responsibility suggests that African American men and women have a job or duty to deal with and take care of each other and their communities. This proposal locates agency—individual and collective—in both its collaborative and adversarial forms—at the center of family and community and other African American institutions. In doing so, the rhetoric of responsibility challenges sexism and stereotypes and other negative understandings and practices that thwart participation and feelings of community ownership that now frame much of contemporary African American communities. After summarizing models for contemplating responsibility within various contexts, I will provide a brief statement to show the relationship between models of responsibility and *Tar Baby* with the intention of drawing similarities between Nordgren's models of responsibility and Morrison's rhetoric of responsibility.

The confluence of Morrison's rhetoric of responsibility and Nordgren's model is most evident in their treatment of responsibility as a customary way of thinking and behaving as individuals and in communities. The various uses of responsibility in *Tar Baby* are reminiscent of Nordgren's tracing of responsibility back to seventeenth-century Europe and its etymological roots to the Latin word "respondeo," which means to have two different but related meanings. Nordgren provides two understandings of the term as "answering" (responding when called to appear before a legal court or tribunal) and "accounting" (as in one owes others due to promises or financial debt). In this sense, respondeo is a special form of accountability or answering to others. While responsibility literally means to answer when one is called to appear in a legal proceeding, it also means to respond, as in accounting for or accountability. Nordgren is more concerned with responsibility in a metaphorical sense that encompasses our responsibility for our actions toward others, as in "We owe things to other and others owe things to us (not always money but can have a direct link to money)," and the owing metaphor, as in "a state of moral obligation to" avoid conduct that might hurt another person (2001, 3). While one might not be hurt by his/her conduct, his/her choices will most likely impact the larger society or community.

The traditional use of responsibility is most evident in *Tar Baby* in the parent and adult-child relationships between Jadine and her aunt Ondine and uncle Sydney, who are also her adoptive parents. Although Jadine choses to believe that her appearance and intelligence earned her Valerian's and Margaret Street's trust and financial support, her aunt and uncle know that the Streets fund Jadine as repayment to them for their maid and butler service. In return, Ondine believes that Jadine should be concerned about more than herself and career. Ondine tells Jadine, "What I want from you is what I want for you. I don't want you to care about me for my sake. I want you to care about me for yours" (Morrison 2004b, 281). Defining responsibility in the traditional sense of "answering for" or "accounting to," Ondine asks Jadine to think about what it means to be a daughter who "cares about me for" her own personal welfare. Here, she is appealing to a traditional understanding of responsibility as being a financial debt or moral obligation that one pays. In this scene, the debt she is being asked to repay is not monetary but a moral one, which is her aunt and uncle's love and sacrifice. However, Jadine doesn't feel this responsibility toward her aunt and uncle, as she tells her aunt, "you want me to pay you back. You worked for me and put up with me. Now it's my turn to do it for you, that's all you're saying" (281). Jadine clearly resists any expectations that she should feel responsible for her family regardless of her relationship to them or their commitment to her.

Nordgren summarizes two traditional approaches for considering issues of responsibility before suggesting his own model. The traditional approaches distinguish between causal and social responsibility while Nordgren's model challenges this by proposing that not only does agency and society shape notions of responsibility but so do biological factors and overwhelming feelings to take responsibility for the state of affairs that one doesn't create. Proponents of the first traditional approach or agential model focus on the acting agent and deemphasize "the relation between individuals and society" (Nordgren 2001, 3). Rather than considering social norms and expectations that dictate or determine responsibility, agential proponents consider individual agency as the determining factor of responsibility. If an individual can show that he or she didn't cause an act to happen or an agent had an exceptional reason for causing a set of circumstances, then he or she is not morally responsible. Besides presupposing that an individual is essentially autonomous in society, proponents of the agential model argue that the "only morally relevant aspect is whether he or she caused or could've prevented the state of affairs or created a situation out of an act of 'omission'" (3). If an individual withheld vital information to influence a decision, then that individual is responsible for the act and situation—regardless of his or her intentions.

Proponents of the agential model don't distinguish between autonomy and "moral responsibility," for they believe that "moral autonomy" is "real responsibility" and is different from responsibility based on social conventions or expectations (or moral blame and praise and "social blame and praise") (3). Moral responsibility is a moral fact to be discovered, although established social norms make it difficult to do so. Son's perspective that Valerian is an imperialist who places his needs above the native inhabitants challenges the notion that an individual can imagine himself as an autonomous subject undefined by discourses in society. He does this when he reflects on Valerian as a capitalist who imagines himself as an autonomous subject with a subjectivity unshaped or impacted by social discourses—they can't control how they are interpreted. In thinking about Valerian, Son ponders Valerian's positionality: "he probably thought he was a law-abiding man, they all did, and they all always did, because they had not the dignity of wild animals who did not care where they defecated but they could defecate over a whole people and come there to live and defecate some more by tearing up the land" (Morrison 2004b, 203).

In contrast to the agential model centralizing autonomy, proponents of the social model argue that individuals within a society or community are responsible for the state of affairs regardless of their role in creating the conditions under consideration. "The individual self is socially constituted . . . the product of social influences. Without a community there is no individual self. And because this is the case, moral responsibility is socially determined" (Nordgren 2001, 4). In this sense, "moral responsibility is a social construction not a simple fact. It is ascribed by the community or a particular social group, not discovered" (4). Proponents of the social model maintain that "moral responsibility is not separate from socially ascribed responsibility" and accountability is never separate from socially inscribed responsibility (4). Individuals are fully responsible for the state of affairs that they don't directly or indirectly cause by an act of omission because social practices of blame and praise are linked to social roles. In other words, if an individual is in a social position where he or she has direct authority or supervision over an individual whose actions engender a crisis, the individual in the authoritarian or supervisory role will be blamed for causing or preventing the event.

This underscores the role of society and community in assigning blame. Nordgren writes that "responsibility is a social construction, not a simple moral fact. It is ascribed by the community or a particular social group, not discovered. The content of responsibility is what one's social position demands. If one does not live up to this standard, one may be blamed" for the act and outcome (4). Although he is a butler, Sydney believes his long-term service and status in the African American community grants him a significant amount of authority in the Street household. Part of his feelings of authority are class related, for he sees himself as progressive and intelligent; thus, he believes he is a "genuine Philadelphia Negro mentioned in the book of that name" who accepts that he has more in common with Valerian than with Son and the island inhabitants (Morrison 2004b, 284). However, when Valerian fires two servants for picking apples from the tree near his compound, Sydney angrily protests about the extra work that befalls him and Ondine, but Valerian's decision stands. Clearly, Sydney learns that community inscription supersedes class status and the responsibility that he feels for Valerian's house and family. Valerian shatters Sydney's class-consciousness by reminding him that he (Sydney) is a butler and his wife (Ondine) is just a "cook" in his house, and his social position in the house endows him with limited authority but a great deal of "blame" for problems there.

Nordgren suggests a model that accounts for the "metaphorical character of the concept of moral responsibility" that earlier models overlooked and builds on the strengths of both models' notions of causal or moral accountability as endemic to determining responsibility (5). He proposes a "modified social model" that underscores that the individual isn't independent of society and that s/he is a combination of social and biological influences. Unlike other models that assign responsibility according to underlining events that lead to an incident or one's ethical duty to intercede in preventing an event, Nordgren's model suggests that "responsibility is always a matter of ascribing or taking responsibility" between individuals and in communities (9). Taking responsibility means active "backward-looking" (individuals are held responsible for their past actions) and "forward-looking" (individuals are held responsible for their future actions). Individuals are always ethically and fundamentally responsible because their actions (regardless of intent) continue decisions of the past and shape the present state of affairs. Nordgren's modified social model suggests that "causal agency is relevant to moral responsibility but doesn't in itself determine it," "moral responsibility is ascribed and assumed by communities and individuals," and "individuals can ascribe or assume a moral responsibility that deviates from established social practices" (7). As a result of their different backgrounds, Son and Jadine have different relationships to African American culture. While Jadine possesses an academic knowledge about the disparities in African American communities, Son has first-hand knowledge that is a result of living in the South and various communities around the world. Unfortunately, regardless of their background, they ascribe to social practices that perpetuate gender oppression within the African American community.

Reading *Tar Baby* alongside Nordgren highlights the strategies that Western philosophers employ to leave out how "the self is affected by social identities such as gender, ethnicity, or race" (Alcoff 2006, 48). "Certainly Western philosophy's sustaining assumption has been that its domain covers only the universal and generalizable; particulars are left to the lowly sociologist" (48). The idea that one can discuss a topic as intricate as responsibility without considering the difference that race, class, and gender make is a frequent mistake in Western philosophical queries. Although he pushes against the philosophical tradition of presenting white subjectivity as an unbiased search for the Truth, Nordgren still theorizes dimensions of responsibility as occurring in an unbiased and homogenous group of scientists. I believe that how one imagines responsibility in a given context does, in fact, also depend on how one feels about the context. In other words, individuals are more likely to feel responsible for institutions they believe are responsible to them. The thought that responsibility can be defined without considering ethnicity and gender is problematic, as seen in race and gender lawsuits, reminding us that many people are denied promotions (not given responsibility) for superficial reasons.

Here is the relationship between Nordgren's moral responsibility and Morrison's rhetoric of responsibility: Nordgren suggests that responsibility is a dynamic activity that one has regardless of how one imagines him or herself. In other words, one can't say, "I am an autonomous person, and, therefore, choose not to have responsibility in a given situation" no more than one can say, "I am socially constructed but can choose when I don't want to have responsibility in a given situation." One always has a responsibility to shape, intercede, or influence events or improve the state of affairs. "We blame or praise someone because of something he or she has done. However, the ascription of responsibility may be forward-looking: In the future we will hold you responsible whatever happens" (Nordgren 2001, 9). Similar to Nordgren, who reflects on the relationship between autonomy, social expectations, and responsibility, Morrison considers responsibility to people and community. Regarding her responsibility to or for African American culture as an expression of self-governance, Morrison writes, "Freedom is choosing your responsibility. It's not having no responsibilities; it's choosing the ones you want" (1994a, 195). Morrison's expression of freedom is in her choice to be responsible to African American people and the community. While Nordgren reflects on responsibility in relation to society, individuals, and academic discourse communities, Morrison embraces the responsibility that she feels for celebrating African American life and addressing issues within the African American community. In short, Morrison's rhetoric of responsibility dictates that African American physical, emotional, and spiritual survival depends on the strength of their communities, which can only be realized through a commitment to the legacy of culture and community building.

MORRISON'S GRAMMAR OF RESPONSIBILITY

Morrison's rhetoric of responsibility suggests that African American men and women consciously or unconsciously locate each other in larger discourses about self-worth as opposed to learning about each other. In other words, they carry presumptions with them about each other that are based in racial stereotypes about African American men and women. While they continue to deal with the legacy of slavery as an assault on African American identity, family, and group consciousness, they are responsible for discovering a way to work together to construct subjectivities that will enable them to withstand the negative ideologies that divide them. Morrison argues that on the road to achieve a strong and unbiased community, they must first work on their own relationships and learn to be accountable for their own gender politics.

Crucial to Morrison's rhetoric of responsibility is how the lack of empathy and color-blind discourses permit African Americans to eschew their responsibilities to challenge sexism within their communities. According to Eduardo Bonilla-Silva, color-blind racism is the dominant racial ideology, as the mechanisms and practices for keeping blacks and other racial minorities at the bottom of the well changed "contemporary racial inequality is reproduced through new racism practices that are subtle, institutional, and apparently nonracial" (2010, 62). As a rhetorical practice, color-blindness considers African Americans' "contemporary status as the product of market dynamics, a naturally occurring phenomena, and intellectual cultural limitations" (2). At the core of color-blind rhetoric is liberalism as a philosophy and practice. According to Bonilla-Silva, as a philosophy, liberalism suggests the means by which the dominant culture promoted equality for the white middle class while excluding subjugated people from political, economic, and social power. As a practice, Bonilla-Silva argues that Europe never extended its belief in liberalism to third world countries under its control during colonization. The first frame, abstract liberalism suggests, the theoretical ways that the dominant culture uses social policies that were intended to desegregate society to oppose any further attempts to foster social and economic equality. For example, the dominant culture ignores "the multiple institutional and state sponsored practices behind segregation and . . . [is] unconcerned about these practices' negative consequences" (28). The second frame, which is naturalization is the rationalization of maintaining the order of society, as opposed to considering how it privileged whiteness at the expense of African Americans. Cultural racism, the third frame, relies on stereotypes "to explain the standing of minorities in society" (28). Stereotypes, such as blacks have too many babies, is why they are oppressed. Lastly, minimalization of it suggests that racism is an issue of the past, African Americans have gained a lot, and society has changed drastically.

Morrison focuses readers' attention on the frames of racism by highlighting the elusive but determining qualities of color-blindness in fiction. She argues that the fixed qualities of language are revealed within binaries and oppositions (whiteness is the opposite of blackness): whiteness "is mute, meaningless, unfathomable, pointless, frozen, veiled, curtained, dreaded, senseless, and implacable" and blackness is "dark, signing, Africanist presence" (1989, 58–59). These fixed qualities determine how the presence of black characters is interpreted in literary texts. Morrison writes,

> I wanted to identify those moments when American literature was complicit in the fabrication of racism, but equally important, I wanted to see when literature exploded and undermined it. . . . Much more important was to contemplate how Africanist personae, narrative, and idiom moved and enriched the text in self-conscious ways, to consider what the engagement meant for the work of the writer's imagination. (1992, 16)

Racialized language shapes American literature and the Africanist presence functions as a subtext in American literary texts. Similar to the postcolonial argument that Edward Said makes about European's textual representations of the Orient, Morrison argues that the presence of blackness in early American fiction provide writers with a standard against which to define themselves and construct white characters. The relationship between color-blindness and Africanism is that they are both rhetorical strategies that overwrite presence. Bonilla-Silva describes this relationship as naturalization. Steeped in discourses about the American dream and the presence of the Other, Jadine's negative attitude toward Son is a constructed narrative about black males grounded in historical stereotypes about their nature. Blinded by the bootstraps ideology (the dominant culture notices and rewards Others for working hard), Jadine underestimates the power and pervasive nature of racist discourses about black males, and she is unaware of the extent to which her own subjectivity is inscribed by stereotypes about them.

Empathy is a key component in Morrison's rhetoric of responsibility. I borrow my definition of empathy from Suzanne Keen's recent book *Empathy and the Novel* in which she defines empathy as "a vicarious, spontaneous sharing of affect, can be provoked by witnessing another's emotional state, by hearing about another's condition or even by reading" (2007, 4). Drawing from research in literary studies and cognitive psychology, Keen distinguishes between empathy and sympathy: "empathy[,] sometimes described as an emotion in its own right, we feel what we believe to be the emotions of others. This phenomenon is distinguished in both psychology and philosophy (though not in popular usage) from "sympathy, in which feelings for another occur" (5). Keen emphasizes the distinction between empathy and sympathy:

Empathy:	*Sympathy:*
I feel what you feel.	I feel a supportive emotion about your feelings.
I feel your pain.	I feel pity for your pain.

Morrison takes on the lack of empathy (not sympathy) between African American men and women by casting two characters who are very much in love but unable to connect or empathize across gender lines because they are either unable or unwilling to understand their relationship from the other gendered positionality. Morrison writes, "It would be nice, I think . . . to . . . have two attractive people . . . resolve their situation and hold hands and walk off into the sunset. . . . But there's something that, to me, is more vital than that—which is some kind of exploration of what the difficulty is in the first place. The problem has been put in the wrong place, as though it's a sexual battle, not a cultural one" (1994a, 134). The empathy is that Morrison understands men and women don't appreciate that it is a cultural battle that plays out along gender lines. The cultural battle Morrison refers to here is also a gendered one: a contest over whose gender suffered more, whose gender is privileged, and who should be the dominant voice.

Arguing that Morrison advocates a gender-neutral rhetoric of responsibility is not to claim that she rejects the notion that genders have different strengths. Morrison sees the value of men and women having multiple responsibilities, as she point out in an 1985 interview: that as a wife and mother she "tried hard to be both the ship and the safe harbor at same time, to be able to make a house and be on the job market and still nurture the children" (197). Thus, men and women shouldn't be asked to make a choice between home or career and that they should simply want to enhance their lives with "additional things rather than [be] conflicted by additional things" (197). Morrison imagines a society where men and women subvert expected gender roles. Furthermore, because gender performances are rarely perfect or absolute, the gaps between them provide spaces within which to enact alternatives. I am suggesting that Morrison's profound desire to shift or subvert gender roles speaks to African American sensibilities. Much is at stake here; and it is more—frankly—than a debate about the legacy of slavery or the place of gender roles in African American consciousness, important though that is. Rather what seems to be enacted is gesturing toward an emancipatory discourse that will give African Americans a way to remember and embrace our historical legacy without falling victim to or reenacting it in our personal lives and romantic and unromantic relationships. The distinction between gender bias language and a rhetoric of responsibility is crucial to mapping the shifting grounds of gender ideology in Morrison's work.

In *Tar Baby,* the lack of empathy and color-blind discourses create a discursive divide between Son and Jadine that manifest as misunderstandings and miscommunications: Son is unable to effectively explain and convince Jadine that she should be concerned with and conscious of the conditions of black people. In contrast, Jadine is unable to understand why Son interrogates systematic racism when he is powerless to change the dominant culture's beliefs and values. Son balks at the idea of working in corporate America because he believes that it perpetuates classism and racism while Jadine resents any suggestion that she should fulfill the traditional roles of womanhood. In presenting a black male character who is doubly defined (black and poor) outside of middle-class America and a black female character who locates herself outside black culture and community, Morrison suggests that the dissonance that African American men and women experience in their relationships is a result of a lack of empathy for each other. Morrison states that

> Many of the problems modern couples have are caused not so much by conflicting gender roles as by the other differences culture offers. That is what the conflicts in *Tar Baby* are all about. Jadine and Son had no problems as far as men and women are concerned. They knew exactly what to do. But they had a problem about what work to do, when and where to do it, and where to live. Those things hinged on what they felt about who they were, and what their responsibilities were in being black. . . . It was not because he was a man and she was a woman that conflict arose between them. (1994a, 147)

Son and Jadine have their own ideas of men's and women's responsibility in relationships. While they both proclaim to have awareness about how discourses function oppressively in the lives of African Americans (Jadine accepts that African American men like Son use it as an excuse to not pursue goals, and Son argues that black women like Jadine circumvent it with sexuality), they are unaware of the extent to which racialized discourses determine their ability to have a relationship. In other words, color-blindness creates tension through the duration of their romance, which distorts how they perceive each other's intentions.

Another example of how the lack of empathy and color-blind discourses create dissonance is when Son criticizes Jadine's lack of knowledge about the various ways European artists appropriated African culture and sensibilities (she thinks "Picasso is better than an Itumba mask. The fact that he was intrigued by them is proof of his genius, not the mask makers" [2004b, 74]). In the midst of an argument with Jadine, Son asks her, "what did they teach you about me? Did they tell you what I was like . . . you 'educated nitwit'?" (265) Son makes a significant point about how academic disciplines manage to separate the African intellectual or the "African body" from the creative expression or the "artwork," an important point that Simon Gikandi argues in "Picasso, Africa, and the Schemata of Difference" (2003, 36). Gikandi writes that Picasso's "oscillation between the African body and artwork appears to be the symptom of a deep and continuous engagement with the continent, the mythologies surrounding it, the fantasies it generated and ultimately the threat it posed to the idea of civilization that the modernist both wanted to deconstruct and yet secure as the insignia of white European cultural achievement" (36). However, cruelly, Son refers to Jadine as an "educated nitwit" (Morrison 2004b, 265). Besides belittling the years she put into studying art history, Son disparages the legacy of African Americans who fought for education: from Frederick Douglass and African Americans who fought to desegregate schools to those who contributed critical revisions to the European intellectual tradition and promoted the African diaspora. Son's perspective that African Americans who excel academically want to be white is culturally inaccurate and often made by conservatives such as John McWhorter, who claims in *Losing the Race* that in African American culture academic success is perceived as acting white. Scholars challenge this belief as being legitimate among children who typically feel isolated by teachers, other students, and administrators.

•

> My brothers . . . never understood they must represent half the world to me, as I represent half the world to them.
>
> —ALICE WALKER, *BROTHERS AND SISTERS* (2002, 203)

In *Tar Baby,* much of the gender politics plays out in the discursive divide of individual and community responsibility: Son and Jadine believe in the sanctity of community but they have different ideas on how to build, support, and protect it and the roles or positions that each person should occupy. Community responsibility is a particularly sensitive area for African Americans because it harkens the historical time when they were barred from mainstream activities and organizations. Civil rights were withheld from African Americans, as they were denied the right to participate actively in the electoral process. Despite the institutional barriers placed in their paths and their struggle to address social injustices and participate in democracy, African Americans historically were depicted as uninvolved and socially irresponsible in mainstream society and popular media. Such assertions are troublesome, as they overlook the many ways in which African Americans engage within their own racial community. Furthermore, the literature fails to account for institutional barriers such as segregation and the denial of voting rights that prevented many from being as involved.

Historically, African Americans have relied on their collective efforts as a racial group to improve their social economic plight in society. Driven by the perception that American institutions are inherently racist and are unlikely to respond to their needs, African Americans have traditionally worked together to address concerns and issues. The impetus for social responsibility among community members is rooted in historical and material circumstances that stress success through collective group efforts. African Americans promote community responsibility as more than simple charity work or volunteering, but instead trumpet it as a means of essential racial uplift or community caring. Evidence of this in *Tar Baby* is observed in Son sending money to Soldier, a friend and father figure, for eight years "to take care of him" (Morrison 2004b, 248). As a gesture of reciprocity, Soldier saves a majority of the money orders just in case Son needs them and also to protect him from anyone who might start talking and "turn the law out on account of that other business" (248). Morrison offers that Son and his friends intentionally instill a collective consciousness and sense of community responsibility through formal and informal efforts and points out that the ethos of community responsibility, which is so heavily stressed within the African American community, is in utter contradiction with larger society's individual ideology.

Although the discourses that separate African American men and women are much more complex than Morrison depicts in *Tar Baby,* her novel is significant since we can use it to contemplate how the discourses circulate in the community and strategies that African American men and women can draw on to negotiate the discursive divide. Also, we can use Morrison's novel to explore gender oppression as not only the primary form of domination for women but also the fundamental process by which African American men are relegated to lower-class status. *Tar Baby* illuminates the intersections of race, class, and gender oppressions and the price for not embracing a rhetoric of responsibility that considers the multiple ways in which all African Americans are menaced by hegemonic masculinity.

The novel opens with Son, a free spirit, stowed away on a boat. Readers develop a context for him from his thoughts about the boat and its occupants. Son disapprovingly comments on the lavishness of the vessel and the vacationing women occupants' attitude that suggest their wealth. By centralizing Son's critical perspective, Morrison equips him with not only a Marxist perspective on wealth, classism, and community but also uses him to represent vernacular strategies for outsmarting symbolisms of power and dominance. Within the first quarter of the book, readers learn that Son is intelligent, resourceful, and reflective—he isn't mean spirited but definitely more concerned with his own self-preservation. Like a trickster figure, who relies on wit and rhetoric to outmaneuver larger and ferocious animals, Son gains the confidence of Jadine and her family before he outsmarts, misleads, and ultimately divides them. He intentionally conceals his identity, for he is a fugitive who has been on the "run for eight years" who relies on "documented identities . . . and a few undocumented ones" to travel from the United States to the Caribbean. Son imagines that he has a true Self to protect. "The him that he never lied to, the one he tucked in at night and the one he did not want to die. The other selves were like the words he spoke—fabrications of the moment, misinformation required to protect Son from harm and to secure that one reality at least" (139). Although Son's full name is William Green, the narrator identifies him throughout the story as Son—as in somebody's son. This nickname presents him as the everyblackman, meaning a representative or spokesperson for the material experiences of all African American men (like Ralph Ellison's *Invisible Man*). On the other hand, by not using Son's given name throughout the novel (and giving him an alias), Morrison participates in the African American vernacular tradition of naming, and she signifies on her novel *Song of Solomon* in which naming marks male protagonists' journeys of responsibility: from illiteracy to literacy, childhood to manhood, and individual to community member. Unlike the protagonist in *Song of Solomon* who realizes a sense of self at the novel's resolution, readers of *Tar Baby* are left to decide if he achieves this.

A theme that resounds throughout Morrison's works is her concern with the tendency to label women as strong or fearless simply because they defy or speak out against social conventions. Morrison celebrates women's ability to become strong, healthy, and successful after suffering extreme misfortune. She writes, "If women just stand up straight for thirty days, everybody goes, Oh! How Brave! I think we are too accustomed to women who don't talk back or who use the weapons of the weak. . . . Naggin. Poison. Gossip. Sneaking around instead of confrontation" (2008b, 78). In contrast to her characters Sethe in *Beloved* and Eva in *Sula,* who represent this resiliency in their willingness to risk their lives to protect their families, Jadine's passion for success and material wealth places her outside of Morrison's definition of women's strength. In contrast to Son's commitment to embracing a quality of life that includes rebuffing middle-class trappings of wealth and privilege, Jadine is determined to conceptualize notions of blackness as fluid and indefinable as opposed to originating from a specific location (like an African American community), region and experience (the American South and slavery), or creative tradition (the vernacular creations and performances). Her elite education has taught her that African culture and its antecedents are primitive culture and at their best are "eighty percent ludicrous and ten percent derivative to the point of mimicry" (2004b, 75). Despite her intellectual certainty that European culture is more complex and sophisticated, she is still insecure about how she should regard her own skin color in a class, country, and profession where blackness is looked upon as intriguing, savage, and beautiful. In her desire to step out of her skin she struggles with "be[ing] only the person inside—not American—not black—just me" (48). Her education taught her to be color-blind and interact with white Americans and Europeans in a non-threatening manner. How to be "stunning, and to convince them she was not as smart as they were. Say the obvious, ask stupid questions, laugh with abandon, look interested, and light up at any display of their humanity if they showed it. Most of it required only charm—occasionally panache" (127). It is from this place of disconnection that she has difficulty relating to Son's struggle for a self-definition that is grounded outside of American capitalism and European colonization. Jadine ideates black male subjectivity, as deficient and disadvantaged as her education has taught her to think about African American culture.

Conceptualizing the Self as an unstable body that one can rename and redefine makes Son and Jadine a potential couple whose commonalities extend to their beliefs that one shouldn't be sentenced to embrace an identity that is imposed on them from the outside. However, this shared belief undermines their romantic relationship, as they believe in self-definition for themselves but not each other. Son's opinions about women are sexist, and he believes that women should be socialized into gender roles within a patriarchal system that places them in subservient positions. Although he is primarily concerned with the domestic sphere, he advocates a similar role for black women in the public realm too. In this way, his views reflect a long and persistent belief that the establishment of patriarchy within black families will withstand racial oppression. Like earlier clergy, politicians, and public intellectuals, Son seeks to address the problems in African American communities by silencing women. In *We Real Cool,* bell hooks argues that black men often complain about the lack of support they receive from black women and how women of all ethnicities conspire "to make it hard for them" (2004, 85). However, she continues, black men's complaints about gender oppression amount "to scenarios of disappointments and failures wherein someone else is to blame" (85). This scapegoat, hooks contends, "is a diversionary tactic. It allows the scapegoater to avoid issues they must confront if they are to assume responsibility for their lives" (85). While I believe that hooks's criticism of black men is a bit harsh (black male oppression didn't originate from only powerful white males), I also think that she is spot on about the importance of them maintaining an awareness of who they identify as their enemies.

Jadine mocks Son after he shares a life philosophy about labor and the American dream that is akin to a material Marxist analysis about individuals dissociated not only from the products they produce but from their own labor as well, and he notes the debilitating effects of what Marxist theorists refer to as alienated labor on the worker and on society as a whole. Son refuses to participate in the marketplace because, although he recognizes how his labor would fulfill his immediate needs, he fails to see how it would benefit his poor rural community and American society (which he sees as explicitly oppressive). As Son tells her a story about earning his first "original dime" for "cleaning a tub of sheephead," Jadine sarcastically sings a line from Porgy and Bess, written by George Gershwin, "got plenty of nuffin" (Morrison 2004b, 169). To Son's comment that "I don't get excited about money," Jadine tells him to get excited about what it can do and forget that "Thoreau crap" about how labor leads to the destruction of the individual and the nation. Not only does Jadine's barb serve as an example of abstract liberalism (ignoring the historical fact that blacks have always worked low-paying jobs), cultural racism (promoting the stereotype that African Americans are lazy), and classism (working- and middle-class individuals prefer to work hard for less money), her offensive dig also suggests that Son romanticizes sloth. In challenging Son to think more critically about education and capitalism as freedom from social oppression and a path to economic freedom, Jadine participates in a gender performance that Quinn Eli describes as a ritual of humiliation. As Eli argues in "A Liar in Love," black females are always the ones to put black masculinity in check via rituals of humiliation to prove their love, commitment, and trust (1995, 110). Jadine's rhetorical stance frustrates Son, leaving him with no alternative but to question her commitment to him and to the African American community. Morrison's text brings to mind the following questions: How much is a black male willing to sacrifice to love and be in love with a black woman? What price does he pay for her love? What does he stand to gain or lose in a love affair? In a very real way, they both are examples of how racialized discourses wall one into their reality.

As a result of her privileged life, Jadine struggles to empathize with the plight of the underclass or oppressed. On the one hand, her recalling of trips from boarding school and later private school reminds her of her working-class background and invites readers to embrace her as an American rags to riches story. Despite her troubled family history, she manages to graduate from college and build a successful career as a model. On the other hand, Jadine's lack of familiarity with African American customs, such as formally greeting older and senior individuals, incites Son and leaves readers wondering about her lack of respect and empathy for the native population that works for Valerian. When Jadine refers to the gardener as Yardman, as opposed to his given name "Gideon," Son admonishes her for being insensitive. It's not that Jadine is responsible for the stripping of the Caribbean or for Valerian's feigned innocence. However, as an educated African American woman, she should show empathy for the devastating effects of oppression on the African diaspora and for unconsciously denying Gideon his given name and seeing him only as a worker. Expressing empathy toward African American men means understanding them as men with dreams and ambitions: what are they like, what do they think about, what or whom do they resemble, and what do they desire or long for? This insight isn't written in textbooks or learned during study abroad programs, for they study cultures and civilizations that have been damaged, ravaged, and ruined. Despite her lack of knowledge about black men, Son still pursues a romantic relationship with Jadine, unaware that he must contend with her elite education and lofty personal and professional goals.

Son's cultural racism is an example of masculine arrogance—men's tendency to blame women for the rhetorical dimensions of hegemonic masculinity without acknowledging the multiple ways that black men are privileged in society. While criticizing Jadine for allowing Valerian to pay for her education and disapproving of the expensive gifts that her boyfriend bought her, he lives for free in Valerian house and allows Valerian to buy him an expensive suit and to pay for his haircut. In addition, he relies on her savings from her lucrative modeling contracts to meet their living expenses in New York. Morrison does not make Son's motives known nor does she suggest that he is aware that his reasoning is circular at best and hypocritical at worst. Morrison leaves the reader wondering about Son's intentions: Does he just like having someone to take care of him (which would suggest his own feelings of entitlement)? Internally, Son grapples with uncertainties and insecurities—perhaps he is afraid of failure, or is emotionally detached—all of which weakens and complicates his relationship with Jadine.

Neither Son nor Jadine represent the ideology of the African American community. Instead, their perspectives are just one of many competing discourses within the African American community about culture building and social responsibility. In *Toni Morrison: Playing with Difference*, Lucille Fultz argues that Morrison presents a variety of black characters against the "pervasive awareness of white society" as a way to highlight difference and multiplicity within African American communities (2003, 12). Illuminating diversity within the African American context, Morrison creates ambiguity in her texts, moments that Fultz identifies as "figurations of racism" (12). Thus, Son's and Jadine's contrasting arguments about race, gender, and community responsibility serve as a reminder that African Americans aren't a monolithic group who speak with one voice. More importantly, these arguments interrogate long-held community values and expectations, which are put to the test when Son takes Jadine to Eloe.

•

> An individual who can't relate to the black community, understand and be understood by her own people, isn't well educated.
>
> —JONNETTA COLE, "CULTURE" (1970, 42)

Undoubtedly Cole's quote describes the discursive divide that I have been outlining throughout this book. On one side is the responsibility to the community and on the other is the desire to be an autonomous subject who decides how one wants to relate to the community. Morrison takes these complex discursive positions to task when she represents Son and Jadine as characters who romanticize their subject positions as totally liberated from the bounds of gender and sexuality, thereby crossing and demolishing lines between masculine and feminine at will. Even their attempts to locate each other in a particular gender role is embedded in a cultural discourse that assigns blame and scapegoats each other for the problems within the community. As Son idealize his hometown Eloe as a community where Jadine can learn interdependence, extended kinship, and collective responsibility, she ridicules Eloe as a place where black women want Son to feel "superior in a cradle, deferring to him" to solve simple and difficult problems (Morrison 2004b, 269). Son and Jadine unfairly blame each other for a social structure that they didn't create, and their privileging of a gender order that further oppresses them indicates the text's attempt to articulate a complex relation to community. To read Son and Jadine as complicit in gender oppression also thwarts and historicizes a narrow cultural model that must always see figures as either man/provider or woman/caregiver and must pathologize any mixing of practices of gender roles.

That Son's and Jadine's history of gender (dis)identification occurs within what are so obviously circumscribed restrictions—the restrictions of a domesticity that is interpenetrated by the limits of their own trajectory, which stops short at a complete rejection of gender roles—may indicate that they are designed to draw readers' attention to the restrictions they place on each other. When they travel to Eloe to escape the New York City streets choked with emasculated men and anxious women, Son is nostalgic about the small rural town that seethes interdependence, extended kinship, and collective responsibility and focuses on how perfect they would be if Jadine would simply embrace the community, while Jadine rejects notions of community responsibility that include an insistence on a communal commitment at the expense of self-discovery. Jadine is unable or unwilling to conceive of a reason to embrace a community subjectivity that challenges her beliefs about black men and culture or that gives her a critical lens to be an African American woman in the world. However, several times in the novel Jadine thinks about herself in relation to the black women; for example, the African woman in the yellow dress whose presence "made her feel lonely . . . and inauthentic," Son's ex-wife Cheyenne who had "the best pussy in Florida," and the women in the small Eloe community who represent a traditional womanhood and femininity that Jadine lacks (48, 254, 257). Encounters with these women (in person and/or her imagination) overwhelm Jadine and engender her own struggle with her subjectivity formation. Concerned with black women as Jadine's Other, Margo Natalie Crawford describes her feelings of uncanniness as "complicated and multilayered. . . . Instead of simply falling in love . . . Jadine finds her aesthetic assumptions shocked and disoriented" (2008, 97). To Jadine, the women in Eloe reflect Son's notions of black womanhood. Although a brief appearance in the book, they offer a meaningful commentary on gender roles: "Paleothitic, she thought. I am stuck here with a pack of Neanderthals who think sex is dirty or strange or something and he is standing here almost thirty year old doing it too. Stupid, she said aloud" (Morrison 2004b, 257). Similar to the women who walk around without purses in the southern town of Shalimar in *Song of Solomon,* the Eloe women perform a femininity and womanhood that isn't defined by individuality at the expense of community advancement. As opposed to expecting the community to bend to their needs or whims, the black women in Eloe accept that they are part of it and that their responsibilities include advancing the community through anti-sexist and anti-patriarchal practices.

Bell hooks describes these anti-patriarchal practices as listening to the voices of self-reflective people who are committed to addressing the ways that patriarchy menaces African American men and women. She suggests that this dedication is in the writings of visionary black men and women who bring a healing message that releases men from the devastating logic of patriarchy. Hooks continues that visionary black men and women bring a healing message to the African American community "that could empower black men" (2004, 140–41). The healing process, according to Kevin Powell (2003) and Terrance Real (2002), creates strong friendships and romantic relationships and addresses what John Bradshaw refers to as soul-murder—"once a person loses contact with his own feelings, he loses contact with his own body" (1996, 216). While hooks's interest is mostly in black men learning a progressive masculinity platform that privileges verbal and written expressions of love as new life strategies for self-definition and discovery, I believe that men and women can benefit from a progressive anti-patriarchal platform that honors intracultural relationships beyond gender lines and that respects self and community responsibility (2004, 19). Emotionally, Son puts himself at risk in wanting to protect and provide for Jadine but remains limited. Son's healing includes articulating his feelings about the events from his life that cause him great emotional pain. "Son told her what she wished to hear about the [Vietnam] war. He could not speak to her or anyone about it coherently so he told her what she wished to hear. Regarding her whole self as an ear, he whispered into every part of her stories of icecaps and singing" (Morrison 2004b, 224–25). Jadine "pours her heart out to him and he to her" (224). They bear witness to each other's experiences—Jadine cried as "she told him about her mother and the awful hat she'd worn to the funeral" and how she did not have many choices after she graduated from high school: "She said she always thought she had three choices: marry a dope king or a doctor, model, or teach at Jackson High" (225). Son and Jadine's struggle to connect suggests the impact and presence of the dominant ideology of color-blindness in relationships between black men and women.

Focusing on men and women proposes an intricate articulation of a complex problem within African American culture and Morrison's fictional text. Morrison's depiction of Son and Jadine captures a constellation of interrelated ideas. Reading Son and Jadine's operations in Morrison's fictive world though

Simone de Beauvoir's *Second Sex,* women are not only Other to men but also to themselves, inasmuch as they have accepted objectifications of them—their essentialist interpretations of femininity and their notions of women's natural inferiority—thus maintaining men in their sovereign masculinity. If we follow this line of inquiry, women play a considerable role in the social exclusion of their own gender by discursively constructing themselves as the Other. This idea comes to the surface when one applies Morrison's theory of American Africanism to her novel. Africanist refers to "a nonWhite, Africanlike presence or persona and its imaginative uses" (1992, 6). By her definition, Africanism functions as a lens for "the connotative and denotative blackness that African peoples have come to signify, as well as the entire range of views, assumptions, readings and misreadings that accompany Eurocentric learning about these people" (6–7). Since I detail the intricacies of Morrison's explanation of Africanist presence in the introduction to this book, I will focus on her suggestion that certain characters act as a foil for the dominant culture or white characters. Africanism as the Othering of Africans elucidates Son's and Jadine's complex relationship to the African American community.

Too often, individuals from vulnerable communities internalize hatred and violence and adopt and apply the gaze of the dominant culture to their lives. What surfaces for those who assume this oppressive stance is antagonism and hostility directed toward oneself and one's community. For example, Jadine operates as the archetypical educated black woman, a self-imposed culture alienation, and a symbol of colorism and its psycho-social effect on African American women. Looking through her camera lens, Jadine appropriates the white gaze. In Eloe, when Son sees Jadine taking pictures of the residents (children, women, and the elderly), he begins to accept the distance between himself and the town and the liberal white intellectual circles Jadine frequents. Jadine positions herself in the small town similar to that of an anthropologist studying a remote African village. Occupying the space of a tourist, Jadine objectifies and stands in judgment of the local residents. She's an observer of a small country town and a recorder of the difference between city and rural life—not a participant. Thus, Son is not figured into Jadine's interests in Eloe, and her photographing highlights the predatory nature of the photographic act and the unequal power relationship on which it is based.

> There is something predatory in the act of taking a picture. To photograph people is to violate them, by seeing them as they never see themselves, by having knowledge of them they can never have; it turns people into objects that can be symbolically possessed. (Sontag 1977, 14)

In the above quote, Susan Sontag refers to the photographic act as a predatory event. When we consider, specifically, photographs taken by Jadine of the children in Eloe or, more generally, photographs taken by a privileged person of economically poor African American children in Eloe, Sontag's point seems even more compelling because the power differential between photographer and human subject is very obvious. As James Faris further explicitly explains the liberty and power a photographer exercises is in his/her unqualified right to take photographs, which privileges the most Western and capitalist of foundations—the absolute right to be able to see anyone, anywhere. It is to stand on power (2003, 264). In a similar point, Christopher Pinney draws an analogy between photography and the exercise of surveillance, as expressed in Michel Foucault's panoptical model of power relations in the modern state. In the panopticon prison, the prisoners are always visible to the wardens in their central observation tower. The wardens know all about the prisoners, but the prisoners are not privy to details about the wardens. The wardens live in a relatively unknown world. In photography, writes Pinney, photographers are invisible behind their cameras, while what they see is rendered completely visible (1997, 76). There is no doubt about the differential power relation between Jadine and the Eloe children. Nor is there any doubt that Son sees the act of taking photographs as a predatory one, an act by which the children are captured and appropriated, an act by which they become a future conversation piece for Jadine.

After leaving Eloe, Jadine's discourse still has traces of symbolic racism (preoccupied with matters of moral character and informed by the virtues associated with the traditions of individualism). At the center of her language is the contention that blacks do not try hard enough to overcome the difficulties they face and that they take what they have not earned. Prejudice is expressed in the language of American individualism (Bonilla-Silva 2010, 6). Embracing the idea of the self-made man, Jadine wants Son to accept the theology of the free market and the moral liberty of the individual to pursue goals and capitalist ambitions. While she acknowledges the difference that race makes to succeeding in a race conscious society (she talks about competing with white women for modeling jobs, doubts her French finance's sincerity—does he want her or any black girl sees that Valerian's generosity doesn't extend to Yardman and Mary), she doesn't consider how the historical discourses about black men disenfranchise them. At what point does one place one's own understanding of needs and desires above what is best for the culture and community building? The answer to who is right or wrong is sought after in a world in which there are no absolute truths or untruths but only assumptions and stereotypes about what each believes to be possibilities for the other: "Each knew the world as it was meant or ought to be. One had a past, the other a future and each one bore the culture to save the race in his hands" (Morrison 2004b, 269). The race and gender politics that plague Son's relationship with Jadine appear to be about which gender suffers more from racism (whose blues are worse) or that black men and women not only experience racial oppression differently but that black women are scathed by social oppression more than men.

Although the novel turns on Jadine's lack of responsibility to African American people and community, the narrative underscores Son's hypocrisy at his eagerness to accuse Jadine of lacking cultural knowledge and insensitivity toward her aunt and uncle, while being oblivious to the ways he naturalizes racialized discourses. Son functions as the representative of an empowered and self-defined black man, as a culture and community protector and symbol of black male sexual politics. Although Son's race disqualifies him from directly inheriting white male patriarchy, he still defines himself within the logic of white masculinity through practices of colorism. Anthony J. Lemelle states that "black masculinity is not outside of the cultural history of white patriarchy nor is it synonymous with white patriarchy. To think in these erroneous ways would be to work in the interests of the structure of domination through a process of mystifying gendered and racial positions in U.S. cultural organization. It would miss the ways that culture produces black males as a separate gender from constitutive of a feminized and hypermasculinized representation in the sociocultural sphere" (2010, 94). Son internalizes white notions of female beauty, which include a preference for African American women with a light complexion, European facial features, and straight hair. Despite voicing his commitment to culture and community responsibility, he (like Jadine) is inscribed in racialized discourse that sees blackness as the inferior antithesis of whiteness and is oblivious to the ways that he perpetuates and naturalizes the color-blindness that he criticizes Jadine of practicing.

Letitia L. Moffitt points to Son's hypocrisy as an example of his complicity in community and racial oppression:

> Whether Son expresses (and Morrison endorses) the values attributed to him . . . as a realistic character in a novel, he does not always act according to his values. He constantly (and convincingly) chastises Jadine for failing to care for her aunt and uncle ("They are the ones who put you through school," he reminds her when she credits Valerian for her education; "You should cook for them" [265]), and yet Son himself has sent only checks, no letters, to the father he has not visited in years. He speaks lovingly of "the fat black ladies in white dresses minding the pie table in the basement church"

> (119), but the two women he has fallen in love with—sexpot Cheyenne and sophisticated, ambitious Jadine—are impossibly at odds with that image. He "insists on Eloe" as being a kind of ideal black community but spends less than a single chapter of the book there (and, at the book's conclusion, seems unlikely ever to return). (Moffitt 2004, 13–14)

By having Son endorse values that he doesn't observe, Morrison proposes to readers that his responsibility to his community and cultural values are thrown in relief when he caters to his own desires. In distinguishing and preferring darker skin colors/hues, Son aligns himself with a discourse of colorism that dates back hundreds of years when slaves with lighter skin colors/hues were favored by the slave master. In *Paradise,* Morrison's characters resist internalizing class and color prejudice, her 8-rock clan hold their blackness as a sign of power and wholesomeness, plainly identifying themselves with "a deep deep level in the coal mines" (2007b, 193). Thus, *Tar Baby* and *Paradise* are Morrison's strongest statements about reversed-value colorism.

Morrison's rhetoric of responsibility becomes even more explicit as Son's behavior escalates from challenging Jadine's values and principles to physically attacking her and referring to her as Valerian's patsy—easily fooled into tricking black men into renouncing black culture and severing ties with their community. Morrison explains the construction of the story as "*Tar Baby* being a black woman and the rabbit a black man. I introduced a white man and remembered the tar. The fact that it was made out of tar and was a black woman, if it was made to trap a black man—the white man made her for that purpose" (1994a, 102). Comparing Jadine to a trickster character, he draws on all the color-blind frames. Through the tale, Son gives a reasonable explanation that appeals to liberalism: the desire for wealth is the American dream; it's natural for educated black women to feel distance from poor black men. She is trying to compensate for her deep feelings of racial inferiority, and he uses the tale to minimize his own racial (and gender) oppression.

My argument's focus on the rhetoric of responsibility in Morrison's novel reveals that while the legacy of racial and gender oppression against African American men and women continues to undermine their romantic relationships, they can address their dissonance by focusing on issues within their culture. In Morrison's words, "The problem has been put in the wrong place, as though it's a sexual battle, not a cultural one. Racism hurts in a very personal way. Because of it, people do all sorts of things in their personal lives and love relationships based on differences in values and class and education and their conception of what it means to be black in this society" (1994a, 133). The crisis is that the responsibility that was at one time the foundation for African American relationships has been replaced with blame, animosity, and competition and that African American men and women "no longer recognize as valuable the notion that they collectively shape the terms of their survival" by their ability to control how they withstand, confront, and survive racism and oppression (hooks 1990, 206). This ability is recoverable through an understanding of how African American men and women have historically been partners or "a friend of each other's mind" in the struggle against racial inequality (Morrison 1987, 272). As friends of each other's mind, African Americans have a cultural understanding of the importance of affirming, supporting, enabling, and empowering one another. In addition, they recognize that within their relationships the goal should be to struggle for self-actualization—a realization of each other as African American men and women who have joint and individual needs.

CODA

Beyond Baldwin and Morrison

FROM SLAVERY to contemporary America, African American men embrace diverse strategies for navigating the discursive divide and the dominant discourses that comprise it. In exploring the discursive divide, I have argued that we must consider the strategies of resistance from the African American rhetorical and folklore traditions that African American men employ as a defense against racial oppression and to build a life for themselves and their families. The dominant culture perpetuates hegemonic masculinity not only as a means to subordinate men but also as a mechanism to consolidate various ideologies to mobilize African American men and women to oppress each other. And it is precisely the inequality, ambiguity, and apprehension attending these strategies that I elaborate on in this book. Baldwin's and Morrison's canons invite an exploration of rhetoric and folklore as acts of resistance against oppressive forces. Such consideration requires attending to the multiple ways that cultural history and gender criticism elucidate the complexity of hegemonic oppression. Moreover, the book's trafficking between the struggles of the present and the historical condition of the past is especially consequential for both assessing the ongoing evolution of African American male subjectivity formation and questioning existing assumptions regarding the status of identity critique as a mode of intervention.

The significance of my approach for exploring black male subjectivity is that it is transportable and can be used to contextualize any inquiry or debate about African American male subjectivity formation. Innocence and romance as dominant discourses that attempt to obfuscate the inner workings of hegemonic masculinity and the discursive divide as the metaphorical space in which black men contend for recognition and liberation in the face of innocence and romance is played out in other texts and contexts. Unlike novels where we are privileged to read the machinations of the characters' minds, media texts (in most cases) don't give the actors' subconscious thoughts. Instead, we are presented with themes, plots, and personalities that remind us of what we see every day, or, what is worse, what prevents us from seeing African American people as complex human beings. Gaining an understanding of African American subjectivity construction requires one to accept themes, plots, and characters as imitations of what is not real—what is instead "make believe" or constructed. Contemporary media texts take on the performance of the subconscious to illustrate the relationship of African American subjectivity to stereotypes.

In my analysis, seemingly unrelated written and visual texts are categorically interrelated. There is a thread of thought that runs through the texts and strings them together. Any notion to confine my approach to thinking through black male subjectivity loses steam once the tie that binds it is detected in written and visual texts. A clear example of this is John Ridley's *12 Years a Slave* and Quentin Tarantino's *Django Unchained*. Both films are concerned with the mental and physical trauma slavery takes on black male subjectivity; however, each director explores black male resistance in very different ways. Based on the 1853 autobiography of the same name by Solomon Northup, *12 Years a Slave* tells the story of Solomon, a free black man, who is kidnapped in 1841, sold into slavery, and forced to labor on plantations in Louisiana for twelve years before being reclaimed by a white friend. Solomon defends himself against the brutality that accompanies enslavement, and he reminds himself daily that he will not sink into despair. In contrast, Tarantino's protagonist, Django Freeman, performs black male resistance as cruel, humorous, and self-destructive. After searching two years for the Mississippi plantation owner who enslaved his wife, Django locates and kills the plantation owner and several of his men. Django is supposed to represent black male resistance. However, I believe that Tarantino's movie depicts black male subjectivity as random acts of violence based solely on revenge as opposed to community survival.

Another context where an understanding of the complex rhetorical function of the discursive divide is fruitful is in the recent murders of African

American men by white private citizens and police officers. The racial dynamics that create a context where African American men are victims of white aggression can be understood within this space, i.e., white men perceiving African American men as stereotypes as opposed to individual men with distinct backgrounds and experiences. In the discursive divide, Trayvon Martin was racially profiled, stalked, and killed by George Zimmerman, who testified that he believed Martin was burglarizing houses in his neighborhood. Unbeknownst to Zimmerman, Martin was walking to his father's house, which was adjacent to the neighborhood Zimmerman lived in. Michael Brown was killed by a white police officer who claimed that he fired his weapon eight times in self-defense, as Brown was the aggressor. Adjudication of the details surrounding the shooting revealed that the police officer's deadly response was a result of his fear of black men, as he describes Brown as physically imposing. Lastly, Eric Garner was choked to death by a police officer during an attempt to arrest him for selling cigarettes outside a convenience store. The police officers's claims that Garner was resisting arrest is refuted by video, showing them aggressively wrestling him to the ground and Garner pleading for his life, "I can't breathe." These murders further confirm the need for a critical lens that engages black men beyond the white and black dialectic.

My exploration suggests that critical discussions about African American male experiences have never been rich and complex enough to encompass their subjectivity, as has often been discussed in response to traditional analysis of class, gender, and nationalism. Critical approaches explain the perceived construction and differences in race, physiology, and personality as well as the arbitrary values given to those features of African American men. However, they do not demonstrate how African American men become aware of the impact of the gulf between the expected performance of their identity and their own subjectivity. I argue that in the places where African American men resist or appear to acquiesce to oppressive conditions, they construct subjectivities that are defiant, defensive, resilient, and self-fashioning. In fiction and nonfiction, acts of rhetorical self-identification function as the hermeneutic for exploring how subjectivity creates a presence within dominant discourses of, primarily, African American and, secondarily, American cultural contexts.

These incidents serve as a reminder that African American identity is still forced to be in the service of the subjectivity of the dominant group regardless of how far society has developed in terms of race relations. Old interrogations of ethnic subjectivity, such as that by David Palumbo-Liu, still have a great deal of currency for thinking about discontents and challenges to subjectivity formation. In "Assumed Identity," Palumbo-Liu describes the challenge of articulating ethnic subjectivity in the context of dominant discourses that have historically and systemically defined them:

> The real question thus is not how to get beyond identity, but rather how to get to it in the first place—how to make the transition from typecasting to a recognizing of, precisely, individual identity? The real difficulty in making this move is that identity is predicated upon a set of behaviors that for racial and other minorities and women, is geared to a set of historical narratives about them precisely as groups, rather than as individuals, and these narratives form the perceptual grid that precedes them in the social discourse of identity. (2000, 765–67)

Ethnic identity is plotted on a complex grid of discourses. Thus, in order to discursively recover subjectivity, one must deconstruct the discourses that have historically constructed the identity of minorities.

Frantz Fanon's preoccupation with analyzing the discursive construction of race in relation to the hermeneutics of science, philosophy, and all other means of rational inquiry as a justification of an irrational act of subjugation, enslavement, and colonization is equally still relevant for thinking about black male subjectivity. Modified by the adjective "black," subjectivity is not simply represented by a private, personal, and psychological dimension of identity. Played out on the larger theater of the world, it represents a mode of antifoundational inquiry into dominant discourses of truth, reason, and natural inheritance. Black subjectivity has been constructed in language by the discursive divide that defines it as the anomaly: neither human nor animal. Dominant discourses (philosophy, psychology, law, among others) have used this language to rationalize its subjection of black male subjectivity because its contested terrain has been the "phenomenon of language . . . for it is implicit that to speak is to exist absolutely for the other" (Fanon 1967, 17). For Fanon, the self-fashioning of the colonial black is the moment the subject is deeply embedded in historical and intellectual contexts. Representations of African American male subjectivity need to be studied in these larger historical and cultural contexts. Fanon's work has functioned as the critical turning point in cultural studies that problematize racial identity construction in the spaces where black subjectivity confronts the machinery of white will to power and domination. His provocative use of the mirror image is often cited as a crucial metaphor for the construction of the racial other, but (as my introduction points out) even a cursory glance at African American intellectual traditions reveals the extent to which African American writers have continually explored their human subjectivity in the face of legitimizing discourses that evoke religious, historical, and biological determinism to prove that African Americans have animal/lower-order qualities.

In many ways, postcolonial theory is useful for articulating how Western subjectivity attempts to overwrite subaltern subjectivities and for theorizing how these subjectivities resist this overwriting. Spivak's argues in "Deconstructing Historiography" that the subaltern illuminates the "contrivance of more positivist models of the subject" (1996, 204). In official histories, the subaltern provides a counter-narrative to the subject's claim that national, political, social, and cultural narratives make up the subjectivities of a nation. In the case of European and American history, the sensibilities of Africans and later African Americans function as the antithesis of Western sensibilities.

In her most famous quote, "Can the subaltern speak?," Spivak lays bare the discursive conditions that need to be understood in order to recover subaltern history from within the context of official histories and from those that claim to speak for the subaltern (for example, native or nationalist histories). This question can be applied fruitfully to the expressive African American man. Can we recover his "voice" from, for example, the *Moynihan Report,* which marks the official social history of the discourses of pathology that continues to construct him? Can we recover black male voices from black feminist work, which equates black masculinity with patriarchy? Can we recover his voice from the native, nationalist histories of Black nationalism and the Civil Rights movement? This is a key problematic that Baldwin and Morrison represent in their texts.

I position Baldwin and Morrison among this group. They conceptualize how the black man is a signifier and has historically occupied a unique discursive position: he represents debates about sex, crime, drugs, welfare, the breakdown of the family, and other political conversations that mark both the definition of African American cultural values and their breakdown. It is this context that Baldwin and Morrison consider while exploring the discourses about black male identity that have historically constructed black men. For these writers, identity in this instance is ideological and is not a viable way to think about black male identity in the context of African American culture. Within the African American intellectual tradition, scholars and writers understand this from Baldwin's *The Evidence of Things Not Seen,* where he speculates that black men signify a "vision, or nightmare" in the consciousness of white men and the "Republic on every level" (1986, 21), to Morrison's *What Moves at the Margins,* where she discusses how black men "are converted into a sexualized spectacle" (2008b, 134), but we need to continue to articulate, as historically and as carefully as we can, the cultural contexts that make black men different from one another. We have stressed continuity and we simultaneously need to stress the specificity of discursive conditions. For Baldwin and Morrison, it is about considering how their African American male characters negotiate the discourses that seek to define them, how they resist them, and how they succeed in making a life for themselves.

My hope for this book is that it is fits within the numerous studies on black male subjectivity and masculinity that challenge hegemonic masculinity. This book represents the third wave of African American cultural studies. The African American male characters in the fiction of Baldwin and Morrison construct their subjectivity with the discourses available to them in order to redefine themselves as fathers, husbands, lovers, or friends. Who they desire to become is different from how they are viewed by society, family, and friends, which makes for contentious relationships within and outside African American cultural contexts. This is the distinction between identity and subjectivity, which is also crucial to my project. Each of the characters find themselves in the discursive divide where they must use discourses that were historically used to oppress them to redefine their subjectivity and negotiate dominant discourses.

I tried to get at this this truth, which is black men know what this society is all about and where this society's priorities lie, but they still seem to retain some faith that it will do right by them. I wanted to get at why we still stay the course. Is it that we really feel like we don't have a choice or is it because we understand the score and we are really marching to the beat of our own drummer? I don't know if we are doing this because we get caught up in our own politics. I was in interested in the network of the discourses that oppress black men and the way they attempt to negotiate them. So much attention is given to how black men are oppressed but not enough to how they get beyond this. I have outlined the ways they maneuver beyond these discourses and thought about how they intrude on black women's subjectivity because, as I stated throughout this book, black men can't succeed without black women and vice versa. This creates issues because black men and women have individual experiences that situate them in gender politics. The challenge then is to further their own political agendas without undermining one another's efforts. This is a difficult task because sometimes men's politics are insensitive to women, which necessitates that women push back against them.

BIBLIOGRAPHY

Abrahams, Roger D. 2006. *Deep Down in the Jungle: Black American Folklore from the Streets of Philadelphia.* New Brunswick, NJ: Aldine Transaction.

Alcoff, Linda Martin. 2006. *Visible Identities: Race, Gender, and the Self.* New York: Oxford University Press.

Alexander, Estrelda Y. 2011. *Black Fire: One Hundred Years of African American Pentecostalism.* Downers Grove, IL: InterVarsity Press.

Alexander, Michelle. 2011. *The New Jim Crow: Mass Incarceration in the Age of Colorblindness.* New York: New Press.

Allen, Shirley S. 1988. "Religious Symbolism and Psychic Reality in Baldwin's *Go Tell It on the Mountain.*" In *Critical Essay on James Baldwin,* edited by Fred L. Standley and Nancy V. Burt, 166–87. Boston: G. K. Hall.

Althusser, Louis. 1994. "Ideology and Ideological State Apparatuses (Notes towards an Investigation)." In *Mapping Ideology.* 2nd ed. Edited by Slavoj Žižek. New York: Verso.

Anderson, Elijah. 2008. *Against the Wall: Poor, Young, Black, and Male.* Philadelphia: University of Pennsylvania Press.

Aristotle. 1927. *The Poetics.* London: Heinemann.

Arobateau, Red Jordan. 2012. *Suzie Q and Other Stories.* New York: Red Jordan Press.

Awkward, Michael. 1995. *Negotiating Difference: Race, Gender, and the Politics of Positionality.* Chicago: University of Chicago Press.

———. 2001. "A Black Man's Place in Black Feminist Criticism." In *Traps: African American Men on Gender and Sexuality,* edited by Rudolph P. Byrd and Beverly Guy-Sheftall, 177–93. Bloomington: Indiana University Press.

Babuscio, Jack. 1993. "Camp and the Gay Sensibility." In *Camp Grounds: Style and Homosexuality,* edited by David Bergman, 19–38. Amherst: University of Massachusetts Press.

Baker, Houston A., Jr. 1984. *Blues, Ideology, and Afro-American Literature: A Vernacular Theory.* Chicago: University of California Press.

———. 1990. *Long Black Song: Essays in Black American Literature and Culture.* Charlottesville: University of Virginia.

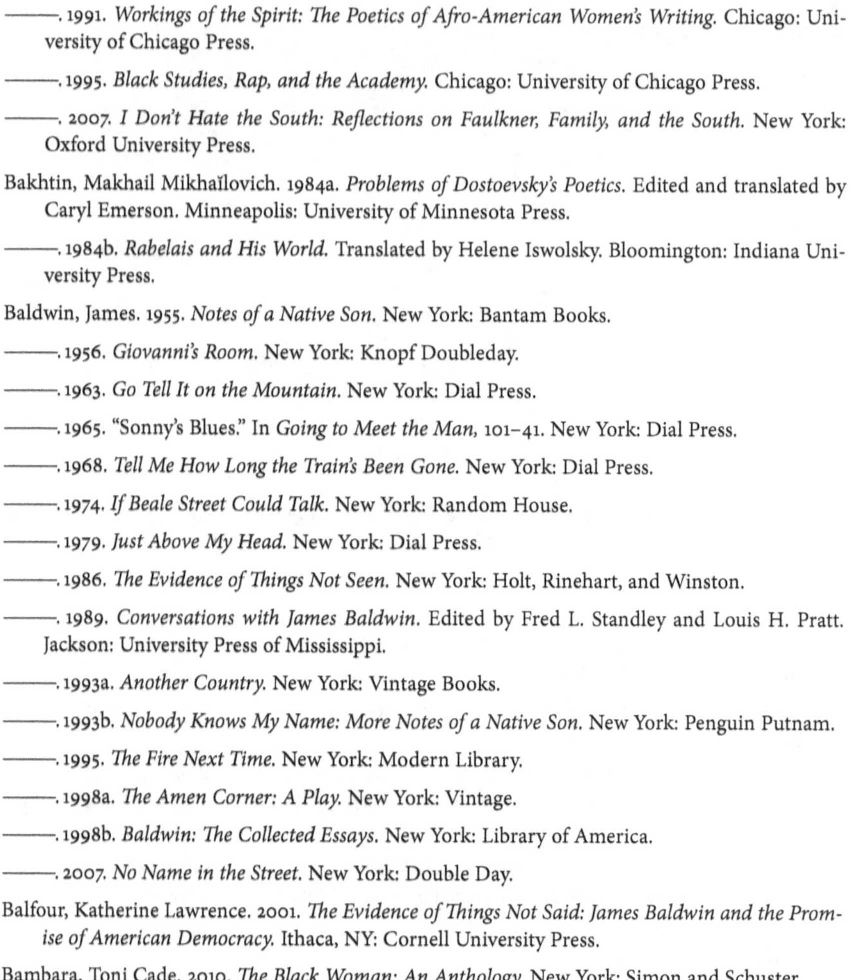

———. 1991. *Workings of the Spirit: The Poetics of Afro-American Women's Writing.* Chicago: University of Chicago Press.

———. 1995. *Black Studies, Rap, and the Academy.* Chicago: University of Chicago Press.

———. 2007. *I Don't Hate the South: Reflections on Faulkner, Family, and the South.* New York: Oxford University Press.

Bakhtin, Makhail Mikhaĭlovich. 1984a. *Problems of Dostoevsky's Poetics.* Edited and translated by Caryl Emerson. Minneapolis: University of Minnesota Press.

———. 1984b. *Rabelais and His World.* Translated by Helene Iswolsky. Bloomington: Indiana University Press.

Baldwin, James. 1955. *Notes of a Native Son.* New York: Bantam Books.

———. 1956. *Giovanni's Room.* New York: Knopf Doubleday.

———. 1963. *Go Tell It on the Mountain.* New York: Dial Press.

———. 1965. "Sonny's Blues." In *Going to Meet the Man,* 101–41. New York: Dial Press.

———. 1968. *Tell Me How Long the Train's Been Gone.* New York: Dial Press.

———. 1974. *If Beale Street Could Talk.* New York: Random House.

———. 1979. *Just Above My Head.* New York: Dial Press.

———. 1986. *The Evidence of Things Not Seen.* New York: Holt, Rinehart, and Winston.

———. 1989. *Conversations with James Baldwin.* Edited by Fred L. Standley and Louis H. Pratt. Jackson: University Press of Mississippi.

———. 1993a. *Another Country.* New York: Vintage Books.

———. 1993b. *Nobody Knows My Name: More Notes of a Native Son.* New York: Penguin Putnam.

———. 1995. *The Fire Next Time.* New York: Modern Library.

———. 1998a. *The Amen Corner: A Play.* New York: Vintage.

———. 1998b. *Baldwin: The Collected Essays.* New York: Library of America.

———. 2007. *No Name in the Street.* New York: Double Day.

Balfour, Katherine Lawrence. 2001. *The Evidence of Things Not Said: James Baldwin and the Promise of American Democracy.* Ithaca, NY: Cornell University Press.

Bambara, Toni Cade. 2010. *The Black Woman: An Anthology.* New York: Simon and Schuster.

Bell, Bernard W. 1998. "*Beloved*: A Womanist Neo-Slave Narrative; or Multivocal Remembrances of Things Past." In *Critical Essays on Toni Morrison's* Beloved, edited by Barbara H. Solomon, 166–76. New York: G. K. Hall.

Bell, Derrick. 2001. "The Sexual Diversion." In *Traps: African American Men on Gender and Sexuality,* edited by Rudolph P. Byrd, and Beverly Guy-Sheftall, 168–76. Bloomington: Indiana University Press.

Bergman, David. 1993. "Strategic Camp: The Art of Gay Rhetoric." In *Camp Grounds: Style and Homosexuality,* edited by David Bergman, 92–109. Amherst: University of Massachusetts Press.

Bhabha, Homi. 1984. "Of Mimicry and Man: The Ambivalence of Colonial Discourse." October 28: 125–33.

———. 2012. *The Location of Culture.* 2nd ed. New York: Routledge.

Bible, The New English. 1972. New York: Oxford University Press.

Blount, Marcellus, and George P. Cunningham. 1996. *Representing Black Men.* London: Routledge.

Bonilla-Silva, Eduardo. 2010. *Racism without Racists: Color-Blind Racism and the Persistence of Racial Inequality in the United States.* Lanham: Rowman & Littlefield.

Bosmajian, Haig Aram, and Hamida Bosmajian. 1969. *The Rhetoric of the Civil-Rights Movement.* New York: Random House.

Bouson, Brooks J. 1999. "Quiet as It's Kept: Shame and Trauma in Toni Morrison's *The Bluest Eye.*" In *Scenes of Shame: Psychoanalysis, Shame, and Writing,* edited by Joseph Adamson and Hilary Clark, 207–36. Albany, NY: SUNY Press.

Bowser, Pearl, and Louise Spence. 2000. "Oscar Micheaux's *Body and Soul* and the Burden of Representation." *Cinema Journal* 39 (3): 3–29.

Bradshaw, John. 1996. *Bradshaw on: The Family: A New Way of Creating Solid Self-Esteem.* Deerfield Beach: Health Communication, Inc.

Bronner, Simon J. 2005. *Manly Traditions: The Folk Roots of American Masculinities.* Bloomington: Indiana University Press.

Brooks, Gwendolyn. 2005. *The Essential Gwendolyn Brooks.* Edited by Elizabeth Alexander. American Poets Projects #19. New York: Library of America.

Brown, Cecil. 2004. *Stagolee Shot Billy.* Cambridge, MA: Harvard University Press.

Butler, Judith. 1990. *Gender Trouble: Feminism and the Subversion of Identity.* New York: Routledge.

———. 1999. "From Interiority to Gender Performatives." In *Camp: Queer Aesthetics and the Performing Subject: A Reader,* edited by Fabio Cleto, 361–69. Ann Arbor: University of Michigan Press.

———. 2014. *Bodies That Matter: On the Discursive Limits of "Sex."* New York: Routledge.

Byrd, Rudolph P., and Beverly Guy-Sheftall, eds. 2001. *Traps: African American Men on Gender and Sexuality.* Bloomington: Indiana University Press.

Byron, Gay L. 2003. *Symbolic Blackness and Ethnic Difference in Early Christian Literature.* New York: Routledge.

Campbell, Bebe Moore. 1995. *Your Blues Ain't Like Mine.* New York: Random House Publishing.

Campbell, James. 1991. *Talking at the Gates: A Life of James Baldwin.* Berkeley: University of California Press.

Carbado, Devon W., Dwight A. McBride, and Donald Weise, eds. 2002. *Black Like Us: A Century of Lesbian, Gay, and Bisexual African American Fiction.* San Francisco: Cleis Press.

Carby, Hazel V. 1999. *Cultures in Babylon: Black Britain and African America.* London: Verso.

Carpenter, Faedra Chatard. 2005. "Robert O' Hara's Insurrection: 'Que(e)rying History.'" In *Black Queer Studies: A Critical Anthology,* edited by E. Patrick Johnson and Mae G. Henderson, 322–47. Durham, NC: Duke University Press.

Carson, Warren J. 2000. "Manhood, Musicality, and Male Bonding in *Just Above My Head.*" In *Re-viewing James Baldwin: Things Not Seen,* edited by Daniel Quentin Miller, 215–32. Philadelphia: Temple University Press.

Charles, John C. 2013. *Abandoning the Black Hero: Sympathy and Privacy in the Postwar African American White-Life Novel.* New Brunswick, NJ: Rutgers University Press.

Christian, Barbara. 2000. "The Race for Theory." In *The Black Feminist Reader,* edited by Joy James and T. Denean Sharpley-Whiting, 11–23. Malden, MA: Blackwell.

Clark, Keith. 2002. *Black Manhood in James Baldwin, Ernest J. Gaines, and August Wilson.* Urbana: University of Illinois Press.

Cleaver, Eldridge. 1999. *Soul on Ice.* St. Louis: Turtleback Books.

Cole, Johnetta B. 1972. "Culture: Negro, Black, and Nigger." *Black Scholar* 1: 40–46.

Coleman, James Wilmouth. 1987. "The Quest for Wholeness in Toni Morrison's *Tar Baby.*" *Black American Literature Forum* 20 (1/2): 63–73.

———. 2001. *Black Male Fiction and the Legacy of Caliban.* Lexington: University Press of Kentucky.

Collins, Patricia Hill. 2000a. *Black Feminist Thought: Knowledge, Consciousness, and the Politics of Empowerment.* New York: Routledge.

———. 2000b. "The Social Construction of Black Feminist Thought." In *The Black Feminist Reader,* edited by Joy James and T. Denean Sharpley-Whiting, 183–207. Malden, MA: Blackwell.

Cone, James H. 1997. *Black Theology and Black Power.* Maryknoll, NY: Orbis Books.

Connell, Raewyn W. 2005. *Masculinities.* 2nd Edition. Berkeley: University California Press.

Courlander, Harold, ed. 1996. *A Treasury of Afro-American Folklore: The Oral Literature, Traditions, Recollections, Legends, Tales, Songs, Religious Beliefs, Customs, Sayings, and Humor of Peoples of African Descent in the Americas.* New York: Marlowe.

Crawford, Margo Natalie. 2008. *Dilution Anxiety and the Black Phallus.* Columbus: The Ohio State University Press.

Crenshaw, Kimberly. 1993. "Demarginalizing the Intersection of Race and Sex: A Black Feminist Critique of Antidiscrimination Doctrine, Feminist Theory, and Antiracist Politics." In *Feminist Legal Theory: Foundations,* edited by D. Kelly Weisberg, 383–95. Philadelphia: Temple University Press.

Cullen, Countee. 1932. *One Way to Heaven.* New York: Harper and Brothers.

de Beauvoir, Simon. 2011. *The Second Sex.* New York: First Vintage Books.

Delany, Samuel R. 2013. *Aye and Gomorrah: Stories.* Phoenix: Orion.

Deleuze, Gilles. 2007. *Difference and Repetition.* London: Athlone Press.

Derrida, Jacques. 1995. *The Gift of Death.* Chicago: University of Chicago Press.

———. 1997. *Of Grammatology.* Translated by Gayatri Chakravorty Spivak. Baltimore: Johns Hopkins University Press.

De Santis, Christopher C., ed. 1995. *Langston Hughes and the Chicago Defender: Essays on Race, Politics, and Culture, 1942–62.* Urbana: University of Illinois Press.

Dievler, James A. 1999. "Sexual Exiles: James Baldwin and *Another Country.*" In *James Baldwin Now,* edited by Dwight A. McBride, 161–83. New York: New York University Press.

Dixon, Melvin. 2013. *Vanishing Rooms.* San Francisco: Cleis Press.

Drums and Shadows: Survival Studies among the Georgia Costal Negroes. 2010. Edited by Georgia Writers Project. Los Angeles: Indo-European Publishing.

Donnan, Hastings, and Fiona Magowan. 2012. "Sexual Transgression, Social Order and the Self." In *Transgressive Sex: Subversion and Control in Erotic Encounters,* edited by Hastings Donnan and Fiona Magowan, 1–24. New York: Berghahn Books.

Douglass, Frederick. 1995. *Narrative of the Life of Frederick Douglass: An American Slave.* New York: Dover.

Du Bois, W. E. B. 1997. *The Souls of Black Folk.* Boston: Bedford Books.

———. 2000. "The Church and the Negro." In *Du Bois on Religion*, edited by Phil Zuckerman, 45–46. Lanham, MD: Rowman & Littlefield.

Dunbar, Paul Laurence. 1960. *The Complete Poems of Paul Laurence Dunbar*. New York: Dodd, Mead.

Dundes, Alan. 1973. *Mother Wit from the Laughing Barrel: Readings in the Interpretation of Afro-American Folklore*. Oxford: University Press of Mississippi.

Durham, Joyce R. 1990. "The City in Recent American Fiction: Listening to Black Urban Voices." *College English* 52 (7): 764–75.

Dyson, Michael Eric. 2001. "When You Divide Body and Soul, Problems Multiply." In *Traps: African American Men on Gender and Sexuality*, edited by Rudolph P. Byrd and Beverly Guy-Sheftall, 308–26. Bloomington: Indiana University Press.

———. 2004. "Homotextualities: The Bible, Sexual Ethics, and the Theology of Homoeroticism." In *The Michael Eric Dyson Reader*, 238–57. New York: Basic Civitas Books.

Eagleton, Terry. 1981. *Walter Benjamin: Or, Towards a Revolutionary Criticism*. London: Verso.

Eckstein, Lars. 2006. *Re-membering the Black Atlantic: On the Poetics and Politics of Literary Memory*. Amsterdam: Rodopi.

Eli, Quinn. 1995. "A Liar in Love." In *Speak My Name: Black Men on Masculinity and the American Dream*, edited by Don Belton, 137–43. Boston: Beacon Press.

Ellison, Ralph. 1980. *Invisible Man*. New York: Vintage Books.

———. 1995a. *The Collected Essays of Ralph Ellison*. New York: Random House.

———. 1995b. *Conversations with Ralph Ellison*. Edited by Maryemma Graham and Amritjit Singh. Oxford: University Press of Mississippi.

———. 1995c. *Shadow and Act*. New York: Knopf Doubleday.

———. 2011. "A Party Down at the Square." In *Flying Home and Other Stories*, 3–11. New York: Knopf Doubleday.

Fabian, Johannes. 1983. *Time and the Other: How Anthropology Makes Its Objects*. New York: Columbia University Press.

———. 2007. *Memory against Culture: Arguments and Reminders*. Durham, NC: Duke University Press.

Fabre, Michel. 1974. "Fathers and Sons in James Baldwin's *Go Tell It on the Mountain*." In *James Baldwin: A Collection of Critical Essays*, edited by Kenneth Kinnamon, 120–38. Englewood Cliffs, NJ: Prentice Hall.

Fanon, Frantz. 1963. *The Wretched of the Earth*. New York: Grove Press.

———. 1967. *Black Skin, White Masks*. Translated by Charles Lam Markmann. New York: Grove Press.

Faris, James C. 2003. *Navajo and Photography: A Critical History of the Representation of an American People*. Salt Lake City: University of Utah Press.

Finney, Brian. 1998. "Temporal Defamiliarization in Toni Morrison's *Beloved*." In *Critical Essays on Toni Morrison's* Beloved, edited by Barbara H. Solomon, 104–16. New York: G. K. Hall.

Foucault, Michel. 1984. *The Foucault Reader*. Edited by Paul Rabinow. New York: Pantheon.

Franklin, John Hope. 2011. *From Slavery to Freedom: A History of African Americans*. Boston: Harvard University Press.

Fultz, Lucille. 2003. *Toni Morrison: Playing with Difference*. Urbana: University of Illinois Press.

Fulwieler, Howard W. 2000. "Belonging and Freedom in Morrison's *Beloved:* Slavery, Sentimentality, and the Evolution of Consciousness." In *Understanding Toni Morrison's* Beloved *and* Sula*: Selected Essays and Criticisms of the Works by the Nobel Prize-Winning Author,* edited by Solomon O. Iyasere and Marla W. Iyasere, 113–46. Troy, NY: Whitston.

Furman, Jan. 1996. *Toni Morrison's Fiction.* Columbia: University of South Carolina Press.

———. 1999. "Male Consciousness: *Song of Solomon.*" In *Toni Morrison's* Song of Solomon, edited by Harold Bloom, 195–208. Philadelphia: Chelsea House.

Gaines, Kevin K. 1996. *Uplifting the Race: Black Leadership, Politics, and Culture in the Twentieth Century.* Chapel Hill: University of North Carolina Press.

Gates, Henry Louis. 1980. *Figures in Black: Words, Signs, and the "Racial" Self.* New York: Vintage International.

———. 1988. *The Signifying Monkey: A Theory of Afro-American Literary Criticism.* New York: Oxford University Press.

Gellert, Lawrence. 1939. *Me and My Captain: Chain Gang Negro Songs of Protest.* New York: Hours Press.

Giddings, Paula. 1984. *When and Where I Enter: The Impact of Black Women on Race and Sex in America.* New York: Morrow.

Gikandi, Simon. 2003. "Picasso, Africa, and the Schemata of Difference." *Modernism/Modernity* 10 (3): 455–80.

Gilman, Sanders L. 1985. *Difference and Pathology: Stereotypes of Sexuality, Race, and Madness.* Ithaca, NY: Cornell University Press.

Gilyard, Keith. 1996. *Let's Flip the Script: An African American Discourse on Language, Literature, and Learning.* Detroit: Wayne State University Press.

———. 2004. "Introduction: Aspects of African American Rhetoric as a Field." In *African American Rhetoric(s): Interdisciplinary Perspectives,* edited by Elaine Richardson and Ronald Jackson, II, 1–20. Carbondale: Southern Illinois University Press.

Giovanni, Nikki. 1997. *Love Poems.* New York: Morrow.

Glenn, Cheryl. 2004. *Unspoken: A Rhetoric of Silence.* Carbondale: Southern Illinois University Press.

Gordon, Edmund W. 2000. "The Myth and Realities of African-American Fatherhood." In *Resilience Across Contexts: Family, Work, Culture, and Community,* edited by Margaret C. Wang and Ronald D. Taylor, 217–32. Mahwah, NJ: Lawrence Erlbaum.

Gramsci, Antonio. 1971. *Selections from the Prison Notebooks of Antonio Gramsci.* New York: International Publishers.

———. 1992. *Prison Notebooks.* New York: Columbia University Press.

Griffin, Farah Jasmin. 1995. *"Who Set You Flowin'?": The African American Migration Narrative.* New York: Oxford University of Press.

Guerrero, Edward. 1990. "Tracking 'The Look' in the Novels of Toni Morrison." *Black American Literature Forum* 24 (4): 761–73.

Guy-Sheftall, Beverly. ed. 1995. *Words of Fire: An Anthology of African-American Feminist Thought.* New York: New Press.

———. 2002. "Response from a 'Second Waver' to Kimberly Springer's 'Third Wave Black Feminism?'" *Signs* 27 (4): 1091–94.

Halberstam, J. Jack. 2012. *Gaga Feminism: Sex, Gender, and the End of Normal.* Boston: Beacon Press.

Haley, Alex. 1976. *Roots: The Saga of an American Family.* Garden City, NY: Doubleday & Company, Inc.

Handler, Richard, and Jocelyn Linnekin. 1984. "Tradition, Genuine or Spurious." *Journal of American Folklore* 97: 273–90.

Haraway, Donna. 1988. "Situated Knowledges: The Science Question in Feminism and the Privilege of Partial Perspective." *Feminist Studies* 14 (3): 575–99.

Harding, Wendy, and Jacky Martin. 1998. "Reading at the Cultural Interface: The Corn Symbolism of *Beloved.*" In *Critical Essays on Toni Morrison's* Beloved, edited by Barbara H. Solomon, 233–46. New York: G. K. Hall.

Harper, Phillip Brian. 1996. *Are We Not Men?: Masculine Anxiety and the Problem of African-American Identity.* New York: Oxford University Press.

Harris, E. Lynn. 1991. *Invisible Life: A Novel.* New York: Knopf Doublesday.

Harris, Othello, and R. Robin Miller. 2006. *Impacts of Incarceration on the African American Family.* New Brunswick, NJ: Transaction Publishers.

Harris, Trudier. 1985. *Black Women in the Fiction of James Baldwin.* Knoxville: University of Tennessee Press.

———. 1991. *Fiction and Folklore: The Novels of Toni Morrison.* Knoxville: University of Tennessee Press.

———. 1998. "*Beloved*: 'Woman Thy Name Is Demon.'" In *Critical Essays on Toni Morrison's* Beloved, edited by Barbara H. Solomon, 127–37. New York: G. K. Hall.

Harris-Perry, Melissa V. 2011. *Sister Citizen: Shame, Stereotypes, and Black Women in America.* New Haven, CT: Yale University Press.

Heidegger, Martin. 1992. *History of the Concept of Time: Prolegomena.* Bloomington: Indiana University Press.

Hemphill, Essex, ed. 2007. *Brother to Brother: New Writings by Black Gay Men.* Washington DC: Red Bone Press.

Henderson, Mae G. 2005. "James Baldwin's *Giovanni Room:* Expatriation, 'Racial Drag,' and Homosexual Panic." In *Black Queer Studies: A Critical Anthology,* edited by E. Patrick Johnson and Mae G. Henderson, 298–322. Durham, NC: Duke University Press.

Hernton, Calvin. 1971. *Coming Together: Black Power, White Hatred and Sexual Hang-Ups.* New York: Random House.

Herskovits, Melville. 1958. *The Myth of the Negro Past.* Boston: Beacon Press.

Heyman, Richard. 1995. "Universalization and its Discontents: Morrison's *Song of Solomon*—A (W)hol(e)y Black Text." *African American Review* 29 (3): 381–92.

Holloway, Karla F. C. 1987. "African Values and Western Chaos." In *New Dimensions of Spirituality: A Biracial and Bicultural Reading of the Novels of Toni Morrison,* edited by Karla Holloway and Stephanie A. Demetrakopoulos, 117–30. New York: Greenwood.

Holmes, David G. 2004. *Revisiting Racialized Voice: African American Ethos in Language and Literature.* Carbondale: Southern Illinois University Press.

hooks, bell. 1984. *Feminist Theory: From Margin to Center.* Cambridge: South End Press.

———. 1990. *Yearning: Race, Gender, and Cultural Politics.* Boston: South End Press.

———. 1995. "Black Women: Shaping Feminist Theory." In *Words of Fire: An Anthology of African-American Feminist Thought,* edited by Beverly Guy-Sheftall, 270–82. New York: New Press.

———. 2004. *We Real Cool: Black Men and Masculinity.* New York: Routledge.

———. 2014. *Talking Back: Thinking Feminist, Thinking Black.* New York: Routledge.

Hubbard, Dolan. 1994. *The Sermon and the African American Literary Imagination.* Columbia: University of Missouri Press.

Hughes, Langston. 1959. *Selected Poems of Langston Hughes.* New York: Vintage Classics Edition.

———. 1963. *The Big Sea: An Autobiography by Langston Hughes.* New York: Hill and Wang.

Hurston, Zora Neale. 1990. *Mules and Men.* New York: HarperCollins.

———. 1997. *The Sanctified Church.* New York: Marlowe.

———. 2006. *Their Eyes Were Watching God.* Harper Collins.

Hutcheon, Linda. 1988. *A Poetics of Postmodernism: History, Theory, Fiction.* New York: Routledge.

Ikard, David. 2007. *Breaking the Silence: Toward a Black Male Feminist Criticism.* Baton Rouge: Louisiana State University Press.

Jackson, Blyden. 1991. "Introduction: A Street of Dreams." In *Black Exodus: The Great Migration from the American South,* edited by Alferdteen Harrison, xi–xviii. Oxford: University Press of Mississippi.

Jacobs, Harriet A. 2009. *Incidents in the Life of a Slave Girl: Written by Herself.* Boston: Thayer & Eldridge.

Jennings, La Vinia Delois. 2008. *Toni Morrison and the Idea of Africa.* New York: Cambridge University Press.

Johansen, Bruce E. 1997. "Race, Ethnicity, and the Media." In *Mass Media and Society,* edited by Alan Wells and Ernest A Hakansen, 513–26. Greenwich, CT: Ablex.

Johnson, Charles. 2001. "A Phenomenology of the Black Body." In *Traps: African American Men on Gender and Sexuality,* edited by Rudolph P. Byrd, and Beverly Guy-Sheftall, 223–35. Bloomington: Indiana University Press.

Johnson, Patrick E. 2005. "'Quare' Studies, or (Almost) Everything I Know About Queer Studies I Learned from My Grandmother." In *Black Queer Studies: A Critical Anthology,* edited by E. Patrick Johnson and Mae G. Henderson, 124–60. Durham, NC: Duke University Press.

Jones, Gayle. 1987. *Corregidora.* Boston: Beacon Press.

Jordan, June, and Houston Baker. 1988. "Black Writers in Praise of Toni Morrison." *New York Times Book Review,* January 24. Late City Final Edition.

Julien, Isaac, and Kobena Mercer. 2007. "True Confessions: A Discourse on Images of Black Male Sexuality." In *Brother to Brother: New Writings by Black Gay Men,* edited by Essex Hemphill, 206–15. Washington DC: Red Bone Press.

Kang, Nancy. 2003. "To Love and Be Loved: Considering Black Masculinity and the Misandric Impulse in Toni Morrison's *Beloved.*" *Callaloo: A Journal of African Diaspora Arts and Letters* 26 (3): 836–54.

Kaufman, Bob. 1967. *Golden Sandals.* San Francisco: City Lights Books.

Keen, Suzanne. 2007. *Empathy and the Novel.* New York: Oxford University Press.

Kenan, Randall. 1992. *Let the Dead Bury the Dead and Other Stories.* New York: Harcourt Brace.

Kent, George E. 1990. *A Life of Gwendolyn Brooks.* Lexington: University Press of Kentucky.

King, Lovalarie. 1998. "The Disruption of Formulaic Discourse: Writing, Resistance, and Truth in *Beloved*." In *Critical Essays on Toni Morrison's* Beloved, edited by Barbara H. Solomon, 272–83. New York: G. K. Hall.

King, Lovalerie, and Lynn Orilla Scott, eds. 2006. *James Baldwin and Toni Morrison: Comparative Critical and Theoretical Essays*. New York: Palgrave Macmillan.

King, Martin Luther, Jr. 1964. *Why We Can't Wait*. New York: Signet Classic.

———. 1994. *Letter from the Birmingham Jail*. San Francisco: Harper.

Kitts, Lenore. 2006. "Toni Morrison and 'Sis Joe': The Musical Heritage of Paul D." *Modern Fiction Studies* 52 (2): 495–523.

Kovel, Joel. 1984. *White Racism: A Psychohistory*. New York: Columbia University Press.

Kristeva, Julia. 1982. *Powers of Horror: An Essay on Abjection*. Translated by Leon S. Roudiez. New York: Columbia University Press.

Kupers, Terry A. 2001. "Rape and the Prison Code." In *Prison Masculinities*, edited by Donald F. Sabo, Terry Allen Kupers, and Willie James London, 113–17. Philadelphia: Temple University Press.

Lash, John S. 1977. "Baldwin beside Himself: A Study in Modern Phallicism." In *James Baldwin: A Critical Evaluation*, edited by Therman B. O'Daniel, 47–55.Washington DC: Howard University Press.

Lee, Spike, dir. 2000. *Bamboozled*. Los Angeles: New Line Cinema. DVD.

Lemelle, Anthony J. 2010. *Black Masculinity and Sexual Politics*. New York: Routledge.

Levin, Hank M., and Clive R. Belfield. 2005. "Families as Contractual Partners in Education." In *Supplementary Education: The Hidden Curriculum of High Academic Achievement*, edited by Edmund W. Gordon, Beatrice L. Bridglall, and Aundra Saa Meroe, 211–37. Lanham, MD: Rowman & Littlefield.

Lincoln, C. Eric, and Lawrence H. Mamiya. 2003. *The Black Church in the African American Experience*. Durham, NC: Duke University Press.

Locke, Alaine LeRoy. 1970. *The New Negro: An Interpretation*. New York: Athenaeum.

Lorde, Audre. 2007. *Sister Outsider: Essays and Speeches*. Berkeley: Crossing Press.

Majors, Richard, and Janet Mancini Billson. 1992. *Cool Pose: The Dilemmas of Black Manhood in America*. New York: Lexington Books.

Malmgren, Carl D. 2000. "Mixed Genres and the Logic of Slavery in Toni Morrison's *Beloved*." In *Understanding Toni Morrison's* Beloved *and* Sula: *Selected Essays and Criticisms of the Works by the Nobel Prize-Winning Author*, edited by Solomon O. Iyasere and Marla W. Iyasere, 190–203. Troy, NY: Whitston.

Manning, Marable, 1995. *Beyond Black and White: Rethinking Race in American Politics and Society*. London: Verso.

Mason, Theodore O., Jr. 1988. "The Novelist as Conservator: Stories and Comprehension in Toni Morrison's *Song of Solomon*." *Contemporary Literature* 29 (4): 564–81.

Mayberry, Susan Neal. 2007. *Can't I Love What I Criticize?: The Masculine and Morrison*. Athens: University of Georgia Press.

Mbalia, Doreathea Drummond. 1991. "*Tar Baby*: A Reflection of Morrison's Developed Class Consciousness." In *Toni Morrison's Developing Class Consciousness*, 67–86. Selinsgrove, PA: Susquehanna University Press.

———. 1999. "*Song of Solomon*: The Struggle for Race and Class Consciousness." In *Toni Morrison's* Song of Solomon, edited by Harold Bloom, 125–40. Philadelphia: Chelsea House.

McBride, Dwight A. 1999. *James Baldwin Now*. New York: New York University Press.

McKay, Claude. 1922. "The Lynching." In *Harlem Shadows: The Poems of Claude McKay*. New York: Harcourt Brace and Company.

McWhorter, John H. 2000. *Losing the Race: Self-Sabotage in Black America*. New York: The Free Press.

Medina, Jose. 2003. "Identity Trouble: Disidentification and the Problem of Difference.'" *Philosophy and Social Criticism* 29 (6): 655–80.

Mitchell, Keith B. 2006. "Femininity, Abjection and (Black) Masculinity in James Baldwin's *Giovanni's Room* and Toni Morrison's *Beloved*." In *James Baldwin and Toni Morrison: Comparative Critical and Theoretical Essays*, edited by Lovalerie King and Lynn Orilla Scott, 261–86. New York: Palgrave Macmillian.

Mitchell-Kernan, Claudia. 1999. "Signifying, Loud-Talking and Marking." In *Signifyin(g), Sanctifin' and Slam Dunking: A Reader in African American Expressive Culture*, edited by Gena Caponi-Tabery, 309–30. Amherst: University of Massachusetts Press.

Moffitt, Letitia L. 2004. "'Finding the Door: Vision/Revision and Stereotype in Toni Morrison's *Tar Baby*." *Critique* 46 (1): 12–26.

Morgan, Joan. 2000. *When Chickenheads Come Home to Roost: My Life as a Hip-Hop Feminist*. New York: Simon & Schuster.

Morrison, Toni. 1970. *The Bluest Eye*. New York: Holt, Reinhart and Winston.

———. 1977. *Song of Solomon*. New York: Knopf.

———. 1987. *Beloved*. New York: New American Library.

———. 1989. "Unspeakable Things Unspoken: The Afro-American Presence in American Literature." *Michigan Quarterly Review* 28 (1): 1–34.

———. 1992. *Playing in the Dark: Whiteness and the Literary Imagination*. Cambridge, MA: Harvard University Press.

———. 1993. "On the Backs of Blacks." *Time*, November 18: 57–59.

———. 1994a. *Conversations with Toni Morrison*. Edited by Danille Taylor-Guthrie. Jackson: University Press of Mississippi.

———. 1994b. *Lecture and Speech of Acceptance, upon the Award of the Nobel Prize for Literature, Delivered in Stockholm on the Seventh of December, Nineteen Hundred and Ninety-Three*. New York: A. A. Knopf.

———. 1995. "The Site of Memory." In *Inventing the Truth: The Art and Craft of Memoir*, edited by William Zinsser, 183–200. New York: Houghton Mifflin.

———. 2004a. *Sula*. New York: Vintage.

———. 2004b. *Tar Baby*. New York: Vintage.

———. 2007a. *Jazz*. New York: Random House.

———. 2007b. *Paradise*. New York: Knopf Double Day.

———. 2008a. *A Mercy*. New York: Knopf Double Day.

———. 2008b. *What Moves at the Margins: Selected Nonfiction*. Edited by Carolyn C. Denard. Oxford: University Press of Mississippi.

Moten, Fred. 2003. *In the Break: The Aesthetics of the Black Radical Tradition.* Minneapolis: University of Minnesota Press.

Moynihan Daniel P. 1965. *The Negro Family: The Case for National Action.* Washington DC: Department of Labor, Office of Policy Planning and Research.

Mullen, Patrick. 2008. *The Man Who Adores the Negro: Race and American Folklore.* Urbana: University of Illinois Press.

Murray, Rolland. 2007. *Our Living Manhood: Literature, Black Power, and Masculine Ideology.* Philadelphia: University of Pennsylvania Press.

Mutua, Athena D. 2006. *Progressive Black Masculinities.* New York: Routledge.

Nakayama, Thomas K., and Robert L. Krizek. 1995. "Whiteness: A Strategic Rhetoric." *Quarterly Journal of Speech* 81 (3): 291–309.

Neal, Mark Anthony. 2006. *New Black Man.* New York: Routledge.

Nero, Charles I. 2000. "Toward a Black Gay Aesthetic." In *African American Literary Theory: A Reader,* edited by Winston Napier, 399–420. New York: New York University Press.

Nordgren, Anders. 2001. *Responsible Genetics: The Moral Responsibility of Geneticists for the Consequences of Human Genetics Research.* Dordrecht, Netherlands: Kluwer Academic Publishers.

Nunley, Vorris L. 2004. "From the Harbor to Da Academic Hood: Hush Harbors and an African American Rhetorical Tradition." In *African American Rhetoric(s): Interdisciplinary Perspectives,* edited by Elaine Richardson and Ronald Jackson, II, 221–41. Carbondale: Southern Illinois University Press.

———. 2011. *Keepin' It Hushed: The Barbershop and African American Hush Harbor Rhetoric.* Detroit: Wayne State University Press.

Nwankwo, Chimalum. 1996. "'I Is': Toni Morrison, the Past, and Africa." In *Of Dreams Deferred, Dead or Alive: African Perspectives on African American Writers,* edited by Femi Ojo-Ade, 171–80. Westport, CT: Greenwood.

Olivier, Laurence. 1982. *Confessions of an Actor.* New York: Orion.

Olson, Barbara K. 1997. "'Come-to-Jesus Stuff' in James Baldwin's *Go Tell It on the Mountain* and *The Amen Corner.*" *African American Review* 31 (2): 295–301.

Oring, Elliot. 1986. *Folk Groups and Folklore Genres: An Introduction.* Logan: Utah State University Press.

Palumbo-Liu, David. 2000. "Assumed Identities." *New Literary History* 31 (4): 765–80.

Patterson, Orlando. 1982. *Slavery and Social Death: A Comparative Study.* Cambridge, MA: Harvard University Press.

Patton, Paul. 2010. *Deleuzian Concepts: Philosophy, Colonization, Politics.* Palo Alto: Stanford University Press.

Peach, Linden. 1999. "Competing Discourses in *Song of Solomon.*" In *Toni Morrison's* Song of Solomon, edited by Harold Bloom, 159–76. Philadelphia: Chelsea House.

Petry, Ann. 1971. *Miss Muriel and Other Stories.* Boston: Houghton Mifflin.

———. 1974. *The Street: A Novel.* New York: Houghton Mifflin Company.

Pinckney, Darryl. 1988. "Blues for Mr. Baldwin." In *Critical Essays on James Baldwin,* edited by Fred L. Standley and Nancy V. Burt, 161–66. Boston: G. K. Hall.

Pinney, Christopher. 1997. *Camera Indica: The Social Life of Indian Photographs.* Chicago: University of Chicago Press.

Plant, Deborah G. 2007. *Zora Neale Hurston: A Biography of the Spirit.* Westport, CT: Greenwood Publishing.

Powell, Adam Clayton, Jr. 1971. *Adam by Adam: The Autobiography of Adam Clayton Powell Jr.* New York: Kensington Publishing Press.

Powell, Anna. 2007. *Deleuze, Altered States and Film.* Edinburgh: Edinburgh University Press.

Powell, Betty Jane. 2000. "'Will the Parts Hold?': The Journey Toward a Coherent Self in *Beloved.*" In *Understanding Toni Morrison's* Beloved *and* Sula*: Selected Essays and Criticisms of the Works by the Nobel Prize-Winning Author,* edited by Solomon O. Iyasere and Marla W. Iyasere, 143–54. Troy, NY: Whitston.

Powell, Kevin. 2003. *Who's Gonna Take the Weight? Manhood, Race, and Power in America.* New York: Three Rivers Press.

Puzo, Mario. 1968. Review of *Tell Me How Long the Train's Been Gone* by James Baldwin. *New York Times,* June 23.

Radford-Hill, Shelia. 2000. *Further to Fly: Black Women and the Politics of Empowerment.* Minneapolis: University of Minnesota.

Read, Andrew. 2005. "'As if Word Magic Had Anything to Do with the Courage It Took to Be a Man': Black Masculinity in Toni Morrison's *Paradise.*" *African American Review* 39 (4): 527–40.

Real, Terrance. 2002. *How Can I Get through to You? Closing the Intimacy Gap between Men and Women.* New York: Scribner.

Reed, Ishmael. 1976. *Flight to Canada: A Novel.* New York: Open Road Media.

———. 1995. *Conversations with Ishmael Reed.* Edited by Bruce Dick and Amritjit Singh. Oxford: University Press of Mississippi.

Reid-Pharr, Robert. 2007. *Once You Go Black: Choice, Desire, and the Black American Intellectual.* New York: New York University Press.

Reinelt, Janelle G., and Joseph R. Roach, eds. 2007. *Critical Theory and Performance.* Ann Arbor: University of Michigan Press.

Rich, Adrienne. 2003. "Compulsory Heterosexuality and Lesbian Existence." *Journal of Women's History* 15 (3): 11–48.

Richards, David A. J. 2005. *Disarming Manhood: Roots of Ethical Resistance.* Athens: Ohio University Press.

Richardson, Elaine B. 2004. "Coming from the Heart: African American Students, Literacy Stories, and the Rhetorical Education." In *African American Rhetoric(s): Interdisciplinary Perspectives,* edited by Elaine Richardson and Ronald Jackson II, 155–69. Carbondale: Southern Illinois University Press.

Richardson, Elaine B., and Ronald L. Jackson II. 2004. *African American Rhetoric(s). Interdisciplinary Perspectives.* Carbondale: Southern Illinois University Press.

Roberts, John. 2011. *From Trickster to Badman: The Black Folk Hero in Slavery and Freedom.* Philadelphia: University of Pennsylvania.

Robeson, Paul. 1958. *Here I Stand.* New York: Othello Associates.

Rodgers, Lawrence Richard. 1997. *Canaan Bound: The African-American Great Migration Novel.* Urbana: University of Illinois Press.

Rodriguez, Junius P. 2007. *Slavery in the United States: A Social, Political, and Historical Encyclopedia.* Santa Barbara: ABC-CLIO.

Roediger, David, ed. 1998. *Black on White: Black Writers on What It Means to Be White.* New York: Knopf Doubleday.

Rosenblatt, Paul. C. 2014. *The Impact of Racism on African American Families: Literature as Social Science.* Burlington, VT: Ashgate Publishing.

Ross, Marlon B. 2000. "Some Glances at the Black Fag: Race, Same Sex Desire, and Cultural Belonging." In *African American Literary Theory: A Reader,* edited by Winston Napier, 498–522. New York: New York University Press.

———. 2004. *Manning the Race. Reforming Black Men in the Jim Crow Era.* New York: New York University Press.

Rubin, David C. 1995. *Memory in Oral Traditions: The Cognitive Psychology of Epic, Ballads, and Counting-out Rhymes.* New York: Oxford University Press.

Samuels, Wilfred D. 1999. "Liminality and the Search for Self in *Song of Solomon.*" In *Toni Morrison's* Song of Solomon, edited by Harold Bloom, 5–28. Philadelphia: Chelsea House.

Schechter, William. 1970. *The History of Negro Humor in America.* New York: Fleet.

Schopp, Andrew. 2000. "Narrative Control and Subjectivity: Dismantling Safety in Toni Morrison's *Beloved.*" In *Understanding Toni Morrison's* Beloved *and* Sula*: Selected Essays and Criticisms of the Works by the Nobel Prize-Winning Author,* edited by Solomon O. Iyasere and Marla W. Iyasere, 204–30. Troy, NY: Whitston.

Scott, Darieck. 1996. *Traitor to the Race.* New York: Plume.

———. 2010. *Extravagant Abjection: Blackness, Power, and Sexuality in the African American Literary Imagination.* New York: New York University Press.

Scott, Emmett Jay. 1920. *Negro Migration During the War.* New York: Oxford University Press.

Scott, Lynn Orilla. 2002. *James Baldwin's Later Fiction: Witness to the Journey.* East Lansing: Michigan State University Press.

Scruggs, Charles. 1995. *Sweet Home: Invisible Cities in the Afro-American Novel.* Baltimore: Johns Hopkins University Press.

Sedgwick, Eve Kosofsky. 1985. *Between Men: English Literature and Male Homosocial Desire.* New York: Columbia University Press.

Shange, Ntozake. 2010. *For Colored Girls Who Have Considered Suicide When the Rainbow Is Enuf.* New York: Simon and Schuster.

Shin, Andrew, and Barbara Judson. 1998. "Beneath the Black Aesthetic: James Baldwin's Primer of Black American Masculinity." *African American Review* 32 (2): 247–61.

Showalter, Elaine. 1987. "Critical Cross-Dressing: Male Feminists and the Woman of the Year." In *Men in Feminism,* edited by Alice Jardine and Paul Smith, 116–32. New York: Methuen.

Sitter, Deborah Ayer. 1998. "The Making of a Man: Dialogic Meaning in *Beloved.*" In *Critical Essays on Toni Morrison's* Beloved, edited by Barbara H. Solomon, 189–204. New York: G. K. Hall.

Smith, Barbara. 1995. "Some Home Truths on the Contemporary Black Feminist Movement." In *Words of Fire: An Anthology of African-American Feminist Thought,* edited by Beverly Guy-Sheftall, 254–68. New York: New Press.

Smith, Valerie. 1999. "*Song of Solomon:* Continuities of Community." In *Toni Morrison's* Song of Solomon, edited by Harold Bloom, 41–56. Philadelphia: Chelsea House.

Smitherman, Geneva. 1986. *Talkin and Testifyin: The Language of Black America.* Detroit: Wayne State University Press.

Sontag, Susan. 1977. *On Photography.* New York: Picador.

Spillers, Hortense J. 2003. *Black, White, and in Color: Essays on American Literature and Culture.* Chicago: University of Chicago Press.

Spivak, Gayatri, 1996. *The Spivak Reader: Selected Works of Chakravorty Spivak.* Edited by Donna Landry and Gerald MacLean. New York: Routledge.

Springer, Kimberly. 2002. "Third Wave Black Feminism?" *Signs: Journal of Women in Culture and Society* 27 (4): 1059–82.

Stallybrass, Peter, and Allon White. 1986. *The Politics and Poetics of Transgression.* New York: Cornell University Press.

Staples, William G. 2000. *Everyday Surveillance: Vigilance and Visibility in Postmodern Life.* Lanham, MD: Rowman and Littlefield.

Stepto, Robert B. 1991. *From Behind the Veil: A Study of Afro-American Narrative.* Urbana: University of Illinois Press.

Sterling, Philip. 1997. "Humor." In *Dictionary of Afro-American Slavery,* edited by Randall M. Miller and John David Smith, 347–48. Westport, CT: Greenwood.

Story, Ralph A. 1999. "An Excursion into the Black World: The 'Seven Days' in Toni Morrison's *Song of Solomon.*" In *Toni Morrison's* Song of Solomon, edited by Harold Bloom, 85–94. Philadelphia: Chelsea House.

Strozier, Robert M. 2002. *Foucault, Subjectivity, and Identity: Historical Constructions of Subject and Self.* Detroit: Wayne State University Press.

Summers, Martin Anthony. 2004. *Manliness and Its Discontents: The Black Middle Class and the Transformation of Masculinity, 1900–1930.* Chapel Hill: University of North Carolina Press.

Tally, Justine, ed. 2007. *The Cambridge Companion to Toni Morrison.* New York: Cambridge University Press.

Taylor, Mark C. 1984. *Erring: A Postmodern A/theology.* Chicago: University of Chicago Press.

———. 2012. *Refiguring the Spiritual: Beuys, Barney, Turrell, Goldsworthy.* New York: Columbia University Press.

Taylor, Yuval, and Jake Austen. 2012. *Darkest America: Black Minstrelsy from Slavery to Hip-Hop.* New York: W. W. Norton & Company.

Thurman, Wallace. 1992. *Infants of the Spring.* Lebanon, MA: Northeastern University Press.

———. 1996. *The Blacker the Berry.* New York: Scribner Paperback Fiction.

———. 2003. *The Collected Writings of Wallace Thurman: A Harlem Renaissance Reader.* New Brunswick, NJ: Rutgers University Press.

Vygostsky, Lev. 1978. *Mind in Society: The Development of Higher Psychological Processes.* Cambridge, MA: Harvard University Press.

Walker, Alice. 1982. *The Color Purple: A Novel.* New York: Harcourt Brace Jovanovich.

———. 1983. *In Search of Our Mothers' Gardens: Womanist Prose.* San Diego: Harcourt Brace Jovanovich.

———. 2002. "Brothers and Sisters." In *These Hands I Know: African-American Writers on Family,* edited by Afaa Michael Weaver, 199–203. Louisville: Sarabande Books.

Wallace, Michelle. 1999. *Black Macho and the Myth of the Superwoman.* New York: Verso.

Watkins, Mel. 1999. *On the Real Side: A History of African American Comedy from Slavery to Chris Rock.* Chicago: Chicago Review Press.

Watson, Veronica T. 2013. *The Souls of White Folk: African American Writers Theorize Whiteness.* Jackson: University Press of Mississippi.

Werner, Craig. 1988. "The Economic Evolution of James Baldwin." In *Critical Essay on James Baldwin,* edited by Fred L. Standley and Nancy V. Burt, 78–93. Boston: G. K. Hall.

Wheatley, Phyllis. 1995. *Poems of Phyllis Wheatley: A Native African and a Slave.* Bedford, MA: Applewood Books.

Whitehead, Colson. 2009. *Sag Harbor: A Novel.* New York: Knopf Doubleday.

Wiegman, Robyn. 2001. "The Anatomy of Lynching." In *A Question of Manhood: A Reader in U.S. Black Men's History and Masculinity.* Vol. 2. Edited by Earnestine Jenkins and Darlene Clark Hine. Bloomington: Indiana University Press.

Wildman, Stephanie M., and Adrienne D. Davis. 1996. "Making Systems of Privilege Visible." In *Privilege Revealed: How Invisible Preference Undermines America,* edited by Stephanie M. Wildman, 7–24. New York: New York University Press.

Willis, Susan. 1987. *Specifying: Black Women Writing the American Experience.* Madison: University of Wisconsin Press.

Wolfe, Joanna. 2004. "'Ten Minutes for Seven Letters': Song as Key to Narrative Revision in Toni Morrison's *Beloved.*" *Narrative* 12 (3): 263–80.

Wright, Richard. 1980. *Native Son.* New York: Knopf Doubleday.

———. 1997. "Blue Print for Negro Writing." In *Within the Circle: An Anthology of African American Literary Criticism from the Harlem Renaissance to the Present,* edited by Angelyn Mitchell, 97–106. Durham, NC: Duke University Press.

Wyatt, Jean. 2000. "Giving Body to the Word: The Maternal Symbolic in Toni Morrison's *Beloved.*" In *Understanding Toni Morrison's* Beloved *and* Sula: *Selected Essays and Criticisms of the Works by the Nobel Prize-Winning Author,* edited by Solomon O. Iyasere and Marla W. Iyasere, 231–57. Troy, NY: Whitston.

Ya Salaam, Kalamu. 2001. "Women's Rights Are Human Rights." In *Traps: African American Men on Gender and Sexuality,* edited by Rudolph P. Byrd, and Beverly Guy-Sheftall, 113–18. Bloomington: Indiana University Press.

Yancy, George. 2008. *Black Bodies, White Gazes: The Continuing Significance of Race.* Lanham, MD: Rowman & Littlefield Publishers.

Yellin, Jean Fagan. 2004. *Harriet Jacobs: A Life.* New York: Basic Civitas Books.

Yingling, Thomas E. 1990. *Hart Crane and the Homosexual Text: New Thresholds, New Anatomies.* Chicago: University of Chicago Press.

Young, Vershawn Ashanti. 2007. *Your Average Nigga: Performing Race, Literacy, and Masculinity.* Detroit: Wayne State University Press.

INDEX

www.ingramcontent.com/pod-product-compliance
Lightning Source LLC
Chambersburg PA
CBHW022357110726
47902CB00002BA/321

* 9 7 8 0 8 1 4 2 5 3 9 0 8 *